OVERRULED

THE LONG WAR FOR CONTROL OF THE U.S. SUPREME COURT

OVERRULED

THE LONG WAR FOR CONTROL
OF THE U.S. SUPREME COURT

DAMON ROOT

First published in 2014 by PALGRAVE MACMILLAN® TRADE in the United States—a division of St. Martin's Press LLC, 175 Fifth Avenue, New York, NY 10010.

Where this book is distributed in the UK, Europe and the rest of the world, this is by Palgrave Macmillan, a division of Macmillan Publishers Limited, registered in England, company number 785998, of Houndmills, Basingstoke, Hampshire RG21 6XS.

Palgrave® and Macmillan® are registered trademarks in the United States, the United Kingdom, Europe and other countries.

ISBN: 978-1-137-27923-1

Library of Congress Cataloging-in-Publication Data

Root, Damon, author.
   Overruled : the long war for control of the U.S. Supreme Court / Damon Root.
      pages   cm
   ISBN 978-1-137-27923-1 (hardback)
   1. United States. Supreme Court. 2. Political questions and judicial power—United States. I. Title.
KF8742.R655   2014
347.73'26—dc23

2014017851

A catalogue record of the book is available from the British Library.

Design by Letra Libre Inc.

First edition: November 2014

10 9 8 7 6 5 4 3 2 1

Printed in the United States of America.

Dedicated to my mother
and to the memory of my father.

CONTENTS

OVERRULED

THE LONG WAR FOR CONTROL OF THE U.S. SUPREME COURT

INTRODUCTION

THE LONG WAR

CAN THE FEDERAL GOVERNMENT MAKE YOU eat your fruits and vegetables? Supreme Court nominee Elena Kagan seemed to think so. It was June 29, 2010, the second day of Kagan's confirmation hearings before the Senate Judiciary Committee, and Republican Tom Coburn of Oklahoma wanted to know whether she thought Congress possessed the constitutional power to force every American to "eat three vegetables and three fruits every day." In response, the future Supreme Court justice laughed and said that while it "sounds like a dumb law,"[1] that did not make it an unconstitutional one. "The [principal] protector against bad laws is the political branches themselves," Kagan said. In other words, if you don't like what your lawmakers have done, take your complaint to the ballot box, not to the courthouse.

It was the classic case for judicial restraint, the idea that judges should defer to the will of the majority and refrain from striking down most democratically enacted laws, even the really dumb ones. As a model for this approach, Kagan cited the example of Supreme Court Justice Oliver Wendell Holmes Jr. "He was this judge who lived . . . in the early twentieth century," Kagan explained. He "hated a lot of the legislation that was being enacted . . . but insisted that if the people wanted it, it was their right to go hang themselves."[2]

Appointed in 1902 by President Theodore Roosevelt, Justice Holmes was one of the Supreme Court's earliest and most influential advocates of judicial restraint or, as he once described it, "the right of a majority to embody their opinions in law."[3] By the time he retired in 1933, Holmes had preached the virtues of judicial deference in dozens of major cases, many of which continue to be cited today. Summarizing his philosophy as a judge in a 1920 letter to the British economist Harold Laski, Holmes declared, "if my fellow citizens want to go to Hell I will help them. It's my job."[4]

That view may sound harsh, but it didn't prevent Holmes from being adopted as a hero by the American left, particularly among the assorted reformers, activists, and politicians laboring under the banner of Progressivism, the turn-of-the-century movement that sought to create a vast new regulatory state to combat the perceived evils of industrial capitalism. Holmes was "a sage with the bearing of a cavalier,"[5] gushed the Progressive journalist Walter Lippmann. New York judge Benjamin Cardozo, who would eventually replace Holmes on the Supreme Court, dubbed him "the philosopher and the seer."[6] His "little side-remarks and comments, falling from his lips casually," contain "stuff sufficient for a treatise or a library."[7] Felix Frankfurter, a protégé of Holmes's and an eventual Supreme Court justice himself, managed to outdo even Cardozo in the praise department. Holmes "is led by the divination of the philosopher and the imagination of the poet," Frankfurter exclaimed. "He is, indeed, philosopher become king."[8] As the Progressives saw it, if more judges would only follow the example set by Holmes, the reform movement would be free to make the government as big and powerful as it needed to be.

So Elena Kagan wasn't just showing off her knowledge of arcane legal history by invoking Holmes before the Senate Judiciary

Committee that day; she had placed herself squarely within a long and venerable legal tradition that seeks to give the government wide control over regulatory affairs while simultaneously preventing most interference from the courts. And as it turned out, Kagan would not be the only Holmesian on the bench.

Almost exactly two years later, on June 28, 2012, Holmes returned to the political stage once more, this time as one of the deciding factors in the biggest legal battle of the modern era, the clash over the constitutionality of President Barack Obama's sweeping health care overhaul, the Patient Protection and Affordable Care Act.

After a year's worth of skirmishing in the lower courts, the Supreme Court was finally set to announce its eagerly anticipated decision on the health care law that morning. Although the case against health care reform was initially dismissed by the president and his allies as a partisan stunt, the legal challenge had slowly gathered steam, winning first at the federal district court level and then, more significantly, at the U.S. Court of Appeals for the Eleventh Circuit, where a federal judge appointed by President Bill Clinton joined the majority in voting against the Obama administration. "We have not found any generally applicable, judicially enforceable limiting principle that would permit us to uphold the [health care law] without obliterating the boundaries inherent in the system of enumerated congressional powers,"[9] the Eleventh Circuit's ruling declared. To top it all off, not only had the Supreme Court recognized the seriousness of the challenge by setting aside three days to hear oral arguments in the case—a modern record—those three days had not appeared to go very well for the federal government.

Indeed, not only had conservative justices like Antonin Scalia and Samuel Alito seemed hostile to the Obama administration's case, which rested principally on the theory that Congress could require every American to buy health insurance as part of its power to regulate interstate commerce, but even the right-leaning moderate Anthony Kennedy, who sometimes votes with the liberals and frequently casts the deciding vote in close cases, appeared to be lining up against the health care law. "When you are changing the relation of the individual to the government in this, what we can stipulate is, I think, a unique way," Kennedy asked Solicitor General Donald Verrilli as a packed courtroom looked on, "do you not have a heavy burden of justification to show authorization under the Constitution?"[10]

The stage appeared to be set for a landmark conservative victory. But then something else happened. In a decision that shocked many observers and infuriated most of the right, Chief Justice John Roberts, a veteran of Ronald Reagan's Justice Department and an appointee of George W. Bush, broke with his usual allies and sided instead with the Court's liberals. Thanks to Roberts, the health care law was upheld by the narrowest of margins: five votes to four.

Why did Roberts do it? He said it was an act of judicial restraint. Starting with the premise that legal statutes are owed a "full measure of deference"[11] by the courts, Roberts proceeded to grant every measure of that deference in his opinion, interpreting the law in such a way that it could pass constitutional muster and avoid bringing down a judicial censor. As an authority for this deferential maneuvering, Roberts turned to none other than Justice Holmes, citing the famous jurist's concurring opinion in the 1927 case of *Blodgett v. Holden,* which declared, "between two possible interpretations of a statute, by one of which it would be unconstitutional and by the other valid, our plain duty is to adopt that which will save the Act."[12]

In other words, Roberts tipped the scale in favor of the government. "It is not our job," declared the chief justice of the United States, taking yet another page from Holmes's playbook, "to protect the people from the consequences of their political choices."[13] Let them go to hell.

To say conservatives were outraged at Roberts would be putting it mildly. The *American Conservative* ran an article on the ruling titled "John Roberts's Betrayal,"[14] while Republican Congressman Jack Kingston of Georgia declared on Twitter, "I feel like I just lost two great friends: America and Justice Roberts."[15]

But Roberts had not actually betrayed legal conservatism; he had simply followed one of two possible conservative paths in the case. Judicial restraint, as Roberts well understood, was not only a touchstone of the Progressive left; it was also a philosophy adopted by many members of the modern right. Conservative icon Robert Bork, for example, the former Yale law professor and federal judge whose failed 1987 Supreme Court nomination had galvanized Republicans and set the stage for future judicial confirmation battles, was an outspoken proponent of granting Holmes-style deference to the elected branches of government. As Bork argued in his bestselling book *The Tempting of America,* the "first principle" of the U.S. system was not individual rights; it was majority rule, which meant that when it came to the vast preponderance of political disputes, the courts should simply butt out. "In wide areas of life," Bork wrote, "majorities are entitled to rule, if they wish, simply because they are majorities."[16]

Bork and other conservatives employed this approach most famously when it came to the issue of abortion. In their view, the Court's 1973 ruling in *Roe v. Wade,* which recognized a woman's constitutional right to an abortion, the Supreme Court had effectively overturned the abortion laws of all fifty states, substituting its judgment for the will of the people in every one of those places. Under the majoritarian deference espoused by Bork (and Holmes before him), each state would be free to set its own abortion policy—including a total prohibition on the procedure—without interference from the federal courts. Judicial restraint would therefore accomplish one of the central goals of modern conservatism: the death of *Roe v. Wade.*

That was the path taken by Roberts in the health care case. The only problem was that very few conservatives wanted to join him for the ride. Instead of seeking judicial deference, they wanted the justices to nullify President Obama's signature legislative achievement and overrule the elected branches of government—something the Supreme Court had not done since the great legal battles over Franklin Roosevelt's New Deal in the 1930s.

This was the other conservative path, the one Roberts refused to take. Like the Bork-Holmes approach, it too has its roots in the legal and political controversies of the late nineteenth and early twentieth centuries. Except this school of thought was not inspired by Holmes, but by the legal figures who opposed him: the conservative and libertarian judges and lawyers who rejected judicial deference and worked instead to strike down many of the laws imposed during the Progressive and New Deal eras.

Foremost among these figures was a man named Stephen Field. A pro-Union Democrat and former California Supreme Court justice, Field was appointed to the U.S. Supreme Court in 1863 by President Abraham Lincoln. During his three decades on the bench, Justice Field would emerge as one of the Supreme Court's first great champions of property rights and economic liberty.

Born in Haddam, Connecticut, in 1816, Field moved west to California in the storied year of 1849. Shortly after disembarking from a steamship at San Francisco Bay, he helped to found the nearby gold rush town of Marysville, where his subsequent experiences now sound like something out of a Wild West adventure. As a practicing attorney, Field made powerful enemies: A notorious local judge named William Turner threatened to shoot him dead in the street after several contentious courtroom exchanges. In response, Field purchased "a pair of revolvers and had a sack-coat made with pockets in which the barrels could lie, and be discharged," as he later recounted in his memoir. "I began to practice firing the pistols from the pockets," Field continued. "In time I acquired considerable skill, and was able to hit a small object across the street."[17] Judge Turner backed down.

Field brought a similar tenacity to his judicial career. On the Supreme Court, he became the driving force behind a legal theory that would come to be known as "liberty of contract." Rooted in the free labor philosophy and self-ownership principles of the antislavery movement, liberty of contract held that the Fourteenth Amendment's guarantee that no person be deprived of life, liberty, or property without due process of law served to protect every individual's "right to pursue a lawful and necessary calling"[18] against arbitrary and unnecessary government interference.

Over the next three decades, Field would expound on this and similar legal concepts in a series of powerful dissenting opinions. By the time he retired in 1897, a majority of the Supreme Court was coming around to his libertarian point of view. That year, a unanimous Court explicitly recognized the right to pursue a calling, enshrining a broad guarantee of economic liberty under the Fourteenth Amendment. During the three decades that followed, the Supreme Court would selectively employ that guarantee against various government regulations until the doctrine was reversed during the height of the New Deal.

Revived over the past four decades by a growing camp of libertarians and free-market conservatives, the aggressive legal approach once associated with Justice Field and his successors has come roaring back to life in the early twenty-first century. Its modern followers have no patience with judicial restraint and little use for majority rule. They want the courts to police the other branches of government, striking down any state or federal law that infringes on their broad constitutional vision of personal and economic freedom, an approach one libertarian theorist has dubbed "principled judicial activism."[19] They are the sworn enemies of Justice Oliver Wendell Holmes. We'll call them the libertarian legal movement.

THE LONG WAR between judicial restraint and judicial action is the central theme of this book. As we'll see, it's a contest that cuts across the political spectrum in surprising ways and makes for some unusual bedfellows. Once the exclusive domain of the Progressive left, for example, judicial deference is now a favored tool of the conservative right. Chief Justice Roberts made that point abundantly clear in his striking 2012 decision to uphold President Obama's health care law. And that's not the only twist in this long, strange trip. The DNA of Justice Field, the late nineteenth-century conservative who said the courts should place certain freedoms beyond the reach of lawmakers, lives on prominently today in the landmark liberal rulings that legalized birth control and eliminated state restrictions on "homosexual conduct."

Because the Fourteenth Amendment is the primary legal battlefield upon which judicial restraint and judicial action have come to blows, this book begins with a brief history of that amendment, followed by a close look at the 1873 case in which the Supreme Court first grappled with its meaning and set the terms for the debate we're still having today. From there I turn to the great courtroom duels over economic regulation that marked the Progressive and New Deal eras, including the cases that inspired Franklin Roosevelt's ill-fated attempt to pack the Supreme Court. I then discuss the sweeping liberal triumphs of the mid-twentieth century, such as *Brown v. Board of Education,* and consider their relationship (if any) to the tenets of judicial deference. Next I introduce Robert Bork, founding father of the contemporary legal right and heir to Progressive hero Oliver Wendell Holmes. After Bork comes the first wave of libertarian insurgents who rose up to take him (and Holmes) down. Finally, I explain how all of these factors came together to produce several of the biggest Supreme

Court battles of our own time: namely, the battles over gay rights, eminent domain, gun control, and health care reform.

What follows is the story of two competing visions, each one with its own take on what role the government and the courts should play in our society. Their fundamental debate, which stretches from the Civil War period to the present, goes to the very heart of our constitutional system.

ONE

"THE RIGHT OF FREE LABOR"

N SEPTEMBER 3, 1848, TO MARK THE tenth anniversary of his escape from slavery, the abolitionist leader Frederick Douglass addressed an open letter to his old master, a man named Thomas Auld. "I have often thought I should like to explain to you the grounds upon which I have justified myself in running away from you," Douglass wrote. The morality was simple. "You are a man, and so am I. . . . In leaving you, I took nothing but what belonged to me, and in no way lessened your means for obtaining an *honest* living."[1]

Born into slavery in Talbot County, Maryland, sometime in February 1818, Frederick Douglass broke free from bondage at the age of twenty, making his way north under a false identity to New York City, where he stopped to get married, and then on to the whaling port of New Bedford, Massachusetts, where he found a job loading ships. Before long he was attending abolitionist meetings and had soon established himself as a force to be reckoned with inside the growing movement to abolish slavery. "Three out of the ten years since I left you, I spent as a common laborer," Douglass wrote to Auld. "It was there I earned my first free dollar. It was mine. I could spend it as I pleased. . . . That was a precious dollar to me."[2]

The story of his first paying job would appear frequently in Frederick Douglass's writings and speeches over the years, and with good reason. At the center of his lifelong struggle for liberty and equality stood the principle of self-ownership, a concept that necessarily included both the freedom to compete in the economic marketplace and the right to enjoy the fruits of those labors. Slavery, as Douglass understood all too well, obliterated such things, robbing its victims not only of the products of their toil, but of their control over their own bodies. Earning that "first free dollar" was therefore a milestone in his life. As he described the event in *My Bondage and My Freedom*, the second of his three autobiographies, "I was now my own master— a tremendous fact."[3]

That tremendous fact of self-ownership, and the shattering repercussions that followed from it, would transform American law during the course of the nineteenth century, first by undermining the legal and moral foundations of the slave system, and then by inspiring a new constitutional order to replace it. The centerpiece of that new order was the Fourteenth Amendment to the U.S. Constitution. Drafted by the Radical Republicans of the thirty-ninth Congress in 1866 and ratified by the states in 1868, it declares: "No State shall make or enforce any law which shall abridge the privileges or immunities of citizens of the United States; nor shall any State deprive any person of life, liberty, or property, without due process of law; nor deny to any person within its jurisdiction the equal protection of the laws." According to the author of those words, antislavery Republican Congressman John Bingham of Ohio, among the liberties now under protection from state abuse was "the right to work in an honest calling and contribute by your toil in some sort to the support of your fellowmen, and to be secure in the enjoyment of the fruits of your toil."[4] In other words, Bingham had sought to enshrine the free labor philosophy of Frederick Douglass within the text of the Constitution. As a corollary, the federal courts would now be empowered to protect such rights from the grasp of predatory state officials.

Yet in 1873, just five years after the Fourteenth Amendment went into effect, a bare majority of the U.S. Supreme Court voted to strip it of that meaning in one of the most consequential rulings in American history, a decision known as *The Slaughter-House Cases*. At issue was an act of the Louisiana legislature granting a private corporation the lucrative authority to operate an exclusive central slaughterhouse for the city of New Orleans for a period of twenty-five years. Although framed as a public health measure, the monopoly law had every appearance of corruption and special-interest favoritism, particularly in the eyes of the hundreds of local butchers whose economic livelihoods were suddenly at risk. It was "an odious and burdensome monopoly . . . against common right and the common interest,"[5] argued the lawyers for the Butchers Benevolent Association, the group whose legal challenge helped spark the case. They had good reason to suspect foul play. As the historian Charles Lofgren would later observe, "legislative bribery had greased passage of the law, with its most immediate beneficiaries—the seventeen participants in the corporation it established—adroitly distributing shares of stock and cash."[6]

The Supreme Court, however, adopted a posture of judicial deference toward the state legislature and its corporate beneficiaries, holding that the new Fourteenth Amendment offered virtually no protection for individual rights against state authority. Government officials remained free to control economic affairs as they saw fit. "The power here exercised" by the state of Louisiana, observed the majority opinion of Justice Samuel F. Miller, "has been, up to the present period in the constitutional history of this country, always conceded to belong to the States."[7] To rule otherwise, Miller asserted, would "fetter and degrade the State governments" by denying them their traditional powers. Furthermore, Miller wrote, the Supreme Court had no business acting as "a perpetual censor upon all legislation of the States."[8] (Twentieth-century conservatives would later employ a similar argument when condemning the Court's rulings against state restrictions on abortion.)

Among the minority of justices who took a dissenting view in *Slaughter-House* was Lincoln appointee Stephen Field. As Justice Field saw it, the protection of free labor principles from the rapacious actions of state lawmakers was *the* central issue in *The Slaughter-House Cases*. The majority opinion of the Court, he believed, had turned the Fourteenth Amendment completely on its head. If a constitutional right was under attack by a state legislature, Field maintained, then the Supreme Court was duty-bound by the new amendment to strike down the offending statute. Judicial restraint was no excuse for judicial surrender. As for the slaughterhouse monopoly before him, Field had little doubt that it deserved a fatal blow from the bench. "It is to me a matter of profound regret that [the monopoly's] validity is recognized by a majority of this court," he wrote in his *Slaughter-House* dissent, "for by it the right of free labor, one of the most sacred and imprescriptible rights of man, is violated."[9] According to Field, "the fourteenth amendment does afford such protection, and was so intended by the Congress which framed and the states which adopted it."[10]

More than 140 years have now passed since the Supreme Court issued its *Slaughter-House* ruling, yet the central issues of the case remain as hotly disputed as ever. Should the courts defer to legislative majorities and allow contested regulations to stand? Or does the Constitution require judicial action in defense of individual liberty, forcing the courts to overrule democratically enacted laws? Those questions have cropped up in almost every major Fourteenth

Amendment case since 1873, from the conflict over state regulation of business to the showdown over state controls on abortion. Indeed, it's no exaggeration to say that *Slaughter-House* lies at the very heart of America's long-running dispute over the scope of the Fourteenth Amendment and the reach of state power, perhaps the most litigated area in all of constitutional law.

To understand today's debate over judicial restraint and the role of the courts, we must first understand the origins of that debate in the bloody age of slavery, the Civil War, and Reconstruction.

"LIBERTY AND FREE COMPETITION"

The idea of free labor has deep roots in Anglo-American history. In 1614, Britain's highest judicial officer, Sir Edward Coke, laid out the basic formulation in the case of *Allen v. Tooley.* At issue was a lawsuit filed against an upholsterer who failed to complete an apprenticeship with the local guild before going into business on his own. In mercantilist England, such guilds typically enjoyed broad control over their respective fields. Yet according to Coke, under both the Magna Carta and the common law, "it was lawful for any man to use any trade thereby to maintain himself and his family."[11] The upholsterer won. Later that year, in *The Case of the Tailors of Ipswich,* Coke deployed the same free labor principles against a royally chartered guild that sought to prevent non-members from working as tailors. "At the Common Law," he declared, "no man could be prohibited from working in any lawful Trade, for the Law doth abhor idleness, the mother of all evil."[12]

Adam Smith would make the same basic point a century and a half later in *The Wealth of Nations,* one of the most influential economic treatises of its day in both Britain and America. "The patrimony of the poor man lies in the strength and dexterity of his own hands," Smith wrote. "To hinder him from employing this strength and dexterity in what manner he thinks proper, without injury to his neighbor, is a plain violation of this most sacred property."[13]

James Madison, the primary architect of the U.S. Constitution, agreed with Coke and Smith. "That is not a just government, nor is property secure under it," Madison wrote, "where arbitrary restrictions, exemptions, and monopolies deny to part of its citizens that free use of their faculties, and free choice of their occupations, which not only constitute their property in the general sense of the word; but are the means of acquiring property strictly so called."[14] President Thomas Jefferson made a similar claim in his first inaugural address, describing "the sum of good government" as a legal order that "shall restrain men from injuring one another, shall leave them otherwise free to regulate their own pursuits of industry and improvement, and shall not take from the mouth of labor the bread it has earned."[15] Of course, Madison and Jefferson were not themselves entirely scrupulous on this point, as the many slaves forced to labor on their respective Virginia plantations might have told you. It would fall to the antislavery activists of the nineteenth century to correct these and other shortcomings of the founding generation.

Those activists had their work cut out for them. By the middle of the nineteenth century, the peculiar institution was deeply embedded in American political and economic life. But despite the daunting task before it, the antislavery movement proceeded to make its case, arguing not only against the evils of human bondage, but in favor of a superior system to replace it: the system of free labor. Those arguments would build directly on the intellectual foundation first established by thinkers such as Coke, Smith, and Madison. The "ever-present motive power" of slavery, announced Massachusetts Senator Charles Sumner, one of the slave system's most persistent foes, was "simply to compel the labor of fellow-men without wages," by "excluding them from that property in their own earnings, which the law of nature allow, and civilization secures. . . . It is robbery and petty larceny, under the garb of law."[16] The abolitionist William Goodell struck a similar note. "Honest labor is despised at the south," he wrote. "The idlers of the south, live upon the unrequited toil of the laborer."[17] "All these distinctions may be resolved into this fundamental difference," declared the *National Era,* a leading abolitionist publication. "The free working man owns himself; the slave is owned by another."[18] As the legal scholar William E. Forbath later observed, "It was the abolitionists who first lent moral sanction and rhetorical energy to the notion that the northern worker's freedom rested simply in self-ownership and the right to sell his own labor."[19]

Slavery's defenders also recognized the potency of these free labor principles and correctly saw them as a threat to their way of life. To the pro-slavery politician John C. Calhoun of South Carolina, for instance, the idea of a universal right to life, liberty, and property was both dangerous and preposterous, a point of view that led Calhoun not only to denounce the abolitionists, but also to attack the celebrated words of the Declaration of Independence. Jefferson's notion that all men are created equal and endowed at birth with certain unalienable rights was "the most dangerous of all political errors,"[20] Calhoun claimed. "For a long time it lay dormant; but in the process of time it began to germinate, and produce its poisonous fruits."[21] Those "poisonous fruits" included the existence of an organized abolitionist movement that had the nerve to take the Declaration of Independence at its word.

The pro-slavery writer George Fitzhugh went even further than Calhoun, arguing that slavery was superior to "liberty and free competition"[22] in all respects. The condition of free labor in an unfettered market, Fitzhugh maintained, was "worse than slavery"[23] because the forces of capitalism routinely exploited the poor and the working class, and left them struggling to make ends meet. "Slavery relieves our slaves of these cares altogether," he bragged in his 1854 bestseller *Sociology for the South, or The Failure of Free Society*. "Slavery is a form, and the very best form, of socialism."[24] As for the notion that "individuals and peoples prosper most when governed least,"[25] Fitzhugh proclaimed it to be a lie: "It has been justly observed that under this system the rich are continually growing richer and the poor poorer."[26] In fact, he declared, far from making the world a better place, "the love of personal liberty and freedom from all restraint, are distinguishing traits of wild men and wild beasts."[27] As the historian Eugene Genovese later explained, "Fitzhugh understood that the South was the battleground for two irreconcilable forces,"[28] slavery and free labor.

George Fitzhugh and Frederick Douglass disagreed about many things, but on this point they were in rare harmony. The slave system was incompatible with the disruptive and individualizing forces unleashed by the principles of free labor, and both men knew it. But where Fitzhugh's defense of slavery led him to praise socialism and assail the free-market ideas of John Locke and Adam Smith, which he denounced as amounting to "every man for himself, and Devil take the hindmost,"[29] Douglass's writings and speeches were steeped in the classical liberal tradition Fitzhugh spurned. Evoking Locke's famous description of private property emerging from man mixing his labor with the natural world, for instance, Douglass pointed to black Americans "plowing, planting and reaping, using all kinds of mechanical tools, erecting houses . . . engaged in all manner of enterprises common to other men,"[30] as proof that they too deserved the full range of natural rights. "Would you have me argue that man is entitled to liberty? That he is the rightful owner of his own body?" Douglass asked. "There is not a man beneath the canopy of heaven that does not know that slavery is wrong *for him*."[31] As for the alleged shortcomings of capitalism, Douglass was prepared to test his luck in the free market. "Give the Negro fair play," he declared, "and let him alone."[32]

"AN ABOLITION WAR"

Those free labor principles found a temporary political home with the formation of the new Republican Party, founded by antislavery activists in 1854. As one leading party member declared in a speech on behalf of Abraham Lincoln's 1860 presidential campaign, "The Republicans stand before the country, not only as the anti-slavery party, but emphatically as the party of free labor."[33]

The Grand Old Party arrived on the scene at a precipitous moment in American history. By 1854 the controversy over slavery had become the single greatest issue in American life—and the disagreements it provoked did not always involve mere words alone. Eleven years before Frederick Douglass wrote to his old master, a pro-slavery mob in Alton, Illinois, had murdered Elijah Lovejoy, publisher of the antislavery *Observer*, killing him while he defended his printing press from destruction. On a moonlit night in May 1856, the radical abolitionist John Brown, along with seven other men, including four of his sons, dragged five pro-slavery settlers from their homes near Pottawatomie Creek, Kansas, and executed them by blade and bullet. "Death for death,"[34] John Brown Jr. later explained. At the same time in many northern cities, abolitionist vigilance committees were forming to harass and oppose the slave catchers—"man stealers" they called them—unleashed by the Fugitive Slave Act of 1850, which stripped suspected runaways (which is to say any black person who fell under any suspicion at any time) of virtually all legal protections, including the right to testify on their own behalf and the right to invoke the writ of *habeas corpus*. To stack the deck even further in favor of slavery, when a suspected fugitive was brought before a government commissioner under the fugitive slave law, the commissioner earned $10 for every individual "returned" to bondage and $5 for every suspect that was set free. The Supreme Court, meanwhile, in its notorious 1857 ruling against the slave Dred

Scott, had set off a national firestorm by declaring that blacks could never be citizens of the United States and that under the principles of the American founding the black man "had no rights which the white man was bound to respect."[35] In sum, the nation was tottering on the brink of civil war. Shortly after Lincoln's election in 1860 and the resulting secession of seven slaveholding states, that war finally came.

For the abolitionists, there was little doubt about what the war's outbreak meant for their cause: The destruction of slavery must become an explicit aim of the U.S. government. As Frederick Douglass put it, "no war but an Abolition war; no peace but an Abolition peace."[36] With the surrender of Confederate General Robert E. Lee at Appomattox Courthouse on April 9, 1865, and the ratification of the Thirteenth Amendment abolishing slavery later that same year, Douglass and his allies appeared to have succeeded on both counts. Unfortunately, that appearance would prove tragically deceptive.

"THEY DO NOT KNOW WHETHER THEY ARE FREE OR NOT"

In the aftermath of the Civil War, the governments of the former Confederate states quickly moved to restore slavery in practice, if not in name, by systematically eliminating or curtailing every possible avenue the freedmen might pursue in the hopes of improving their lives or securing their rights. Known as the "Black Codes," these laws and regulations targeted everything from the freedmen's right to self-defense to their ability to seek paying work outside of the plantation system. Mississippi set the pace in the spring of 1865 when a state convention instructed the legislature to enact new laws to guard "against any evils that may arise from their sudden emancipation."[37] Alabama and Georgia soon passed similar resolutions. With the arrival of the Black Codes, it became clear what sort of "evils" those lawmakers intended to guard against.

"Every freedman, free negro, and mulatto," declared the Mississippi Black Code, was required to provide written evidence every January of a "lawful home or employment,"[38] or else face the charge of vagrancy, which in turn allowed the state to sentence them to long terms of forced labor, often on the plantations of their former masters. Florida's law "in relation to Contracts of Persons of Color" placed similar controls on black economic mobility, including by criminalizing "willful disobedience of orders, wanton impudence, or disrespect to his employer or his authorized agent, failure to perform the work assigned to him, idleness, or abandonment of the premises,"[39] also punishable by forced labor. Unlike the free labor system of the North, where an absent or impudent worker risked getting fired and having to find a new job, the Black Codes basically re-shackled the former slaves to their former masters, using criminal punishment enforced by state officials to keep the plantation system running as before.

Freedmen seeking economic independence faced no shortage of government-sponsored treacheries. Under South Carolina's Black Code, for example, blacks intending to work as artisans or mechanics had to pay an annual licensing fee of $10, a sum that did not come easily to most former slaves; those who wanted to work as shopkeepers or peddlers had to pay $100 annually and also persuade a white district judge of their "skill and fitness."[40] In North Carolina, if at least one party to the sale of an animal or good worth more than $10 happened to be black, a white person was legally required to witness the sale, making economic transactions impossible for the freedmen in certain locales.

The right to acquire and use property was similarly restricted. Opelousas, Louisiana, openly declared, "No negro or freedman shall be permitted to rent or keep a house within the limits of the town under any circumstances." The same ordinance also prevented blacks from living anywhere in town unless "in the regular service of some white person or former owner, who shall be held responsible for the conduct of said freedman." As for any would-be entrepreneurs hoping to earn a living in that unwelcoming place, "No freedman shall sell, barter, or exchange any articles of merchandise"[41] without written permission from an employer or town official. To put it mildly, such permission was not readily forthcoming from local whites. According to Joseph E. Roy, a white Chicago clergyman who toured the South extensively between October and December 1865 on behalf of the American Home Missionary Society, "A few [white] persons whom I met would admit that [blacks] had the right to acquire property . . . but the great mass of the people were opposed to their having a chance to gain possession of real estate."[42] Overall, Roy reported, "a great many cruelties are practiced on the colored people."[43]

Southern blacks readily confirmed Roy's dismal findings. "A party of twelve or fifteen men go around at night searching the houses of colored people, turning them out and beating them," one black man testified before Congress in February 1866. "I was sent here as a delegate to find out whether the colored people down there cannot have protection." They "are willing to work for a living," he continued. "All they want is some protection and to know what their rights are . . . they do not know whether they are free or not."[44] Richard R. Hill, a former slave living in Hampton, Virginia, knew perfectly well that his old masters were plotting against him. "They have said that, and it seems to be a prevalent idea," Hill declared. If the whites had their way, Hill said, "their old laws would still exist by which they would reduce [the freedmen] to something like bondage. That has been expressed by a great many of them."[45] Government officials openly expressed that same bigoted agenda. In Florida, the legislative committee charged with preparing the state's Black Code praised slavery as a "benign"[46] institution and announced, "we have a duty to perform—the protection of our wives and children from threatened danger, and the prevention of scenes which may cost the extinction of an entire race."[47]

In reality, of course, it was the freedmen who faced danger at the hands of state officials and their vigilante enforcers, a dire situation made worse by the fact that most Black Codes stripped African Americans of their right to keep and bear arms for self-defense. Mississippi, for instance, made it a crime for blacks "to keep or carry firearms of any kind, or any ammunition, dirk, or bowie knife,"[48] while Florida made it "unlawful for any Negro, mulatto, or person of color to own, use, or keep in possession or under control any bowie-knife, dirk, sword, firearms, or ammunition of any kind," unless licensed by a probate judge, "under a penalty of forfeiting them to the informer, and of standing in the pillory for one hour, or be whipped not exceeding thirty-nine lashes, or both."[49]

In short, the freedmen were besieged on all sides by hostile government forces that robbed them of their liberty, prevented them from exercising their economic rights, and deprived them of virtually all methods of meaningful self-defense. To say that this state of affairs violated the bedrock free labor principle of self-ownership would be a severe understatement. In the words of Alexander Dunlap, a free black living in Williamsburg, Virginia, in 1866, "We feel in danger of our lives, of our property, and of everything else."[50] Against this backdrop of state-sanctioned violence and exploitation, the Fourteenth Amendment to the U.S. Constitution was born.

"EVERY SECURITY FOR THE PROTECTION OF PERSON AND PROPERTY"

On December 5, 1865, the Republican-dominated thirty-ninth Congress was gaveled into session in Washington, D.C. Its first and primary order of business was to put a stop to the mounting outrages occurring in the South. To that end, congressional Republicans pursued a two-front strategy: First, they sought passage of a sweeping federal civil rights bill to protect both the freedmen and their white Unionist allies from abuse by the former Confederates; second, they drafted a new constitutional amendment to give that legislation force and provide further protections for individual rights against harmful state actions. First up was the Civil Rights Act of 1866, enacted in April over the veto of President Andrew Johnson. A groundbreaking proposal, the law held that all persons born on U.S. soil were citizens of the country (thereby repudiating *Dred Scott*'s holding that blacks could never be citizens), and that such citizens, "of every race and color . . . shall have the same right, in every state and territory . . . to make and enforce contracts, to sue, be parties, and give evidence, to inherit, purchase, lease, sell, hold, and convey real and personal property, and to full and equal benefit of all laws and proceedings for the security of persons and property, as is enjoyed by white citizens."[51] Put differently, state and local governments were required to respect the fundamental rights of all Americans, particularly economic rights, or else be held accountable by federal authorities, including the federal judiciary.

To its opponents the bill looked to be an unprecedented and unacceptable attack on states' rights. President Johnson said as much in his veto message to Congress, where he denounced the Civil Rights Act as a "stride towards centralization."[52] Democratic Senator Willard Saulsbury of Delaware concurred and raised an even more specific objection. The law would give blacks "every security for the protection of person and property which a white man has," he complained, including the right of armed self-defense. "In my state for many years," Saulsbury went on, "there has existed a law of the state based upon and founded in its police power, which declared that free negroes shall not have possession of firearms or ammunition. This bill proposes to take away from the states this police power."[53]

Indeed it did. The whole point of the Civil Rights Act was to protect the freedmen (and their white Unionist allies) from mistreatment via the Black Codes and similar provisions, a category of legislation that plainly included the gun control measure so cherished by Senator Saulsbury. The chief question was whether Congress actually possessed the legitimate authority to enforce it. In other words, did the opponents of the Civil Rights Act have a point about its constitutionality?

When the Constitution was first modified in 1791 to include the batch of amendments known to us today as the Bill of Rights, the various protections spelled out in the first eight of those amendments, such as freedom of speech and the keeping and bearing of arms, were understood to apply solely against the federal government, not against the states. The language of the First Amendment was quite explicit on this point. "Congress shall make no law," it begins, thereby leaving state legislatures free to censor the press or establish their own religions, as some did, including several slaveholding states that made it illegal to possess abolitionist literature. Other states basically duplicated various phrases from the Bill of Rights in their own state constitutions. The point is that it was up to the states themselves to make that determination, without federal oversight. The Supreme Court reinforced that original understanding in the 1833 case of *Barron v. Baltimore*, where Chief Justice John Marshall held that the Bill of Rights "must be understood as restraining the power of the General Government, not as applicable to the States."[54] On top of that, it was widely understood that each state possessed significant regulatory authority of its own, known as the police powers, to protect the health, welfare, and safety of all persons within its borders. Leaving such extensive power solely in the hands of the states was part of the original system of American federalism.

So it was by no means a legal certainty in 1866 that Congress possessed the lawful power to protect civil rights from infringement by state and local officials. Congressional Republicans divided unevenly over the question, with most believing they did enjoy the power to enforce the Civil Rights Act (particularly given the outcome of the late war), while a few prominent skeptics argued otherwise. Foremost among the skeptics was Ohio Representative John Bingham, a skilled lawyer and member of the congressional Joint Committee on Reconstruction. His qualms led him to draft Section One of the Fourteenth Amendment. Among other reasons, Bingham knew that the proposed amendment would guarantee the constitutionality of the 1866 Civil Rights Act.

THE MEANING OF THE FOURTEENTH AMENDMENT

"When John Bingham arrived in Congress," observed one legal scholar, "he brought with him the idealistic goals of northern Ohio Republicans and their abolitionist, Liberty Party, and Free Soil predecessors, who had been fighting for racial equality for the previous three decades."[55] The Fourteenth Amendment was the fruit of that long fight. "No State," it declares, in language written by Bingham, "shall make or enforce any law which shall abridge the privileges or immunities of citizens of the United States; nor shall any State deprive any person of life, liberty, or property, without due process of law; nor deny to any person within its jurisdiction the equal protection of the laws." As Bingham would tell the House of Representatives in his final speech in support of the amendment in May 1866, its purpose was to provide a check against the "many instances of State injustice and oppression," referring to the Black Codes and similar restrictions, and "to protect by natural law the privileges or immunities of all the citizens of the Republic and the inborn rights of every person within its jurisdiction whenever the same shall be abridged or denied by the unconstitutional acts of any State."[56]

To understand the meaning of what Bingham wrote in the Fourteenth Amendment—indeed, to understand the meaning of any constitutional provision—it's necessary to look at both the text in question and the history surrounding it. As we've seen, the historical events that produced the Fourteenth Amendment include the rise of the antislavery movement, the free labor principles that movement espoused, the outrages perpetrated after the Civil War under the Black Codes and other discriminatory state laws, and the desire of antislavery Republicans such as Bingham to correct those postwar injustices while simultaneously enshrining the free labor philosophy as the supreme law of the land.

That's the history. What about the text? In addition to granting U.S. citizenship to all persons born on American soil (with a few exceptions), the Fourteenth Amendment contains three principal clauses designed to protect individual rights: the Privileges or Immunities Clause, the Due Process Clause, and the Equal Protection Clause. Of those three, it was the first one, the Privileges or Immunities Clause, that was supposed to do the lion's share of the work. But a question immediately arises: What are the privileges and immunities of a U.S. citizen?

The short answer is that they are the same sort of individual rights that have long been associated with the Declaration of Independence, the Constitution, and the natural rights philosophy that shaped both documents. According to the legal scholar Michael Kent Curtis, author of the leading Fourteenth Amendment history, *No State Shall Abridge,* the text of the amendment must be understood "in light of the anti-slavery crusade that produced it."[57] For Congressman Bingham and his Republican allies, the paramount goal was securing civil rights for all Americans, regardless of color, against abusive state governments, while at the same time returning the Constitution to its original purpose as "a document protecting liberty."[58]

To that end, Bingham relied on language widely associated with the natural rights tradition of American constitutionalism. As Curtis documented in his study, "the words *rights, liberties, privileges,* and *immunities* seem to have been used interchangeably"[59] in political and legal writing throughout America and Britain in the eighteenth and nineteenth centuries. James Madison and other founders, for example, frequently treated the words as synonymous. In his 1789 speech proposing the addition of the Bill of Rights to the Constitution, Madison referred to "freedom of speech" and "rights of conscience" as the "choicest privileges of the people."[60] The famed English jurist William Blackstone endorsed a similar reading in his influential 1765 *Commentaries on the Laws of England,* where he referred to "privileges and immunities" as a mix of liberties and rights. As Curtis explained, Blackstone "had divided the rights and liberties of Englishmen into those 'immunities' that were the residuum of natural liberties and those 'privileges' that society had provided in lieu of natural rights."[61] In other words, immunities are natural rights while privileges are civil rights.

What then are the rights and liberties (privileges and immunities) of a U.S. citizen? As a guidepost, Bingham and other framers of the Fourteenth Amendment pointed to Supreme Court Justice Bushrod Washington's influential 1823 Circuit Court opinion in *Corfield v. Coryell,* in which he remarked that "it would perhaps be more tedious than difficult to enumerate"[62] the full extent of the privileges and immunities secured by Article Four, Section One of the Constitution, which reads, "The Citizens of each State shall be entitled to all Privileges and Immunities of Citizens in the several states." Nonetheless, Justice Washington went ahead and specified a few, including, "Protection by the government; the enjoyment of life and liberty, with the right to acquire and possess property of every kind, and to pursue and obtain happiness and safety." In short, things that "are, in their nature,

fundamental; which belong, of right, to the citizens of all free governments."[63] Justice Stephen Field later drew on that same language in
his 1873 *Slaughter-House* dissent, in which he too spoke of the rights
belonging "to the citizens of all free governments."[64]

At a minimum, then, the privileges and immunities of citizens
were understood by Bingham and his colleagues to include the rights
to own property, to make contracts, to testify in court, to bring lawsuits, and to enjoy personal security, all of which are found in both
Corfield and in the Civil Rights Act of 1866. But that was not the
end of it. According to Republican Senator Jacob Howard of Michigan, who introduced the Fourteenth Amendment in the Senate and
spearheaded its passage through that chamber, while the full extent
of the privileges and immunities of citizenship "cannot be fully defined in their entire extent and precise nature" (thus paraphrasing
Corfield), they certainly include "the personal rights guarantied and
secured by the first eight amendments of the Constitution," including the right to freedom of speech, the right to keep and bear arms,
and the right to be free from unreasonable search and seizure. As
Howard told the Senate in a widely reprinted speech, "the great object of the first section of this amendment is . . . to restrain the power
of the States and compel them at all times to respect these great
fundamental guarantees."[65]

Similar arguments were made as state lawmakers gathered to vote
on the Fourteenth Amendment's ratification. In Pennsylvania, for example, one Republican welcomed the proposed amendment as a victory for those who favored securing "civil rights to every individual
born in the land" over those "opposed to giving this security to civil
liberty and civil right."[66] Opponents of ratification often expressed
that same understanding of the amendment's meaning—indeed, that
was the whole reason they opposed it. According to one critic in New
Hampshire's ratification convention, the Fourteenth Amendment

represented "a dangerous infringement upon the rights and independence of the states."[67]

To summarize, the text of the Fourteenth Amendment, the historical context that shaped it, and the statements of support made by those who drafted it, voted for it, and ratified it, all point in the same direction: It was designed to make state and local governments respect a broad range of fundamental individual rights, including both those rights spelled out in the Bill of Rights and those economic liberties essential to safeguarding the principles of free labor.

Which brings us back to *The Slaughter-House Cases* of 1873, where the Supreme Court rejected this textual and historical evidence on every count. What happened?

"A VAIN AND IDLE ENACTMENT"

Slaughter-House presented the Supreme Court with two related questions. First, what's the proper scope of state regulatory power? And second, what's the meaning of the Fourteenth Amendment? In his decision for the majority, Justice Samuel F. Miller answered both questions after first adopting a posture of judicial restraint. The state of Louisiana enjoys broad regulatory powers, he argued, and the federal courts have no business getting in the way. To hold that the Privileges or Immunities Clause somehow now prevented Louisiana from granting a private corporation the exclusive contract to run a big city slaughterhouse "radically changes the whole theory of the relations of the State and Federal governments to each other and of both these governments to the people," a result Miller could not and would not abide. It would make the Supreme Court "a perpetual censor upon all legislation of the States."[68] Instead, Miller argued, the Privileges or Immunities Clause protected only a very narrow (and for the most part inconsequential) set of federal rights, such as the right to access federal waterways and the right to visit the seat of the federal government. The independent slaughterhouse operators of New Orleans were out of business and out of luck.

Justice Stephen Field challenged Miller on every point. In a long dissent joined by three other members of the Court, including Chief Justice Salmon P. Chase, a veteran antislavery lawyer and former treasury secretary under President Lincoln, Field made the case for the Supreme Court as a chief guardian of individual liberty under the Fourteenth Amendment. There is no doubt, Field began, that the state of Louisiana possesses a legitimate police power that "extends to all regulations affecting the health, good order, morals, peace, and safety of society." But the slaughterhouse law in question did not fit that bill. As Field saw it, the Louisiana statute contained "only two provisions which can properly be called police regulations." One required that all slaughtering be performed downstream from the city, so as not to pollute the water supply; the other required that all animals be inspected before slaughter. Those two regulations passed muster. The rest of the law, however, "is a mere grant" of special privilege to a private corporation "by which the health of the city is in no way promoted."[69]

Field then took aim at Miller's ahistorical reading of the Fourteenth Amendment. Citing a range of evidence, including the controversy over the Black Codes, the congressional debates over the Civil Rights Act and the Fourteenth Amendment, and Justice Washington's influential opinion in *Corfield v. Coryell*, Field maintained that the Privileges or Immunities Clause did in fact place substantive limits on state power, such as requiring lawmakers to respect the civil rights of all Americans. "Clearly among these," he wrote, "must be placed the right to pursue a lawful employment in a lawful manner, without other restraint than such as equally affects all persons."[70] Yet, thanks to Miller's cramped reading, Field observed, the Fourteenth Amendment had been reduced to "a vain and idle enactment, which accomplished nothing and most unnecessarily excited Congress and the people upon its passage,"[71] an outcome Field found ludicrous in light of the evidence plainly before him.

It was a strong dissent, firmly rooted in the text and history of the Fourteenth Amendment—but it was still a dissent. Louisiana and its corporate partners won the case. The Supreme Court had declared the Privileges or Immunities Clause to be dead on arrival.

FROM *SLAUGHTER-HOUSE* TO LIBERTY OF CONTRACT

Although it failed to command a majority in *The Slaughter-House Cases*, Field's dissent would lay the foundation for future victories. Over the following three decades, Field sharpened and expanded his *Slaughter-House* arguments in a series of influential opinions, mostly filed in dissent, but with some carrying the force of law. In them, he advanced three interlocking ideas: First, that the Fourteenth Amendment protects economic liberty, including the free labor right "to pursue a lawful employment in a lawful matter," soon to be shorthanded to "liberty of contract"; second, that government regulations are only permissible if they represent a legitimate and verifiable effort to protect the health, welfare, or safety of the public; and third, that it is both necessary and proper for the courts to police government actions in order to distinguish between legitimate regulations and illegitimate infringements on liberty. By the time Field retired in 1897 at the age of eighty-one, a majority of the Supreme Court was beginning to follow his approach.

The writing was on the wall as early as 1885. That year the New York Court of Appeals—the state's highest court—employed language that might have been ghostwritten by Field himself in order to strike down a state law banning the manufacture of margarine, or oleomargarine as the food product was then known. "No proposition is more firmly settled," that court held, "than that it is one of the fundamental rights and privileges of every American citizen to adopt and follow such lawful industrial pursuit, not injurious to the community, as he may see fit."[72] One year later, in the case of *In re Tie Loy*, a federal circuit court in California bypassed the *Slaughter-House* majority entirely and instead relied in part on Field's dissent to overturn an economic regulation for violating the Fourteenth Amendment right to labor in an "honest, necessary, and in itself harmless calling," a right the federal court described as "one of the highest privileges and immunities secured by the Constitution to every American citizen, and to every person residing within its protection."[73]

At the Supreme Court, meanwhile, Field was busy reading the precepts of free labor into the Fourteenth Amendment's guarantee that no person be deprived of life, liberty, or property, without due process of law, effectively keeping the original purpose of the Privileges or Immunities Clause alive through its neighbor, the Due Process Clause. In time, that approach would come to be known as substantive due process, referring to the idea that the Due Process Clause guarantees more than just fair procedure and in fact protects various substantive rights as well. And surprisingly enough, a state law targeting margarine would once again figure prominently in the evolution of this constitutional doctrine into a handy tool used by the courts to invalidate state and federal laws.

"A HEALTHY AND NUTRITIOUS ARTICLE OF FOOD"

If the idea of waging a major Supreme Court battle over the fate of a popular food product like margarine sounds funny now, it was no joke in the late nineteenth century. Margarine was invented in 1869 by a French chemist named Hippolyte Mège-Mouriès, whose own spark of innovation came courtesy of French Emperor Napoleon III, the sponsor of a major contest seeking an affordable alternative to butter, which Mouriès entered and won. In the words of one food writer, Mouriès "produced a substance very like butter, although his primitive product lacked flavour and colour." Nonetheless, it "was an immediate commercial success despite the disdain of those who regarded it as a cheaper and inferior substitute."[74] Among the loudest voices raised in disdain were those of American dairy farmers. They feared the competition and, in the words of historian Paul Moreno, "clamored for the suppression of the new rival."[75] The dairy industry's clamorous lobbying paid off in the states of New York and Pennsylvania, where margarine bans soon went into effect.

The Supreme Court entered the mix in 1888 when it heard oral argument over the constitutionality of the Pennsylvania ban in the case of *Powell v. Pennsylvania*. According to state officials, prohibiting the manufacture and sale of margarine was necessary "for the protection of the public health, and to prevent adulteration of dairy products,"[76] though of course the unstated true purpose of the law was to protect dairy farmers from unwelcome economic competition. Nonetheless, thanks to the principle of judicial deference, Justice John Marshall Harlan said he had no choice but to take those officials at their word. "Every possible presumption is in favor of the validity of a statute,"[77] he declared. For those persons hoping to manufacture, sell, or consume "wholesome oleomargarine as an article of food," Harlan's opinion contained a distasteful message: "Their appeal must be to the legislature, or to the ballot-box, not to the judiciary."[78]

Field just shook his head in disbelief. The purpose of the government's regulatory power, he responded in dissent, was to protect "the health of the people,"[79] not to use flimsy pretexts in order to prevent the manufacture or sale "of a healthy and nutritious article of food."[80] The courts must "examine into the real character of the act," he argued, not simply "accept the declaration of the legislature as conclusive."[81] Having performed such basic scrutiny on the regulation before him, Field was left with no choice but to nullify the bogus law. "It de-rives no validity by calling itself a police or health law," he announced. "It is nothing less than an unwarranted interference with the rights and liberties of the citizen."[82] The government should congratulate the makers of a healthy and affordable new food product, he observed, not hound them out of business with baseless regulations.

EXPANDING LIBERTY'S REACH

In the eyes of many critics, Justice Field's real agenda had nothing to do with individual liberty and everything to do with aiding and abet-ting the forces of industrial capitalism. The influential political scientist Robert Green McCloskey, for instance, once described Field as a heart-less reactionary who put property before people while on the Supreme Court. Field's commitment to "the legal and theoretical fictions of 'laissez faire,'"[83] McCloskey argued, made it "more and more difficult" for him "to recognize that human rights have any real standing in the scale of social values."[84]

To be sure, Field was no angel. In the 1873 case of *Bradwell v. Illinois*, for instance, he joined the majority in upholding that state's power to prevent women from practicing law, effectively forbidding a brilliant woman named Myra Bradwell from exercising her free labor right to earn a living as a licensed attorney. Field did not always prac-tice the libertarian philosophy he liked to preach.

Nor did Field shy away from casting his vote in favor of the rich and powerful. Take the 1877 case of *Munn v. Illinois*. At issue was one of the so-called Granger Laws, a series of regulations passed through-out the Midwestern states at the urging of organized farm labor groups such as the Grange. In *Munn*, the state legislature had set maximum storage rates for fourteen massive privately owned grain elevators lo-cated at the port of Chicago. According to local farmers, the law was necessary in order to level the playing field and save them from ruinous price gouging.

Writing for the majority, Chief Justice Morrison Waite agreed with that assessment and upheld the price-fixing scheme as a legitimate exercise of the state's police powers. When private property is "affected with a public interest,"[85] it becomes open to greater government intervention, Waite argued. The grain elevators "stand . . . in the very gateway of commerce and take toll from all who pass"; they "exercise a sort of public office,"[86] a de facto monopoly. Besides, Waite said, striking a pose of judicial deference, even if there was something funny about the regulation, "for protection against abuses by the legislature, people must resort to the polls, not the courts."[87]

Writing in dissent, Field accused the majority of turning a blind eye to government overreach. The right to property under the Due Process Clause must refer to more than just "title and possession,"[88] he said. It necessarily includes the right to use and dispose of one's property, to set rates of compensation, and to profit. Yet under what he saw as the Court's perverse rationale in *Munn,* Field charged, "whenever one devotes his property to a business which is useful to the public," that usefulness carried the risk of forfeiting constitutional protection and leaving the property subject to previously unacceptable forms of state control. "If this be sound law . . . all property and all business in the State are held at the mercy of a majority of its legislature."[89] As for the grain elevators, they are "not nuisances," their operation "of receiving and storing grain infringes upon no rights of others, disturbs no neighborhoods, infects not the air, and in no respects prevents others from using and enjoying their property."[90] Because the regulation served no legitimate public purpose, he concluded, it should have been struck from the books.

To say the least, Field's dissent in *Munn* showed little sympathy for the farmers who felt themselves getting squeezed by high prices at the port of Chicago. But that's not to say his economic opinions always came down on the side of the big guy. In *Slaughter-House*, for instance, Field sided with small-scale butchers against a state-backed corporation wielding monopoly powers. In *Powell*, he opposed the dairy industry's successful effort to prevent upstart competitors from entering the marketplace and selling a harmless food product. But perhaps nothing better illustrates how Field's jurisprudence could serve to expand liberty's reach than a pair of cases arising out of California's notoriously xenophobic crackdown on Chinese immigrants in the latter half of the nineteenth century.

Among his responsibilities as a Supreme Court justice, Field was required to "ride circuit," meaning he spent a certain part of the year hearing cases as a federal appellate court judge. His circuit covered his adopted home state of California. In that capacity, Field encountered the case of *Ah Kow v. Nunan*. At issue was a San Francisco ordinance of 1876 requiring all male prisoners in the county jail to have their hair "cut or clipped to an uniform length of one inch from the scalp." Ostensibly a public health measure, the law's true purpose was to humiliate and harass those male Chinese immigrants who wore their hair in long braided ponytails, also known as "queues." Indeed, throughout the Bay Area, the law was commonly referred to as the "queue ordinance."

Employing the same scrutiny he later applied to Pennsylvania's margarine ban, Field cut to the heart of the matter. The notion of a "hostile and spiteful"[91] law such as the queue ordinance serving any sort of legitimate regulatory function "is notoriously a mere pretense," he declared. The law's only purpose was to punish the Chinese, and everybody knew it. "When we take our seats on the bench we are not struck with blindness," he observed, "and forbidden to know what we see as men."[92] He nullified the law.

Three years later, Field brought the same scrutiny to yet another San Francisco law rooted in anti-Chinese animus. Under the terms of a municipal ordinance of 1882, anyone seeking to operate a laundry business within city limits had to first obtain "the consent of the board of supervisors, which shall only be granted upon the recommendation of not less than 12 citizens and taxpayers in the block in which the laundry is proposed to be established, maintained, or carried on."[93] In this case, the law's true targets were those entrepreneurial Chinese immigrants who had established themselves in the laundry business. Writing once again for a majority of the Circuit Court, Field voided the law.

He began with the "miserable pretense" offered by the city as justification for its exercise of the police power. Government-issued licenses may certainly be required "where the nature of the business demands special knowledge or qualifications," Field held, but they may not be required "as a means of prohibiting any of the avocations of life which are not injurious to public morals, nor offensive to the senses, nor dangerous to the public health and safety,"[94] such as the non-dangerous and non-offensive business of washing, ironing, and pressing clothes.

Furthermore, he argued, the city's requirement that a business owner receive permission from his neighbors serves no conceivable public health purpose; it simply subjects one person's ability to exercise a basic economic freedom to "the favor or caprice of others."[95] Indeed, Field noted, the petitioner in the case was more than happy to pay any necessary fees required by the city, yet on account of the "great antipathy and hatred toward the people of his race,"[96] he found it impossible to find twelve neighbors willing to endorse his business. The Fourteenth Amendment was designed to outlaw that very sort of discriminatory economic regulation, Field maintained, and he put the amendment to precisely that use by striking down the law

A LIBERTARIAN LEGACY

Justice Stephen Field sat on the Supreme Court for thirty-three years, a busy stretch of history that ran from the height of the Civil War to the pre-dawn of the twentieth century. And while he often voted in dissent, that heterodox position did not stop him from leaving his mark on the law. Several months before his retirement in 1897, a unanimous Supreme Court adopted the core premise of his 1873 *Slaughter-House* dissent, holding that a Louisiana statute forbidding state residents from buying insurance through the mail from an out-of-state company violated the Fourteenth Amendment right to liberty of contract. "In the privilege of pursuing an ordinary calling or trade, and of acquiring, holding, and selling property, must be embraced the right to make all proper contracts in relation thereto,"[97] declared the opinion of Justice Rufus Peckham in *Allgeyer v. Louisiana.*

For once, Justice Field sided quietly with the majority. Unfortunately for him, the hard-fought victory would not last long.

TWO

THE DEVIL
AND OLIVER
WENDELL HOLMES

ON SEPTEMBER 17, 1862, TWO GREAT armies met in battle in and around the quiet town of Sharpsburg, Maryland. For Confederate General Robert E. Lee, who had marched his formidable Army of Northern Virginia into the Union-controlled border state just two weeks earlier, the goal was nothing short of total victory. Invading the North and menacing the enemy on its own soil, Lee wrote to Confederate President Jefferson Davis, would demolish northern morale, solidify the case for Southern independence, and "enable the people of the United States to determine at their coming elections whether they will support those who favor a prolongation of the war, or those who wish to bring it to a termination."[1] The stakes were equally high for Union Maj. General George B. McClellan, now forced to reorient his massive Army of the Potomac in order to meet the invading Southern host. "Destroy the rebel army if possible,"[2] instructed Abraham Lincoln.

The resulting clash of arms would prove to be the single bloodiest day of the entire Civil War. By the time the smoke cleared after
twelve hours of hard, brutal fighting, some 23,000 men were dead,
wounded, or missing. "The air was full of the hiss of bullets and the
hurtle of grapeshot,"[3] recalled one Union soldier who survived the
ordeal. At the center of the Confederate battle line, in a sunken farm
road now remembered as the Bloody Lane, Southern soldiers were
outflanked and massacred by the score. As the historian Shelby Foote
later described it, "Quite suddenly, as if they had tumbled headlong
by the hundreds out of the sky, dead men filled whole stretches of the
road to overflowing."[4]

It was a day of death and horror, with staggering casualties on both
sides of the Antietam Creek, the winding local waterway that gave
the battle its now-storied name. Among the thousands of wounded
men littering the ground that day, shot through the neck and left for
dead, was twenty-one-year-old Oliver Wendell Holmes Jr., captain of
the Twentieth Massachusetts Regiment and future associate justice of
the U.S. Supreme Court. "It don't seem to have smashed my spine,"
Holmes wrote home to his mother, "or I suppose I should be dead or
paralyzed or something."[5]

It was not the young officer's first brush with death. Two months
earlier, at the Battle of Ball's Bluff in northern Virginia, Holmes was
shot twice in the chest, causing his mouth to fill with blood. "The
first night I made up my mind to die & was going to take that little
bottle of laudanum as soon as I was sure of dying with any pain,"[6] he
reported home. He suffered a third and final wound one year later at
the Battle of Chancellorsville, also in Virginia, where he was shot in
the foot. "I've been chloroformed & had bone extracted," he informed
his mother, "probably shant lose foot."[7]

To read Holmes's wartime correspondence today is to receive a
guided tour through these and other depths of that terrible inferno.

"Swollen bodies already fly blown and decaying,"[8] he reported in one letter to his family, "Lowell is probably dead bowels cut,"[9] he noted in another. "It's odd how indifferent one gets to the sight of death," he told his mother in December 1862, "perhaps, because one gets aristocratic and don't value much a common life."[10]

The Civil War had a profound impact on the young man who would later become one of America's most famous and influential jurists, and it was not a pretty one. As it does for many young soldiers, the experience of combat obliterated Holmes's youthful idealism. "I am not the same man,"[11] he informed his parents in May 1864. But the disillusion went far deeper than that. As the historian Louis Menand memorably put it, "The war did more than make him lose those beliefs. It made him lose his belief in beliefs."[12] Gone forever was the young abolitionist who left Harvard two months before graduation in order to enlist on behalf of a grand cause. In his place was a man who scorned all mention of lofty principle. "I don't talk much of rights," Holmes would declare, "as I see no meaning in the rights of man except what the crowd will fight for."[13]

In a sense, the Civil War transformed Oliver Wendell Holmes into a democrat of the very purest sort. The majority must get its way, he came to believe, regardless of whether or not minorities got trampled in the process. "It is no sufficient condemnation of legislation that it favors one class at the expense of another," he argued in the *American Law Review*, for all laws are "necessarily . . . a means by which a body, having the power, put burdens which are disagreeable to them on the shoulders of somebody else."[14] He made the same majoritarian point with even greater force in a letter to Harvard professor and future Supreme Court Justice Felix Frankfurter. "A law should be called good if it reflects the will of the dominant forces of the community," Holmes maintained, "even if it will take us to hell."[15] The Civil War may not have taught Holmes that might makes right, but it did teach him that might was the one thing that truly mattered, both on and off the battlefield.

That stark worldview permeated his legal opinions, leading Holmes to embrace an extreme form of judicial restraint that required judges to bow down routinely to the wishes of lawmakers and elected officials. Sometimes that deference to government authority was oblique, as when Holmes led the Supreme Court in brushing away the First Amendment in order to uphold the 1918 conviction of left-wing activist Eugene Debs, arrested under the Espionage Act of 1917, a notorious piece of legislation that made it a federal offense to interfere with American involvement in World War I. What was Debs's crime? He gave an antiwar speech to a crowd of socialists out for an afternoon picnic. Such was Holmes's commitment to deference that he allowed so dubious a prosecution to stand.

Other times Holmes's submission to state power was unmistak-able. "We have seen more than once that the public welfare may call upon the best citizens for their lives," Holmes observed in 1927, allud-ing to his own Civil War experience. "It would be strange if it could not call upon those who already sap the strength of the State for these lesser sacrifices."[16]

So wrote Justice Holmes in the notorious case of *Buck v. Bell*, where the "lesser sacrifice" in question was the state of Virginia's desire to forcibly sterilize seventeen-year-old Carrie Buck, "a feeble minded white woman," as Holmes described her, "the daughter of a feeble minded mother . . . and the mother of an illegitimate feeble minded child."[17] Raped and impregnated by the nephew of her foster mother, Buck had been committed to a state institution for the "socially inad-equate" by her foster parents. After a cursory review of the alleged facts of the case, Holmes deferred to the questionable judgment of state officials on every count and ruled in favor of the eugenics law: "Three generations of imbeciles are enough."[18]

If Justice Stephen Field was the Supreme Court's first great champion of judicial action in the cause of limited government and individual rights, then Justice Oliver Wendell Holmes was his nemesis, the Court's first great advocate of judicial deference to lawmakers and to the will of the majority. Whereas Field urged the courts to "examine into the real character"[19] of the laws that came before them and to strike down those democratically enacted statutes that violated fundamental liberties or exceeded the reach of legitimate government powers, Holmes preached a very different sort of gospel, telling his fellow judges to respect "the right of a majority to embody their opinions in law,"[20] even when such an act of restraint would mean sending the whole country straight to the devil.

It's hard to imagine two judicial philosophies with a greater gulf between them. And although Field's retirement in 1897 prevented the two men from clashing face-to-face on the Supreme Court, their dueling approaches would still collide repeatedly throughout Holmes's long tenure on the bench, which lasted from 1902 until 1932. During those three decades, as Field's libertarian vision gradually started winning important cases, Holmes registered his objections in a series of increasingly disgruntled dissents. These great legal battles, waged over issues ranging from economic regulation to civil liberties to racial equality, would shape the course of American law in the twentieth century, with repercussions still felt today.

LIBERTY OF CONTRACT

The opening shots rang out in 1905 in the landmark case of *Lochner v. New York*. The *Lochner* story had begun ten years earlier with the passage of a sweeping reform bill by the New York State Legislature targeting sanitary and working conditions in the Empire State's baking industry. The Bakeshop Act, as the 1895 law came to be known, was a thoroughgoing

piece of work, covering everything from ventilation and drainage to the
terms under which state inspectors would give or withhold their stamps of
approval. In addition, the law also placed strict new limits on the relationship between employers and employees. Henceforth, no bakery workers
were permitted to work more than ten hours per day or sixty hours per
week, including overtime, unless those bakers happened to own the business or be related to the owner.

That last part was a tip-off that the maximum hours law was designed with something other than just health and safety concerns in
mind. After all, if the well-being of workers or consumers was really
at stake, why offer any sort of exemption from the saving regulation?
In his recent history of the case,[21] the legal scholar David Bernstein
pointed to a more plausible explanation. The origins of the ten-hour
law, Bernstein argued, are found in an economic conflict between
unionized New York bakers, who labored in large shops and lobbied
intensely for the working hours limit, and their non-unionized, mostly
immigrant competitors, who tended to work longer hours in smaller
old-fashioned bakeries. As the *Baker's Journal,* the weekly publication
of the bakers' union, put it in an editorial, "cheap labor . . . from
foreign shores"[22] threatened the livelihood of all card-carrying members. The imposition of a ten-hour day, therefore, "would not only
aid those unionized bakeries who had not successfully demanded that
their hours be reduced," Bernstein noted, "but would also drive out of
business many old-fashioned bakeries that depended on flexible labor
schedules."[23] For their part, state officials seemed to share the union's
hostility to immigrant workers. "It is almost impossible to secure or
keep in proper cleanly condition the Jewish and Italian bakeshops,"
one state inspector reported in 1898. "Cleanliness and tidiness are entirely foreign to these people."[24] Meanwhile, the state's large corporate bakeries, as Bernstein's research discovered, mostly sided with the
union and tacitly supported the Bakeshop Act. That counterintuitive

position makes sense when you consider that the new regulations helped to undermine their competition as well.

Among that competition was a German immigrant named Joseph Lochner, who operated a small family-run bakery in Utica, New York, with his wife and a handful of employees. As Lochner saw it, the maximum hours provision went too far and violated both his rights and the rights of his workers to settle on the basic terms of employment. With the backing of the New York Association of Master Bakers, a trade group comprised of small-scale proprietors, Lochner brought the legal challenge that eventually landed him before the U.S. Supreme Court and added his name to the annals of constitutional history.

Heading into the courtroom in 1905, his odds of success appeared mixed at best. Although the Supreme Court had said that the Fourteenth Amendment protected the right to make labor contracts free from unnecessary government interference in the 1897 case of *Allgeyer v. Louisiana,* where Justice Field's "right of free labor"[25] was enshrined as the right to liberty of contract, the Court had also recently upheld several reform-minded state laws, including a Tennessee requirement that coal miners be paid in cash, not in company script, and a Utah statute limiting mine workers to an eight-hour day. That second case, *Holden v. Hardy,* seemed particularly relevant to the *Lochner* dispute, and New York officials readily cited it as a legal precedent when urging the Supreme Court to uphold their own state's working-hours limit.

But a five-justice majority of the Supreme Court took a different view. The Bakeshop Act's ten-hour provision "is not, within any fair meaning of the term, a health law,"[26] declared Justice Rufus Peckham for the majority. It was an illegitimate interference with the right to liberty of contract under the Fourteenth Amendment, and therefore must be struck down. Following the same template as Field's *Slaughter-House* dissent, Peckham began with a discussion of the proper reach of government power. There is no question that the states possess the lawful authority "to prevent the individual from making certain kinds of contracts,"[27] he observed. As an example, Peckham pointed to the law sustained in *Holden*. In that case, the dangerous and extreme conditions present in an underground coal mine justified the state's placing certain limits on the hours of work. Similarly, Peckham continued, the Bakeshop Act's many provisions dealing directly with public health and workplace safety, such as "inspection of the premises," "furnishing proper washrooms and waterclosets," "providing proper drainage, plumbing, and painting," "height of the ceiling," and "cementing or tiling of floors,"[28] were all perfectly legitimate exercises of the state's police powers.

But Peckham drew the line at the ten-hour provision. "A law like the one before us involves neither the safety, the morals, nor the welfare, of the public," he argued. "Clean and wholesome bread does not depend upon whether the baker works but ten hours per day or only sixty hours a week."[29] Furthermore, unlike the mine workers in the *Holden* case, whose risky jobs justified additional state action, "the trade of a baker has never been regarded as an unhealthy one,"[30] meaning New York bakers already enjoyed sufficient protections thanks to the other regulations put in place by the Bakeshop Act. Given the facts of the case, Peckham concluded, the freedom of employer and employee "to contract with each other in relation to their employment, and in defining same, cannot be prohibited or interfered with, without violating the Federal Constitution."[31]

"THE NATURAL OUTCOME OF A DOMINANT OPINION"

Writing in dissent, Justice Oliver Wendell Holmes rejected every aspect of Peckham's ruling. Sixty-four years old at the time, and a twenty-year veteran of the Supreme Judicial Court of Massachusetts, where he had served a stint as chief justice, Holmes was by then a well-known advocate of judicial restraint. His *Lochner* dissent both solidified and enhanced that reputation. Just over 600 words long, the dissent is packed with memorable phrases and has been cited countless times by a seemingly endless parade of judges, lawyers, academics, and journalists seeking to buttress their own arguments in favor of a deferential Court. "This case is decided upon an economic theory which a large part of the country does not entertain," Holmes proclaimed at the outset. And that questionable theory—"the liberty of the citizen to do as he likes"—had no business replacing the majority's right "to embody their opinions in law." As Holmes quipped, "The Fourteenth Amendment does not enact Mr. Herbert Spencer's Social Statics."[32]

He was right about that, though not quite in the way he meant. Born in 1820, Herbert Spencer was a polymath English philosopher whose writings dealt with everything from politics to sociology to evolution. *Social Statics* (1851) was his second book and first big hit. In it, Spencer laid out what he called his "Law of Equal Freedom," which he considered to be the first principle necessary to establish a "correct system of equity." It held: "Every man has freedom to do all that he wills, provided he infringes not the equal freedom of any other man."[33] That sweeping credo would not be out of place in the most radical of free-market manifestos, and indeed, Spencer was regarded as the late nineteenth century's leading proponent of full-throated laissez-faire. That's why Holmes cast him as the villain in his *Lochner* dissent. He wanted to paint the majority as a bunch of wild-eyed libertarians hellbent on subverting democracy.

But as Peckham's majority opinion had made clear, judicial protection for the right to liberty of contract required nothing so revolutionary as Spencer's Law of Equal Freedom. Consider again the eight-hour law for miners upheld in *Holden* and reaffirmed in *Lochner* (even as the *Lochner* Court rejected the ten-hour law for bakers). There is no way to reconcile that outcome with the basic premise of *Social Statics*. What business is it of the state, Spencer might have asked (he died in 1903), if a miner wanted to risk his life by working longer hours for extra money? The public was placed in no danger by his actions, so why not let the worker put himself in harm's way for a bigger payday? The *Lochner* majority, on the other hand, described the law as a valid safety measure enacted on behalf of vulnerable employees. In short, the *Lochner* ruling did not enact Mr. Herbert Spencer's *Social Statics*.

But the Court's libertarian tendencies were not the only thing bothering Holmes about the outcome of the case. "I think that the word 'liberty,' in the Fourteenth Amendment, is perverted," he declared, "when it is held to prevent the natural outcome of a dominant opinion." Put differently, the people of New York had a broad power to pass whatever laws they deemed fit, and the Supreme Court had no license to nose around in their affairs. The Constitution, Holmes claimed, "is not intended to embody a particular economic theory, whether of paternalism and the organic relation of the citizen to the State or laissez-faire."[34] As he saw it, the *Lochner* majority had committed a grievous error not only by striking down a labor law, but by reading the Fourteenth Amendment as a tool for supervising state affairs in the first place. And as it happened, Holmes was not the only prominent public figure to think so.

PROGRESSIVE DEMOCRACY

Historians generally date the Progressive era as beginning sometime in the early 1890s and concluding sometime in the early 1920s. It takes its name from the assorted politicians, lawyers, and reformers who advocated, seized, and wielded a vast new array of regulatory powers in those days, and it is characterized by their broad view that government should become the primary engine of social change. To that end, the Progressives conceived or enacted many of the most transformative laws of the late nineteenth and early twentieth centuries, from antitrust statutes to the creation of the Federal Reserve banking system to the outlines of what we now consider to be the basic social safety net.

A quarrelsome and morally righteous bunch, the Progressives did not agree with each other on everything. Many of them favored the prohibition of alcohol, for example, seeing the demon rum as a monster unleashed to the detriment of American society; other Progressives, however, failed to see the harm in a working man taking a drink or two, especially after a long day toiling in a factory or walking the picket line. But they did agree on one thing: The *Lochner* decision, which arrived smack dab in the middle of Progressivism's heyday, felt like a slap to the collective face. And that's not just because *Lochner* struck down a regulation championed by organized labor. Like Holmes, the Progressives also hated *Lochner* because the ruling used the Fourteenth Amendment to thwart the will of a state legislature.

That last sentence might sound peculiar in the context of today's legal debates, in which liberalism is so closely associated with the use of the Fourteenth Amendment as a tool against state laws. Indeed, from desegregation to abortion, the Fourteenth Amendment has been inseparable from many of modern liberalism's biggest legal causes. But today's liberals are not carbon copies of their Progressive grandparents. Consider the modern campaign on behalf of gay marriage. When the Supreme Court heard arguments in 2013 over California's Proposition 8, a ballot initiative that had amended the state constitution in order to forbid same-sex unions, the lawyers challenging Prop 8 sought to use the Fourteenth Amendment's guarantee of equal protection to overrule the wishes of those voters and thereby legalize gay marriage— precisely the sort of Fourteenth Amendment jurisprudence Holmes spent his career arguing against. In the next chapter, we'll see how modern liberals learned to stop worrying and love judicial activism

(just as modern conservatives learned to stop worrying and love judicial restraint). But at this point in the story, the Progressives remain
firmly on the side of majority rule and extremely hostile to almost any
claim of individual liberty raised against state governments under the
Fourteenth Amendment.

Take Herbert Croly, the widely read journalist and author who in
1914 founded Progressivism's flagship magazine, *The New Republic*. In
his influential book *Progressive Democracy*, Croly maintained that the
meaning of both the Due Process and Equal Protection Clauses of the
Fourteenth Amendment was "ambiguous and elastic" at best. "These
rules had certainly never been framed for the purpose of curbing
legislative action,"[35] Croly flatly asserted. Yet thanks to a conspiracy
of judges, he went on, "the police power of the state legislatures was
emasculated; and the system of government by Law at the hands of a
judicial aristocracy was perfected."[36]

The celebrated Harvard law professor James Bradley Thayer, who
served as a mentor to Oliver Wendell Holmes, championed an equally
restrictive view of judicial power. According to Thayer, democratically
enacted statutes should only be struck down in those rare instances
"when those who have the right to make laws have not merely made
a mistake, but have made a very clear one,—so clear that it is not
open to rational question."[37] In practical terms, this approach virtually
eliminated the need for judicial review. But Thayer had no problem
with that result, since he saw little reason for judges to ever intrude
on the "wide margin of consideration" that must be accorded "to the
practical judgment of a legislative body."[38]

Felix Frankfurter, who went on to advise President Franklin Roosevelt during the New Deal and later joined the Supreme Court as a
Roosevelt appointee, not only agreed with Thayer, he took the position one step further, arguing in an unsigned *New Republic* editorial
that the Due Process Clause should be stripped from the Constitution

entirely. "We have had fifty years of experiment with the Fourteenth Amendment," Frankfurter wrote, and what that experiment proved to him was that "no nine men are wise enough and good enough" to enjoy such powers of judicial review. "The due process clauses ought to go."[39]

Even Louis Brandeis, the Progressive lawyer and Supreme Court justice best remembered today for his civil libertarianism and early championing of privacy and "the right to be let alone,"[40] favored granting broad deference to state lawmakers in most aspects of life. Brandeis even pointed to Holmes's infamous ruling in *Buck v. Bell,* which upheld the forced sterilization of a teenager, as a permissible example of a state government "meeting modern conditions by regulations."[41]

And then there is the most famous Progressive of them all: Theodore Roosevelt. It should come as perhaps no surprise to find the bombastic ex-president at the forefront of the roiling debate over the courts. Roosevelt began warming to the subject as early as 1908, when he criticized the Supreme Court for having a pro-corporate bias, and then again in 1910, when he denounced *Lochner* as an attack on "popular rights" in a speech before the Colorado legislature. "Such decisions, arbitrarily and irresponsibly limiting the power of the people," Roosevelt declared, "are of course fundamentally hostile to every species of real popular government."[42]

But the Rough Rider really hit his stride two years later with an essay titled "Judges and Progress" written for the Progressive magazine *The Outlook,* where he was listed prominently on the masthead as a contributing editor. Referring repeatedly to "the Bakeshop Case," Roosevelt argued that if such judicial shenanigans did not stop immediately, the people would be left with no choice but to strip the courts of their independence and subject judicial decisions (and judges) to recall by popular vote. "If a majority of the people, after due deliberation, decide to champion such social and economic reforms as those

we champion," Roosevelt wrote, "they have the right to see them enacted into law and become a part of our settled government policy."[43]
The people, he emphasized, "must ultimately control its own destinies,
and cannot surrender the right of ultimate control to a judge."[44]

In essence, the Progressives had declared war on the Fourteenth
Amendment. And their brazen assault did not go unnoticed. Among
the sharpest critics of their approach was the journalist H. L. Mencken,
who took aim at Progressive legal thinking while reviewing a book-
length collection of Justice Holmes's dissenting opinions. "Over and
over again, in these opinions," Mencken observed, Holmes "advocated
giving the legislature full head-room, and over and over again he pro-
tested against using the Fourteenth Amendment to upset novel and
oppressive laws, aimed frankly at helpless minorities."[45] That's not responsible judging, Mencken argued, it's a gross dereliction of basic
judicial duty. "If this is Liberalism," he declared, "then all I can say is
that Liberalism is not what it was when I was young."[46]

In truth, it's no secret why the Progressives adopted Justice Holmes
as their legal standard-bearer. His belief in virtually unchecked majority rule lined up perfectly with their own plans to bring industrial
society under government supervision and control. But as Mencken
observed, that approach did leave something to be desired when it
came to the plight of unpopular groups. What happened when the
majority was willing to steamroll over minority rights and the courts
were not willing to stop it?

IN RESTRAINT OF LIBERTY

When President Woodrow Wilson led the United States to war against
Germany in 1917, he did so in the name of making the world safe for
democracy. But the former head of Princeton University was also worried
about certain dangers lurking much closer to home. "There are citizens

of the United States, I blush to admit," Wilson announced, "who have poured the poison of disloyalty into the very arteries of our national life. . . . [T]he hand of our power should close over them at once."[47]

The hand of power moved swiftly. On the national level, Congress responded to Wilson's fears by passing the Espionage and Sedition Acts, vaguely worded federal laws that effectively criminalized most forms of antiwar speech and activism. Indeed, it was the Espionage Act that landed the socialist leader Eugene Debs in federal prison for the harmless "crime" of giving a speech. But the crackdown on the radical left was just one part of Wilson's push for homeland security, as German-born Americans and their families quickly discovered.

"Before 1914," the historian David M. Kennedy has written, "the Germans had been probably the most esteemed immigrant group in America, regarded as easily assimilable, upright citizens. Now they found themselves the victims of a brainless fury that knew few restraints."[48] In retrospect, some of that wartime fury now appears comical, such as when self-professed American patriots rejected the use of German-derived words and began referring to their hamburgers as "liberty sandwiches," or when the city of Pittsburgh banned the music of Beethoven on account of the composer's German heritage. But it was no laughing matter in April 1918 when a mob near St. Louis snatched up a young man of German descent named Robert Prager, stripped him, wrapped him in an American flag, and murdered him before a crowd of several hundred onlookers. "In spite of excesses such as lynching," observed the *Washington Post*, in a report filed after several of the mob's alleged ringleaders were acquitted of Prager's killing, "it is a healthful and wholesome awakening in the interior of the country."[49]

"Witch hunt" would be a more accurate term for it. Across the nation, Americans of German descent suffered a catalogue of abuses, ranging from loyalty oaths administered at government jobs to discriminatory treatment by state officials to violent attacks by vigilantes. In Nebraska, the state legislature got in on the act with a law banning both public and private school teachers from instructing young children in a foreign language. Although it did not say so explicitly, the statute's primary target was the state's system of Lutheran parochial schools, where both teachers and students commonly spoke German. One such instructor, Robert Meyer, who taught the Bible in German at a school run by the Zion Evangelical Lutheran Congregation, challenged the statute for violating his rights. He started out in state court, but the Nebraska Supreme Court soon ruled against him. "The salutary purpose of the statute is clear," that Court held. "The legislature had seen the baneful effects of permitting foreigners, who had taken residence in this country, to rear and educate their children in the language of their native land."[50] Meyer then appealed his loss to the U.S. Supreme Court, where, in a notable rejection of democracy, he won.

The Due Process Clause of the Fourteenth Amendment, declared the opinion of Justice James C. McReynolds, clearly secured Meyer's right to earn a living by teaching the Bible in his native tongue, no matter what a majority of his neighbors happened to think about it. By the same token, it also covered the right of parents to educate their children in a foreign language. The Fourteenth Amendment's protection of liberty "denotes not merely freedom from bodily restraint," McReynolds explained, "but also the right of the individual to contract, to engage in any of the common occupations of life, to acquire useful knowledge, to marry, establish a home and bring up children, to worship God according to the dictates of his own conscience, and generally to enjoy those privileges long recognized at common law as essential to the orderly pursuit of happiness by free men."[51]

Today, *Meyer v. Nebraska* is largely remembered as an early victory for civil liberty against mob rule, which it surely was. Yet it was also a victory for economic liberty against overreaching regulation. Notice the shades of both *Corfield v. Coryell* (the Circuit Court case cited by the Fourteenth Amendment's authors) and Stephen Field's *Slaughter-House* dissent in McReynolds's sweeping invocation of liberty. What's more, McReynolds's unabashedly libertarian ruling cited the precedent set in *Lochner v. New York*. In *Meyer*, civil and economic liberty did not just rest side-by-side, they were deeply entwined in every aspect of the case.

So of course Justice Holmes cast a dissenting vote. In his view, the anti-German majority ought to have its way. "I am unable to say the Constitution of the United States prevents the experiment being tried,"[52] Holmes explained in a companion case, *Bartels v. Iowa*, which dealt with a similar state ban on foreign-language teaching. As Holmes saw it, the Fourteenth Amendment offered no impediment to a state legislature's ability to "experiment" with limiting the language of its young citizens. Among the leading Progressives who sided with Holmes was Felix Frankfurter, who said he would rather see the language ban remain in force instead of "lodging that power in those nine gents at Washington."[53]

Holmes's dissent in *Meyer* was an ugly lesson in how judicial restraint could allow state-sanctioned discrimination to thrive. But no case from that era illustrates this lesson better than *Buchanan v. Warley*, in which the Supreme Court was confronted with a popularly enacted Jim Crow law segregating residential housing blocks by race. Before we turn to the facts of that landmark case, however, let's take the opportunity to meet one of the main figures responsible for bringing it about: Moorfield Storey, the libertarian lawyer who argued and won *Buchanan* before the Supreme Court in his capacity as the first president of the National Association for the Advancement of Colored People (NAACP). If today's libertarian legal movement had a patron saint, Moorfield Storey would be it.

THE LIBERTARIAN LAWYER

Born in Roxbury, Massachusetts, in 1845, Moorfield Storey presents a direct link in time between the free labor philosophy of the nineteenth century and the libertarian constitutionalism that emerged in the twentieth. A fierce critic of imperialism, militarism, and executive power,[54] Storey was a founder and president of the Anti-Imperialist League, which opposed U.S. annexation of the Philippines after the Spanish-American War of 1898 and counted Mark Twain, Andrew Carnegie, and President Grover Cleveland among its members. An advocate of free trade, liberty of contract, and the gold standard, Storey also helped organize the independent National Democratic Party, also known as the Gold Democrats, who fought the anti-gold populist William Jennings Bryan's Democratic presidential bid in 1896.[55] An individualist and anti-racist, Storey led the NAACP to its first major Supreme Court victory in *Buchanan v. Warley*.

But before all of that, Storey got his initial start in public life back in 1868 when he served as the personal secretary to Senator Charles Sumner, the legendary Massachusetts abolitionist whose fiery attacks on the peculiar institution inspired one of the most notorious events in congressional history. In 1856, a pro-slavery Congressman named Preston Brooks beat Sumner senseless on the floor of the Senate over Sumner's insulting characterizations of the slaveholding South. Severely injured by the attack, Sumner would spend three years recuperating before he was finally able to return to Congress. Storey, who later wrote an incisive biography[56] of Sumner's life and career, would remain under the influence of his old boss's abolitionist principles for the rest of his life.[57]

Storey put those principles to good use when the case of *Buchanan v. Warley* reached the Supreme Court in 1917. At issue was a Louisville, Kentucky, ordinance segregating residential housing blocks by race. Enacted "to prevent conflict and ill-feeling between the white

and colored races,"[58] the law made it illegal for blacks to live on ma-
jority-white blocks and for whites to live on majority-black blocks. To
test the law, William Warley, the head of the Louisville chapter of the
NAACP, arranged to buy property on a white block from a white real
estate agent named Charles H. Buchanan, also an opponent of the law.
When Warley "learned" that he could not live on the property he was
purchasing, he refused to complete payment. Buchanan then sued,
but the Kentucky courts ruled against him, upholding the ordinance.
NAACP president Storey, joined by Louisville attorney Clayton B.
Blakely, took the case to the Supreme Court.

In their brief, Storey and Blakely denounced residential segregation as a racist interference with economic liberty. The Louisville law
"prevents the plaintiff from selling his property for the only use to
which it can be put," they wrote. "It thus destroys, without due process
of law, fundamental rights attached by law to ownership of property."
Furthermore, the law's true purpose was not "to prevent conflict and
ill-feeling," as it claimed, but rather "to place the negro, however in-
dustrious, thrifty and well-educated, in as inferior a position as possible with respect to his right of residence, and to violate the spirit of
the Fourteenth Amendment without transgressing the letter."[59] Were
such a restriction upheld, they argued, "an attempt to segregate Irish
from Jews, foreign from native citizens, Catholics from Protestants,
would be fully as justifiable."[60] Among the legal authorities cited by
the brief is none other than the *Lochner* case, then the Court's most
famous decision protecting economic liberty from state legislation.

In its *Buchanan* brief, the state of Kentucky took a dimmer view
of property rights and economic liberty. Advocating judicial restraint,
the state argued that the Court should defer to local judgment and stay
out of the matter entirely. "Whether the legislation is wise, expedient,
or necessary, or the best calculated to promote its object," the brief
argued, "is a legislative and not a judicial question."[61] Furthermore,

"the injury [to property rights] is merely incidental to the city's right to segregate, and does not warrant the overthrow of police regulations." As for Storey and Blakely's contention that the law forced blacks to inhabit the city's worst neighborhoods, "the improvement of the negro's condition is limited only by his own character and efforts."[62]

The Supreme Court disagreed. "Property is more than the mere thing which a person owns," Justice William Day held for the unanimous body. "It is elementary that it includes the right to acquire, use, and dispose of it."[63] Accepting Storey's argument that the ordinance was racist in intent, Justice Day held that the Fourteenth Amendment "operate[s] to qualify and entitle a colored man to acquire property without state legislation discriminating against him solely because of color."[64]

Storey was justifiably thrilled at the victory. "I cannot help thinking it is the most important decision that has been made since the *Dred Scott* case," he wrote to NAACP disbursing treasurer and fellow Gold Democrat Oswald Garrison Villard (the grandson of abolitionist William Lloyd Garrison), "and happily this time it is the right way."[65] W. E. B. Du Bois, editor of the NAACP newsletter, *The Crisis,* heartily agreed, crediting *Buchanan* with "the breaking of the backbone of segregation."[66] In fact, as one legal scholar has argued, "though it was not used to its full potential, *Buchanan* almost certainly prevented governments from passing far harsher segregation laws [and] prevented residential segregation laws from being the leading edge of broader anti-negro measures."[67]

It was a major triumph for individual rights under the Fourteenth Amendment and also the first significant victory for the young NAACP, which went on to become the most influential civil rights organization in the country. And once again, Justice Oliver Wendell Holmes wrote a dissenting opinion, except this time he decided not to file it and instead voted silently with the majority (for reasons that remain unknown). In the draft of that dissent, however, Holmes took his usual majoritarian position. He began by suggesting that the Supreme Court should dismiss the suit unless the NAACP provided "some evidence that this is not a manufactured case." Turning next to the constitutional merits, he maintained that Kentucky had every authority to regulate property in this manner. "The value of property may be diminished in many ways by ordinary legislation as well as by the police power," he wrote. An earlier draft of the dissent also contained this sentence, later removed by Holmes from the final, unpublished draft: "The general effect of the ordinance is supposed to be beneficial to the whites for the same reasons that make it bad for the blacks."[68] In other words, as Holmes had put it on an earlier occasion, "It is no sufficient condemnation of legislation that it favors one class at the expense of another,"[69] since all legislation boils down to one group imposing its will on other groups. All things considered, the unpublished dissent was a prime example of Holmes's typical deference to lawmakers. The only surprise is that he failed to practice the judicial restraint he normally preached and instead went along quietly with *Buchanan*'s libertarian approach. Perhaps even Holmes had to flinch at the idea of casting a lone vote in favor of Jim Crow.

HOLMES AND THE NEW DEAL

In 1931, to celebrate the occasion of Justice Oliver Wendell Holmes's ninetieth birthday, Harvard law professor Felix Frankfurter put together a book-length collection of tributes to his friend and mentor. Published by the New York firm of Coward-McCann, *Mr. Justice Holmes* featured contributions from a virtual who's who of Progressive intellectuals, all lined up in honor of the elder jurist. The philosopher John Dewey, for example, celebrated Holmes as "the most distinguished of the legal thinkers of our country."[70] Federal Appeals Court Judge Learned Hand praised Holmes for "the capaciousness of his learning, the acumen of his mind . . . his freedom from convention."[71] Benjamin Cardozo, who would soon take Holmes's place on the Supreme Court, said he "gives us glimpses of things eternal"[72] and is "the greatest of our age in the domain of jurisprudence, and one of the greatest of the ages."[73] Frankfurter himself simply gushed, "to quote from Mr. Justice Holmes' opinions is to string pearls."[74]

It was a glowing salute to one of Progressivism's guiding lights. But Holmes would receive a far greater homage over the coming decade as his long campaign on behalf of judicial restraint and majority rule came to be championed by one of the most powerful figures in American history. Franklin Delano Roosevelt entered political life in the shadow of his famous fifth cousin, Theodore, whom he consciously emulated at every step of his career. Like the Rough Rider before him, FDR served as governor of New York and assistant secretary of the Navy, all before finally settling in at the White House, where he adopted Theodore's muscular and nationalistic brand of Progressivism as his own. When it came to his relationship with the courts, however, FDR would finally break the mold, exhibiting an even greater hostility toward the judiciary than his famously pugnacious cousin ever did.

"BOLD, PERSISTENT EXPERIMENTATION"

Franklin Roosevelt had good reason to be wary of the Supreme Court as the New Deal got rolling in 1933. For one thing, not only was *Lochner* still on the books, it had received an unexpected boost in the 1923 case of *Adkins v. Children's Hospital,* in which a majority of the justices struck down a minimum wage law for women from the District of Columbia on the grounds that it violated the right to liberty of contract secured under the Due Process Clause of the Fifth Amendment. (Because D.C. is a federal enclave, the Due Process Clause of the Fourteenth Amendment, which limits state action, did not apply. The Fifth Amendment's due process limits on federal power, however, did.) "The right to contract about one's affairs is a part of the liberty of the individual protected by this clause," observed the majority opinion of Justice George Sutherland. That fact "is settled by the decisions of this Court and is no longer open to question."[75] A former Republican senator from Utah, Sutherland was a longtime champion of women's rights[76] who had introduced the legislation in the Senate (originally drafted by Susan B. Anthony) that would become the Nineteenth Amendment, which established female suffrage. "In view of the great—not to say revolutionary—changes that have taken place," Sutherland argued in *Adkins,* referring to that amendment, "we cannot accept the doctrine that women of mature age . . . may be subjected to restrictions upon their liberty of contract which could not lawfully be imposed in the case of men under similar circumstances."[77]

Then, in 1932, the Court delivered another significant blow against government regulation. At issue in *New State Ice Co. v. Liebmann* was an Oklahoma statute from 1925 granting a handful of companies the exclusive authority to manufacture, sell, and distribute ice. Under the terms of the law, anyone who wanted to enter the ice business had to first justify their plans to the government by providing "competent testimony and proof showing the necessity for the manufacture, sale or distribution of ice"[78] at all proposed locations. In other words, upstart ice vendors faced the unenviable and perhaps impossible task of securing the state's permission to compete against a state-sanctioned ice monopoly.

Oliver Wendell Holmes had retired from the Supreme Court by that point, but Progressive Justice Louis Brandeis, an appointee of President Woodrow Wilson, was still around, and as he saw it, the Court should have let the Oklahoma legislature handle its own internal affairs. "It is one of the happy incidents of the federal system," Brandeis wrote in dissent, "that a single courageous State may, if its citizens choose, serve as a laboratory, and try novel social and economic experiments without risk to the rest of the country."[79] Writing for the majority, Justice Sutherland offered a direct rebuttal to Brandeis's dissent. "In our constitutional system," Sutherland shot back, "there are certain essentials of liberty with which the state is not entitled to dispense in the interests of experiments."

In fact, Sutherland observed, just one year earlier, in the case of *Near v. Minnesota*, the Court had nullified (with Brandeis's full support) that state's defamation law as a violation of the First Amendment. "In [*Near*] the theory of experimentation in censorship was not permitted to interfere with the fundamental doctrine of the freedom of the press," Sutherland pointed out. "The opportunity to apply one's labor and skill in an ordinary occupation with proper regard for all reasonable regulations is no less entitled to protection."[80]

For FDR, who was fond of justifying his New Deal policies as a response to the public's demands for "bold, persistent experimentation,"[81] Sutherland's opinion in *New State Ice Co.* stood as a troubling omen indeed. But then the Supreme Court threw a curveball in 1934 by charting a very different course in yet another test of state regulatory power. The case of *Nebbia v. New York* arose from a 1933 law creating a Milk Control Board to oversee the state's dairy industry. In order to eliminate what it described as the evils of price-cutting, that board set the minimum price of milk throughout the state at nine cents a quart. In Rochester, a grocer named Leo Nebbia ran afoul of the law by selling two quarts of milk and a five-cent loaf of bread for the combined low price of 18 cents. When his case finally reached the U.S. Supreme Court, a five-to-four majority voted against him.

"A state is free to adopt whatever economic policy may reasonably be deemed to promote public welfare, and to enforce that policy by legislation adapted to its purpose,"[82] declared the majority opinion of Justice Owen Roberts. Pointing to the Court's 1877 opinion in *Munn*

v. Illinois, which upheld a law setting the storage rates for grain elevators (over the dissent of Justice Stephen Field) on the grounds that the
business was "affected with a public interest,"[83] Roberts argued that
the state of New York had a similar public interest in keeping a tight
grip on its dairy industry and the essential foodstuffs it produced. Furthermore, Roberts maintained, so long as "the laws passed are seen to
have a reasonable relation to a proper legislative purpose," the Court
should defer to the legislature and assume that "the requirements of
due process are satisfied."[84]

With the New Deal about to enter its third year, and with several
high-profile challenges to federal regulation working their way through
the legal system, the question now troubling FDR was whether the Supreme Court would treat his regulatory experiments with the judicial
deference of *Nebbia* or with the strict judicial scrutiny of *New State Ice
Co.* He got his answer in the spring of 1935. Unfortunately for Roosevelt, it was not the one he was hoping for.

ANOTHER *SLAUGHTER-HOUSE* CASE

When Franklin Roosevelt delivered his first inaugural address on March
4, 1933, he promised to counteract the suffering caused by the Great
Depression while also bringing runaway capitalism to heel. "This Nation
asks for action, and action now,"[85] Roosevelt declared. The centerpiece
of his action-packed agenda would be the National Industrial Recovery
Act (NIRA) of 1933. Hailed by FDR as "the most important and far-
reaching legislation ever enacted by the American Congress,"[86] the NIRA
represented nothing less than an attempt to centrally plan the bulk of
the U.S. economy, relying on the joint cooperation of big business, organized labor, and the federal government to manage economic affairs
from top to bottom. The result was more than 500 "codes of fair competition," with an additional 10,000 administrative orders to give them extra

force. Those codes sought to control everything from wages to prices to the amount of products that could be legally produced or sold. In some cases, whole trades or industries were required to limit their output in order to collectively raise the price of their offerings—in effect, a government-sanctioned cartel. In other instances, the codes reached down to the smallest aspects of local commerce. In Jersey City, New Jersey, for instance, a Hungarian immigrant dry cleaner named Jacob Maged was thrown in jail for three months because he pressed a suit for 35 cents rather than charging the 40-cent minimum set by the New Deal codes.

Meanwhile, in nearby Brooklyn, New York, a small kosher slaughterhouse run by a group of brothers by the name of Schechter ran into their own problems with federal authorities. Among other requirements, the NIRA-promulgated "Code of Fair Competition for the Live Poultry Industry of the Metropolitan Area in and about the City of New York" imposed a strict new rule known as "straight killing." In essence, it forbade slaughterhouse operators from allowing their customers to pick out their own live animals and have them slaughtered while they waited. In addition to facing charges of "destructive price-cutting," the Schechter brothers stood accused of allowing "selections of individual chickens taken from particular coops and half-coops."[87] They had put low prices and customer choice before the edicts of the New Deal.

Their case presented two major constitutional issues. First, the Schechters and their lawyers argued that the NIRA represented an illegal delegation of lawmaking power from the legislative to the executive branch. Under the Constitution, Congress makes the laws and the president enforces them. But with the frequent use of executive orders as part of the NIRA, it seemed as if the president was now acting as a lawmaking power unto himself.

Second, and arguably most important for the future of the New Deal, the Schechters questioned whether federal lawmakers had the authority to enact the NIRA in the first place. As justification for the 1933 law, Congress had cited its authority to regulate interstate commerce under the constitutional provision known as the Commerce Clause. According to President Roosevelt and the New Dealers on Capitol Hill, the Great Depression was a national problem that required a national solution. In practice, that meant Congress sometimes needed to manage purely local activities in order to control the larger national marketplace. The Supreme Court would consider both questions when it heard arguments in the case of *Schechter Poultry Corp. v. United States* in May 1935.

"THIS BUSINESS OF CENTRALIZATION"

According to Article One, Section Eight of the U.S. Constitution, Congress possesses the authority "to regulate commerce with foreign nations, and among the several states, and with the Indian tribes." According to the Schechter brothers, the federal government overstepped this limited grant of power by trying to regulate the local economic activity occurring inside their Brooklyn slaughterhouse.

To the horror of FDR and his allies, that position ruled the day when the Supreme Court finally delivered its eagerly anticipated decision in the *Schechter* case on the morning of May 27, 1935, soon to be dubbed "Black Monday" by despondent New Deal supporters.

The Supreme Court handed down a total of three opinions that Monday morning, each one unanimous, and each one against the New Deal. First, in an opinion by Justice Louis Brandeis, the Court invalidated[88] the 1934 Frazier-Lemke Act, which had modified federal bankruptcy law in order to make it easier for farmers to buy back their farms after foreclosure. Second, in *Humphrey's Executor v. United States,* the Court held that President Roosevelt had exceeded the scope of his authority by firing (for political reasons) a member of the Federal

Trade Commission without senatorial approval. The FTC "cannot in any proper sense be characterized as an arm or an eye of the executive,"[89] the ruling held.

But the main event was *Schechter,* and it turned out to be the biggest and most resounding defeat of them all. The National Industrial Recovery Act must be struck down in its entirety, declared the unanimous opinion of Chief Justice Charles Evans Hughes, otherwise "there would be virtually no limit to the federal power, and, for all practical purposes, we should have a completely centralized government."[90] For starters, the act rested on an illegitimate delegation of lawmaking power to the executive. Furthermore, because the slaughter and sale of kosher chickens in Brooklyn had, at best, an entirely indirect impact on interstate commerce, the Commerce Clause offered no constitutional basis for any federal regulation of such activity. "If the commerce clause were construed to reach all enterprise and transactions which could be said to have an indirect effect upon interstate commerce," Hughes wrote, "the federal authority would embrace practically all the activities of the people, and the authority of the State over its domestic concerns would exist only by sufferance of the federal government."[91] In what many observers took to be a direct rebuke to the president himself, Hughes added, "extraordinary conditions do not create or enlarge constitutional power."[92]

When he learned the news, Roosevelt could barely contain his disbelief. "Where was Cardozo? Where was Stone?" he asked his advisers, naming two of the Court's left-leaning members. "What about old Isaiah?"[93] he demanded, employing the nickname of Justice Louis Brandeis. All three of those liberal justices had voted against him.

No president likes to lose at the Supreme Court, but Roosevelt seemed to have been uncharacteristically naive about his prospects when it came to the fate of the National Industrial Recovery Act. For one thing, the law had always faced strong criticism from the

Progressive left. The muckraking journalist John T. Flynn, for instance, who had written an economics column for *The New Republic* and authored books with titles like *Trusts Gone Wrong!*, frequently characterized the NIRA as an example of the government climbing into bed with big business. "Curiously," Flynn would write, "every American liberal who had fought monopoly, who had demanded the enforcement of the anti-trust laws, who had denied the right of organized business groups, combinations and trade associations to rule our economic life, was branded as a Tory and a reactionary [by the New Dealers] if he continued to believe these things."[94]

New Deal adviser Rexford Tugwell, a member of FDR's original "Brain Trust," would later acknowledge the merit of such criticism. "The detractors of that sort of planning called it price-fixing, and they had a point," Tugwell wrote in his 1968 memoir. "But it was price-fixing in the public interest. At the same time it was thoroughly inconsistent with orthodox progressivism which held that fixing prices should be forbidden as conspiratorial."[95] Raymond Moley, a fellow Brain Truster and co-architect of the NIRA, was even blunter in his assessment of the law's rise and fall. "Planning an economy in normal times is possible only through the discipline of a police state," Moley would write. "Economic planning on a national scale in a politically free society involves contradictions that cannot be resolved in practice. The bones of the [NIRA] should be a grim reminder of this reality."[96]

As for Justice Brandeis, he wasted little time before letting FDR know exactly where the New Deal had gone wrong. An old-school Progressive, "old Isaiah" had long warned about the dangers of corporate monopoly. As a reform-minded young lawyer, Brandeis had first made his name with a book under his belt titled *The Curse of Bigness*. And as he saw it now, the NIRA looked like more of the same old trouble. "This is the end of this business of centralization," Brandeis told New Deal adviser Thomas Corcoran shortly after the *Schechter* ruling came down. "I want you to go back and tell the President that we're not going to let this government centralize everything."[97]

THE COURT-PACKING PLAN

FDR waited four days before going public with his response to the Court's ruling. "The implications of this decision are much more important than almost certainly any decision of my lifetime or yours, more important than any decision probably since the *Dred Scott* case," he announced at a press conference. Turning to the specifics of the opinion, Roosevelt said the Court's error came from trying to square the large-scale requirements of modern government with the out-of-date limits imposed by the Constitution's Commerce Clause. "The country was in the horse-and-buggy age when that clause was written," Roosevelt declared. His administration favored a different method of legal interpretation, he explained, one that would "view the interstate commerce clause in the light of present-day civilization."[98]

Today, that approach is better known (at least to its critics) as "living constitutionalism." Essentially, it holds that the Constitution should be viewed as an inherently flexible document, able to adjust to the changing needs of the times. Among the earliest proponents of this view was a young Woodrow Wilson, who argued in his 1885 book *Congressional Government* that the Constitution must be able to "adapt itself to the new conditions of an advancing society." "If it could not stretch itself to the measure of the times," Wilson wrote, the Constitution "must be thrown off and left behind, as a bygone device."[99]

In private, FDR was far more interested in ditching the Supreme Court as a bygone device, though he did not permit himself the luxury of making that suggestion at his 1935 press conference. When asked by a reporter about the next move in his showdown with the Court, Roosevelt cryptically replied, "We haven't got to that yet."[100]

It would take several more defeats before Roosevelt finally went on the attack. The worst of those defeats came in 1936. First, in the case of *United States v. Butler,* the Court, by a five-to-four vote, effectively nullified the Agricultural Adjustment Act of 1933. Several months later, in a move seen by many reformers as a dangerous reaffirmation of the *Lochner* decision, the Court struck down a New York minimum wage law on the grounds that it interfered with the individual liberty secured by the Fourteenth Amendment. It was the "sacred right of liberty of contract again,"[101] fumed New Deal adviser Harold Ickes. The time had come, Ickes and his allies agreed, for something to be done about the Supreme Court.

The solution was FDR's notorious and ill-fated court-packing plan. The idea itself was not new. Theodore Roosevelt basically floated the concept in 1912 as part of his campaign for the popular recall of *Lochner*-style opinions. "Either the recall will have to be adopted," TR had said, "or else it will have to be made much easier than it now is to get rid, not merely of a bad judge, but of a judge who, however virtuous, has grown so out of touch with social needs and facts that he is unfit longer to render good service on the bench."[102]

Cousin Franklin not only embraced that idea, he spent tremendous political capital in a failed attempt to make it the law of the land. On February 5, 1937, after he had been safely reelected to a second term, FDR submitted to Congress his proposal for reorganizing the federal judiciary. At the center of the controversial bill was a provision granting Roosevelt (and all future presidents) the power to appoint one new federal judge to match every sitting judge that had served at least ten years and had not retired or resigned within six months of turning seventy years of age. Under the plan, FDR could add as many as forty-four new federal judges and, most important, up to six new Supreme Court justices.

"A lower mental or physical vigor leads men to avoid an examination of complicated and changed conditions," FDR explained. "Little by little, new facts become blurred through old glasses fitted, as it were, for the needs of another generation."[103] It was a disingenuous argument, to say the least. The Court's oldest sitting justice at that time was none other than Progressive hero Louis Brandeis. And although Roosevelt may have had his differences with the eighty-year-old justice over *Schechter* and the other "Black Monday" cases, Brandeis was an otherwise reliable vote in favor of liberal reform. Nor did "old Isaiah" show any signs of slowing down with age. In reality, of course, it was no secret to anybody what Roosevelt's true motives were. He wanted to appoint a fresh slate of liberal justices who were ready, willing, and able to practice judicial deference and uphold future New Deal legislation.

Unhappily for the president, the plan backfired spectacularly. Brandeis, offended at both the personal insult and the frank attack on the independence of the judiciary, maneuvered behind the scenes to bring about the bill's defeat. Most significantly, he put the bill's chief congressional opponent, Democratic Senator Burton K. Wheeler of Montana, in touch with Chief Justice Charles Evans Hughes, who had prepared a memo, signed by himself, Brandeis, and Justice Willis Van Devanter, testifying that the Supreme Court was completely on top of its workload and was in no need of any young blood to pick up the non-existent slack. During testimony on the court-packing proposal before the Senate Judiciary Committee, Senator Wheeler unveiled that memo to great effect. Thwarted by such legislative maneuverings, not to mention by the broad public opposition to his apparent tinkering with a co-equal branch of government, Roosevelt failed to garner the necessary votes and the court-packing plan went down to defeat in the Senate.

THE NEW DEAL REVOLUTION

Although FDR lost the court-packing skirmish, there's no doubt that he won the larger battle for control of the Supreme Court. By 1937 the anti– New Deal coalition centered on four justices—dubbed the "Four Horsemen" by their political foes. There was James C. McReynolds, author of the Supreme Court's libertarian ruling in *Meyer v. Nebraska,* which struck down that state's ban on teaching children in a foreign language; Willis Van Devanter, a one-time railroad lawyer and appointee of President William Howard Taft; Pierce Butler, the Court's only Catholic, and the lone dissenter from Justice Holmes's pro-eugenics ruling in *Buck v. Bell;* and George Sutherland, the intellectual leader of the group and the author of the Court's libertarian rulings in *Adkins v. Children's Hospital,* which struck down a minimum wage law for women, and *New State Ice Co. v. Liebmann,* which voided a state-sanctioned ice monopoly.

But as every court watcher knows, the magic number at the Supreme Court is five, not four. And in the late 1930s, that crucial fifth vote was in the hands of Justice Owen Roberts, a former U.S. attorney and appointee of President Calvin Coolidge. In 1936, Roberts had provided the fifth vote needed to strike down New York's minimum wage law. That same year, he authored the Court's opinion nullifying the Agricultural Adjustment Act. But Roberts had also broken stride with the Horsemen on several other occasions, most notably in the 1934 case of *Nebbia v. New York,* where he authored the majority opinion upholding the state's regulation of dairy prices and reaffirming the conviction of a local grocer for selling low-priced milk. That ruling was a paragon of judicial deference and a taste of things to come. With all eyes now focused on FDR's showdown with the Supreme Court, the question of the hour was whether Roberts would side with the Four Horsemen or with the New Deal when the next test of economic regulation reached the bench.

The country got its answer on the morning of March 29, 1937, promptly dubbed "White Monday" by the Washington press corps. By a vote of five to four, with Roberts siding with the liberals and the Horsemen united in dissent, the Supreme Court upheld a Washington state minimum wage law for women under the principle of judicial restraint in *West Coast Co. v. Parrish*. "The Constitution does not speak of freedom of contract," announced the majority opinion of Chief Justice Hughes. "It speaks of liberty and prohibits the deprivation of liberty without due process of law." And as far as the Supreme Court was now concerned, "regulation which is reasonable in relation to its subject and is adopted in the interests of the community is due process."[104] Besides, Hughes added, striking a note of paternalism, "What can be closer to the public interest than the health of women and their protection from unscrupulous and overreaching employers?"[105]

In other words, liberty of contract was now finished as a viable legal argument. Justice Sutherland, author of the suddenly defunct majority opinion in *Adkins v. Children's Hospital*, filed a blistering dissent accusing his colleagues in the majority of a cowardly retreat from basic judicial principles. "The meaning of the Constitution does not change with the ebb and flow of economic events,"[106] Sutherland wrote. To say "that the words of the Constitution mean today what they did not mean when written—that is, that they do not apply to a situation now to which they would have applied then—is to rob that instrument of the essential element which continues it in force as the people have made it until they, and not their official agents, have made it otherwise."[107]

Sutherland was outraged, but whether he liked it or not, the tide had turned decisively against him. Just two weeks later, on the morning of April 12, the same five-vote liberal majority—Charles Evans Hughes, Owen Roberts, Louis Brandeis, Benjamin Cardozo, and Harlan Fiske Stone—sustained the constitutionality of the National

Labor Relations Act, popularly known as the Wagner Act in tribute
to its chief advocate, Senator Robert Wagner of New York. At issue
in *National Labor Relations Board v. Jones & Laughlin Steel Corp.* was
the scope of congressional power under the Commerce Clause, the
very issue that had previously spelled doom for the National Industrial
Recovery Act in 1935.

The question now before the Court was whether a dispute between the Jones & Laughlin Corporation and its unionized steel workers inside the state of Pennsylvania counted as interstate commerce
for the purposes of the new federal labor law. The Court held that it
did, thereby validating the constitutionality of the New Deal's most
extensive labor regulation. To begin, wrote Chief Justice Hughes, the
Court must acknowledge its own fundamentally deferential role in
the political structure. Our job "is to save, and not to destroy. We
have repeatedly held that, as between two possible interpretations of a
statute, by one of which it would be unconstitutional and by the other
valid, our plain duty is to adopt that which will save the act."[108] (Chief
Justice John Roberts would employ that same argument seven decades
later to save President Barack Obama's health care law.) Turning to the
labor law at issue, Hughes found no difficulty in construing it as a permissible exercise of congressional power. "Although activities may be
intrastate in character when separately considered," Hughes wrote, "if
they have such a close and substantial relation to interstate commerce
that their control is essential or appropriate to protect that commerce
from burdens and obstructions, Congress cannot be denied the power
to exercise that control."[109]

All told, it was one of the most striking turnarounds in legal history. In less than a decade, the Supreme Court had not only rendered
liberty of contract a dead letter, it had embraced a sweeping form of
judicial deference toward state and federal legislation while also greatly
expanding congressional power by allowing federal lawmakers to reach

activities that would previously have been seen as off-limits under the Commerce Clause. As the legal historian William E. Leuchtenburg would put it, "From 1937 on, the relationship among the branches of government shifted dramatically, as an era of 'judicial supremacy' gave way to deference by the Supreme Court."[110]

When it came to government regulation of the economy, Americans would now be living in the world envisioned by Justice Oliver Wendell Holmes.

THREE

"ROBERT BORK'S AMERICA"

N JULY 1, 1987, PRESIDENT RONALD REA-gan introduced the American people to the man he had selected to replace retiring Justice Lewis Powell on the U.S. Supreme Court. Robert Bork "is recognized as a premier constitutional authority," Reagan announced, with the nominee standing by his side. A former solicitor general of the United States, a distinguished former professor of law at Yale University, and a sitting judge on the prestigious U.S. Court of Appeals for the District of Columbia Circuit, Bork did indeed come well qualified for the position. Furthermore, Reagan continued, Bork is "widely regarded as the most prominent and intellectually powerful advocate of judicial restraint," which the president described as the view "that under the Constitution it is the exclusive province of the legislatures to enact laws and the role of the courts to interpret them." As a justice, Reagan concluded, Robert Bork "will bring credit to the Court and his colleagues, as well as to his country and the Constitution."[1]

Less than an hour later, Senator Edward "Ted" Kennedy of Massachusetts, a prominent liberal Democrat, took to the floor of the Senate to offer a very different take on Reagan's pick. "Robert Bork's America," Kennedy declared, "is a land in which women would be forced into back-alley abortions, blacks would sit at segregated lunch counters, rogue police could break down citizens' doors in midnight raids, schoolchildren could not be taught about evolution, writers and artists would be censored at the whim of government, and the doors of the Federal courts would be shut on the fingers of millions of citizens for whom the judiciary is often the only protector of the individual rights that are the heart of our democracy."[2]

Although Bork would later spend five grueling days in September sparring with Kennedy and other members of the Senate Judiciary Committee over his legal views, the basic script for his entire confirmation process had been set on that first fateful day. Following Reagan's lead, Bork's Republican supporters characterized him as the heir to a long and noble tradition of responsible judging, a tradition firmly rooted in the judicial deference favored by the turn-of-the-century Progressive movement. "I would ask the committee and the American people to take the time to understand Judge Bork's approach to the Constitution," said Republican Senator Bob Dole of Kansas. "That approach is based on 'judicial restraint,' the principle that judges are supposed to interpret the law and not make it. Now, Judge Bork did not invent this concept," Dole continued. "It has been around for a long time. One of the most eloquent advocates was Oliver Wendell Holmes."[3]

Bork's Democratic opponents, meanwhile, followed Kennedy's example and zeroed in on the ways Bork's jurisprudence threatened to overturn landmark liberal rulings and upset the current political balance. "As I understand what you have said in the last 30 minutes," said Senator Joseph Biden, a Democrat from Delaware and chairman of the Senate Judiciary Committee, who was then questioning Bork about whether or not the Constitution secured a right to privacy, "a State legislative body, a government, can, if it so chose, pass a law saying married couples cannot use birth control devices."[4]

Bork would repeatedly object to that characterization of his views, but there was no denying that Biden had a point. If the Supreme Court had followed Bork's restrained approach to legislative determinations in the 1965 case of *Griswold v. Connecticut,* it never would have invalidated that state's ban on the use of birth control devices by married couples. Similarly, if the Court had followed Bork's deferential approach eight years later in *Roe v. Wade,* Texas's anti-abortion restriction would still be on the books and women would not enjoy a nationally protected right to terminate a pregnancy.

But Bork's supporters on the other side of the aisle also had a point. Reagan and Dole were right: Bork *was* a principled advocate of judicial minimalism. Bork not only opposed what he saw as the Court's liberal activism in *Griswold* and *Roe,* he also rejected what he saw as the conservative activism of *Lochner v. New York,* the same case denounced by Progressive luminaries such as Holmes, Felix Frankfurter, and Theodore Roosevelt. Indeed, during his confirmation hearings, Bork took pains to remind his Democratic interrogators "that there was a time when the word 'liberty' in the Fourteenth Amendment was used by judges to strike down social reform legislation." Those conservative and libertarian judges, Bork argued, "were wrong because they were using a concept to reach results they liked, and the concept did not confine them, and they should not have been using that concept."[5]

It was a sentiment worthy of Justice Holmes himself. Yet not only did Bork's ode to legal Progressivism fail to win him any additional Democratic supporters, it almost certainly helped doom his already troubled nomination, which eventually went down to defeat in the Senate by a vote of 58–42. That's because American liberals had long

ago abandoned the sort of all-encompassing judicial deference espoused by Holmes and his followers. Instead, modern progressives like
Kennedy and Biden took their cues from a new breed of liberal jurist,
best represented by figures such as Chief Justice Earl Warren and Associate Justice William O. Douglas. Those justices had led the mid-
twentieth-century Supreme Court through what has been dubbed
a "rights revolution," a busy stretch during which state actions were
routinely overturned in the name of voting rights, privacy rights, abortion rights, the rights of criminal defendants, and many other rights
besides. Put differently, in the half century that fell between the presi-
dencies of Franklin Roosevelt and Ronald Reagan, the American left
had learned to stop worrying and love judicial activism.

FOOTNOTE FOUR

The story of this sweeping liberal transformation begins in the most
humble of places: a footnote. In 1938, hot on the heels of its famous
about-face on the question of liberty of contract versus judicial restraint,
the Supreme Court considered the constitutionality of a federal statute
charged with depriving entrepreneurs of their economic freedom. At
issue in *United States v. Carolene Products Co.* was a federal law forbidding the interstate shipment of so-called filled milk, which is basically
a milk product made with oil rather than milk fat. Because filled milk
looks like normal milk or cream while containing a cheaper non-dairy
ingredient, the dairy industry viewed the product as a competitor and
lobbied successfully for the restriction. Adopting a deferential posture,
the Supreme Court concluded that Congress must have had its reasons for passing the Filled Milk Act, and therefore voted to sustain
the ban over the objections of the Carolene Products Company, which
had hoped to earn a profit by shipping the foodstuff across state lines
for sale. When it came to "regulatory legislation affecting ordinary

commercial transactions," the Court declared in its *Carolene Products* ruling, "the existence of facts supporting the legislative judgment is to be presumed."[6] In other words, judges should give lawmakers the benefit of the doubt and vote to uphold the overwhelming preponderance of economic regulations.

Lawyers today know this approach as the "rational-basis test," and, in the words of *Black's Law Dictionary*, it "is the most deferential of the standards of review that courts use in due-process and equal-protection analysis."[7] Essentially, the rational-basis test requires judges to respect the wisdom of the elected branches and to examine the details of a law only if it seems to lack any conceivable connection to a legitimate government interest. Thus in *Carolene Products*, because Congress did have a legitimate interest in monitoring the interstate milk market, and because the regulation in question did not appear to be a completely nonsensical way to advance that interest, the Supreme Court made no attempt to determine whether or not Congress had any verifiable scientific evidence for declaring filled milk to be "an adulterated article of food, injurious to the public health."[8] Had the justices looked further, they might have discovered that filled milk was a perfectly safe (and affordable) alternative to whole-fat milk, as countless consumers could have attested then and could still attest now.

Armed with the rational-basis test, the Supreme Court proceeded to grant overwhelming deference to a range of regulatory measures. In the 1948 case of *Goesaert v. Cleary*, for example, the Court upheld a Michigan law forbidding women from working as bartenders unless they happened to be "the wife or daughter of the male owner" of a licensed establishment. "We cannot cross-examine either actually or argumentatively the mind of Michigan legislators nor question their motives," declared the opinion of Justice Felix Frankfurter. "Since the line they have drawn is not without a basis in reason," he continued, "we cannot give ear to the suggestion that the real impulse behind this legislation was an unchivalrous desire of male bartenders to try to monopolize the calling."[9]

Similarly, in the 1954 case of *Williamson v. Lee Optical Inc.*, the Court unanimously upheld an Oklahoma law requiring a prescription from an ophthalmologist or optometrist before an optician was allowed to fit or duplicate eyeglass lenses. Among other results, the law served to ban the longstanding practice of getting an optician to fit old lenses into new frames without a prescription, thereby costing the consumer extra money by mandating a pointless trip to the eye doctor. "The Oklahoma law may exact a needless, wasteful requirement in many cases," admitted Justice William O. Douglas in his opinion for the Court. "But it is for the legislature, not the courts, to balance the advantages and disadvantages of the new requirement."[10] Furthermore, the ruling added, in what would become shorthand for the Court's new deferential regime, "It is enough that there is an evil at hand for correction, and that it *might* be thought that the particular legislative measure was a rational way to correct it."[11]

Nine years later, in the case of *Ferguson v. Skrupa*, the Court relied in part on *Lee Optical* to uphold a state law criminalizing "the business of debt adjustment," essentially a middleman-type position that acts as a paid broker between debtors and collectors. "The Kansas debt adjusting statute may be wise or unwise. But relief, if any be needed, lies not with us but with the body constituted to pass laws for the State of Kansas," declared the majority opinion of Justice Hugo Black, a former New Deal senator from Alabama and Supreme Court appointee of Franklin Roosevelt, who also tacked on this quote from Justice Holmes for good measure: "A state legislature can do whatever it sees fit to do unless it is restrained by some express prohibition in the Constitution of the United States or of the State."[12] Ten years later, in the case of *Lehnhausen v. Lake Shore Auto Parts Co.*, the Court would tip the scales even further in favor of the government, holding that in all

cases dealing with economic regulations, "the burden is on the one attacking the legislative arrangement to negative every conceivable basis
which might conceivably support it."[13]

Yet at the same time that the Supreme Court was committing
itself to this near-total submission to lawmakers on the economic
front, the justices were testing the bounds of greater judicial action
in other realms. As justification for this bifurcated approach, they
pointed back to the fine print in the 1938 *Carolene Products* case. In
Footnote Four of that opinion, Justice Harlan Fiske Stone explained
that while the courts must now presume all economic regulations to
be constitutional, "more exacting judicial scrutiny" would still be appropriate in other types of cases. For example, Stone agued, the Court
should not automatically defer to a law that appeared to run afoul of
"a specific prohibition of the Constitution, such as those of the first
ten amendments." In addition, Stone wrote, judicial deference would
be equally inappropriate when the law at issue appeared to impact the
right to vote or to otherwise impede the "political processes" normally
employed by citizens to vindicate their rights. Finally, Stone argued,
"prejudice against discrete and insular minorities" may also require a
"more searching judicial inquiry."[14] According to Footnote Four, in
other words, the Supreme Court need not after all commit itself to the
practice of judicial restraint in all cases.

To the members of the burgeoning civil rights movement, the call
for enhanced judicial scrutiny on behalf of voting rights and "discrete
and insular minorities" sounded exactly right. Under the leadership
of talented lawyers such as future Supreme Court Justice Thurgood
Marshall, the NAACP Legal Defense Fund was then asking the courts
to breathe real life into the Fourteenth Amendment by securing equal
treatment under the law for African Americans throughout the realm
of Jim Crow. That strategy famously paid off with the Supreme Court's
historic 1954 ruling in *Brown v. Board of Education of Topeka, Kansas,*

one of the greatest legal victories for racial equality since libertarian NAACP president Moorfield Storey won *Buchanan v. Warley* back in 1917. Under *Brown,* racial segregation in public schools was ruled to be "inherently unequal"[15] and therefore unconstitutional under the Equal Protection Clause.

Brown, and the line of desegregation cases that followed it, inspired a harsh backlash throughout the country, with segregationists and their allies denouncing the "judicial tyranny" of the Supreme Court and calling for the impeachment of Chief Justice Earl Warren, who authored the unanimous majority opinion. But *Brown* also had its critics on the left, a fact that is sometimes forgotten today. Foremost among them was Judge Learned Hand, recently retired from his position as chief judge of the U.S. Court of Appeals for the Second Circuit. Considered by many legal observers to be the greatest judge never to sit on the Supreme Court, Hand was an undisputed icon of the Progressive movement, a revered jurist and scholar whose career stretched back to the great battles over the role of the courts that raged during the *Lochner* era.

Born in Albany, New York, in 1872, Hand studied law at Harvard and went on to serve as a key adviser to Theodore Roosevelt's 1912 Progressive Party campaign for the presidency. One year later, Hand himself appeared on the Progressive ticket as a candidate for the chief judgeship of New York's highest court. In 1914, he joined Herbert Croly in founding *The New Republic,* where he regularly contributed articles and editorials advocating Progressive political and legal theories until his appointment to the Second Circuit in 1924, where he would spend the next three decades. When he died in 1961, the *New York Times* responded with a front-page obituary describing him as "the greatest jurist of his time."[16]

In February 1958, at the age of eighty-seven, Hand was invited back to Harvard to deliver the celebrated Oliver Wendell Holmes

Lecture, an annual event featuring a distinguished legal speaker. In his remarks, delivered over three nights and later published as a short book titled *The Bill of Rights,* Hand's theme was the fundamental illegitimacy of judicial review and what he saw as the troubling rise of liberal judicial activism by the current Supreme Court, including its recent decision in *Brown v. Board of Education.* He began with a critique of the "patent usurpation" whereby the Supreme Court had transformed itself into "a third legislative chamber."[17] As he explained, such activism was inappropriate no matter what value was at stake. "I can see no more persuasive reason for supposing that a legislature is *a priori* less qualified to choose between 'personal' than between economic rights,"[18] he announced. As for the constitutional protections spelled out in the Bill of Rights and the Fourteenth Amendment, "we may read them as admonitory or hortatory, not definite enough to be guides on concrete questions."[19] As Hand saw it, the individualistic language of the Constitution was no license for judges to go meddling around with the democratic process.

Turning next to *Brown,* Hand argued that the problem with the Supreme Court's ruling was that the justices had substituted their own values for those of the Kansas authorities. That, he said, was precisely what conservative justices had previously done in order to strike down the economic reforms they disapproved of during the Progressive and New Deal periods. *Brown,* he informed his increasingly disquieted audience, was guilty of the same judicial sins that had marred *Lochner* and other liberty of contract cases, and must therefore be rejected as such. "There can be no doubt," he declared, "that the old doctrine seems to have been reasserted."

Indeed, Hand went on, in the aftermath of *Brown* and other aggressive liberal rulings by the Warren Court, "I do not know what the doctrine is as to the scope of these clauses," meaning the Due Process and Equal Protection Clauses of the Fourteenth Amendment.

"I cannot frame any definition that will explain when the Court will assume the role of a third legislative chamber and when it will limit its authority."[20] It was judicial power run amok.

To conclude his lecture, Hand made one final, personal plea for the Court to adopt the method of judicial deference he had been championing for nearly half a century. "For myself," he said, "it would be most irksome to be ruled by a bevy of Platonic Guardians, even if I knew how to choose them, which I assuredly do not. If they were in charge, I should miss the stimulus of living in a society where I have, at least theoretically, some part in the direction of public affairs."[21]

In time, those eloquent words would come to be celebrated as one of the most powerful statements ever made in favor of judicial restraint. But that eloquence did little to make the bitter pill of Hand's message any easier to swallow in 1958, especially for the many young liberals in his audience who had cheered *Brown* as among the Supreme Court's finest rulings. As Hand biographer Gerald Gunther later put it, "Warren Court admirers could dismiss the most vocal critics of the Court as extremists; yet here was the nation's most highly regarded judge . . . apparently joining the Court's enemies."[22]

INTO THE THICKET

Nor would Hand be the only Progressive veteran to line up against the new liberal order. Felix Frankfurter, the influential Harvard professor, protégé of Oliver Wendell Holmes, and New Deal adviser to President Franklin Roosevelt, had been rewarded for his accomplishments when FDR elevated him to the Supreme Court in 1939. But then something unexpected happened. As his colleagues began to adopt the Footnote Four framework and apply heightened judicial scrutiny in cases dealing with civil liberties and voting rights, Frankfurter, for the first time in his professional life, found himself increasingly out of step with the liberal consensus. By the time he retired in 1962, many young reformers had come to regard Frankfurter as one of the Supreme Court's leading reactionaries, and not as any sort of progressive at all.

Frankfurter got his first taste of the Supreme Court's new direction in a pair of cases dealing with the question of whether public schools may require their students to salute the American flag as part of a daily exercise that included the Pledge of Allegiance. The first of those cases originated in Pennsylvania, where two children, aged ten and twelve, both practicing Jehovah's Witnesses, had refused to salute the flag and were therefore expelled. Their father challenged the law on their behalf, arguing that it interfered with the children's religious liberty.

Frankfurter saw the matter quite differently. In fact, he thought it was an open-and-shut victory for the local school board. "The courtroom is not the arena for debating issues of educational policy," he declared for the majority in the 1940 case of *Minersville School District v. Gobitis.* One of the main purposes of public education, Frankfurter said, was to instill notions of patriotism and democracy in young Americans. And it was simply beyond the legitimate purview of the federal courts to second-guess local determinations made in the service of that basic objective. To rule otherwise, he maintained, "would in effect make us the school board for the country."[23] If a family of Jehovah's Witnesses (or any other sect) wanted to secure greater accommodations for their religious beliefs, they should do so "in the forum of public opinion and before legislative assemblies rather than to transfer such a contest to the judicial arena."[24]

Yet just three years later, thanks in part to a change in the Court's composition, Frankfurter found himself on the losing side of a nearly identical dispute in the case of *West Virginia State Board of Education v. Barnette.* Once again, some young Jehovah's Witnesses had refused to participate in their public school's mandatory flag salute ceremony on religious grounds. But this time the Supreme Court ruled in the students' favor, holding that the state government had trespassed on their constitutional rights. "To sustain the compulsory flag salute," observed the majority opinion of Justice Robert Jackson, "we are required to say that a Bill of Rights which guards the individual's right to speak his own mind left it open to public authorities to compel him to utter what is not in his mind."[25]

Frankfurter was furious about being overturned, and he made no effort to hide it in his dissent. "Responsibility for legislation lies with legislatures, answerable as they are directly to the people," he announced. "This Court's only and very narrow function is to determine whether, within the broad grant of authority vested in legislatures, they have exercised a judgment for which reasonable justification can be offered."[26] Pointing to his own identity as a Jewish American, Frankfurter tartly noted that while he knew a thing or two about the plight of religious minorities, that knowledge still gave him no license as a judge to stamp his own feelings on the Constitution. "As appeal from legislation to adjudication becomes more frequent, and its consequences more far-reaching, judicial self-restraint becomes more, and not less, important," he warned his colleagues, "lest we unwarrantably enter social and political domains wholly outside our concern."[27]

Frankfurter would repeat that same warning with even greater volume two decades later in what turned out to be his final opinion as a justice, a long and bitter dissent from the landmark 1962 voting rights decision in *Baker v. Carr*. Hailed by Chief Justice Earl Warren as "the most vital decision"[28] handed down during his tenure on the bench, *Baker* dealt with the thorny issue of how a state government apportions its legislative districts in the wake of a census. The case originated in Tennessee, where the plaintiffs charged Secretary of State Joseph Cordell Carr with stacking the deck in favor of rural voters at the expense of the state's growing urban population by failing to properly redraw the boundary lines for the ninety-five districts that comprised the Tennessee General Assembly. According to the challengers, the state government was effectively denying urban residents a fair share of political power and thereby violating the basic principle that the Supreme Court would ultimately recognize as "one person, one vote." For its part, Tennessee argued that the federal courts lacked jurisdiction to hear the case, and added that the issue of legislative apportionment was a "political question" that the Supreme Court had no business trying to solve.

Writing for a six-to-two majority, Justice William Brennan ruled against the state. While he did not pass judgment on the constitutionality of Tennessee's current apportionment scheme, Brennan made it clear that the challengers had every right to bring suit and that the federal courts were within their rights to settle the matter in a future case. "The complaint's allegations of a denial of equal protection present a justiciable constitutional cause of action upon which appellants are entitled to a trial and a decision," he held. "The right asserted is within the reach of judicial protection under the Fourteenth Amendment."[29] Two years later, in *Reynolds v. Sims,* Chief Justice Warren went further and nullified Alabama's lopsided districting plan, ruling that representation in a state legislature must closely track the state's actual population. "Legislators represent people, not trees or acres,"[30] he declared.

In a previous redistricting case, Felix Frankfurter had urged the Supreme Court to avoid the matter entirely as a basic act of judicial restraint. "Courts ought not to enter this political thicket,"[31] he famously wrote. Finding himself on the losing side of *Baker,* Frankfurter doubled down on that deferential position. The Court's ruling, he declared in dissent, was "a massive repudiation of the experience of our whole past" brought about by the assertion of a "destructively novel judicial power."[32] The Court had simply gone too far. "There is not under our Constitution a judicial remedy for every political mischief, for every undesirable exercise of legislative power,"[33] he argued. Yet thanks to the majority's holding, the federal courts were now empowered "to devise what should constitute the proper composition of the legislatures of the fifty States,"[34] a result he found both offensive and unworkable. "In a democratic society like ours," Frankfurter maintained, "relief must come through an aroused popular conscience that sears the conscience of the people's representatives,"[35] not through the courts.

To say the least, it was not an opinion destined to win Frankfurter any new fans on the American left. Indeed, as one historian recently put it, "With time, it came to seem impossible that a justice who opposed judicial enforcement of voting rights could be considered liberal."[36] The same thing might be said about the West Virginia flag-salute case, now considered a touchstone in the advancement of civil liberties. Yet there stood Frankfurter, one of the last lions of the Progressive legal movement, attacking his liberal colleagues for their judicial activism on both counts.

What changed? Certainly not Frankfurter—he remained faithful to the majoritarian jurisprudence of his youth. Back in 1924, outraged over the use of the Fourteenth Amendment to overturn state regulations, he had called for the repeal of the Due Process Clause in an unsigned editorial written for *The New Republic.* Now, in the twilight of Jim Crow, Frankfurter was still urging the federal courts to butt out of state affairs and let local citizens and their elected representatives chart their own political futures. He saw Footnote Four as an escape hatch, one that let federal judges roam free once more to strike down state and federal legislation.

"PENUMBRAS, FORMED BY EMANATIONS"

The growing tension between Progressive restraint and liberal activism finally exploded when the Supreme Court grappled with the hot-button issue of reproductive privacy. In Connecticut, under a statute dating back to 1879, it was a crime to use "any drug, medical article or instrument for the purpose of preventing conception,"[37] as well as to assist, counsel, or otherwise aid any person in the use of such devices. Birth-control advocates had previously tried to get the Supreme Court to consider the merits of the contraceptive ban on two separate occasions, and had been rebuffed both times. First, in the 1943 case of *Tileston v. Ullman,* the Court ruled that the challenger lacked the requisite legal standing to bring suit. Then, in 1961's *Poe v. Ullman,* the Court said that because no one had actually been prosecuted for violating the law, the case was not yet "ripe" enough for adjudication.

But all that changed with the 1965 case of *Griswold v. Connecticut.* Two agents of the state's Planned Parenthood League, one of whom was a doctor, had been duly charged with dispensing birth-control information and devices to married couples. The Supreme Court saw its opportunity to rule on the matter and tackled the case head-on.

The result was a fractured ruling that continues to spark debate. At the heart of the case was a deceptively simple question: Does the Constitution protect a right to privacy that covers the freedom of married couples to use birth control? A majority of the Court held that it did, but then quickly divided over precisely how the Constitution managed to do it. Writing for a five-justice majority, Justice William O. Douglas argued that while the right to privacy is not specifically enumerated in the text of the document, various textual provisions do nonetheless protect certain aspects of privacy, such as the Fourth Amendment's guarantee against unreasonable searches and seizures and the Fifth Amendment's protection against self-incrimination. Furthermore, Douglas argued, those "specific guarantees in the Bill of Rights have penumbras [shadows], formed by emanations from those guarantees that help give them life and substance."[38] Taken together, the "penumbras" and "emanations" of these "fundamental constitutional

guarantees" create a distinct "zone of privacy"[39] that is itself a constitutional right worthy of judicial protection. "Would we allow the police
to search the sacred precincts of marital bedrooms for telltale signs of
the use of contraceptives?" he asked. "The very idea is repulsive to the
notions of privacy surrounding the marriage relationship."[40]

   In a separate concurrence, Justice Arthur Goldberg, joined by
Chief Justice Earl Warren and Justice William Brennan, agreed that
the law "unconstitutionally intrudes upon the right of marital privacy," but instead rested the case more squarely on the language of
the Ninth Amendment, which holds, "The enumeration in the Constitution of certain rights shall not be construed to deny or disparage
others retained by the people." As Goldberg saw it, privacy was clearly
among those unenumerated rights retained by the married people of
Connecticut. "Although the Constitution does not speak in so many
words of the right of privacy in marriage," he wrote, "I cannot believe
that it offers these fundamental rights no protection."[41]

   Meanwhile, two other justices, John M. Harlan and Byron White,
each filed their own separate concurring opinions that rejected the
penumbras approach entirely and ruled against the law solely under
the Due Process Clause of the Fourteenth Amendment. In short, the
Court's liberal majority very much wanted to recognize a constitutional right to privacy, but the justices could not reach any sort of
broad agreement over the proper method for doing so.

   Why the disarray? Consider again the central proposition of Footnote Four from the 1938 *Carolene Products* decision. It said that the
Supreme Court may only engage in "exacting judicial scrutiny" when
the law under review appears to violate a specific provision of the Constitution, interfere with the political process, or discriminate against
"discrete and insular minorities." Simply put, Connecticut's intrusion
on marital privacy failed[42] to clearly satisfy any one of those three separate tests, leaving the justices scrambling for a fix.

Douglas in particular struggled to meet the requirements of Foot-note Four. Keep in mind that *Carolene Products* was written in large part as a reaction to cases such as *Lochner v. New York,* which struck down a maximum working hours law for bakery employees, and *Adkins v. Children's Hospital,* which struck down a minimum wage law for women. In each of those cases, the Supreme Court had nullified an economic regulation for violating the unenumerated right to liberty of contract, a right the Court first located in the Fourteenth Amendment's guarantee that no person be deprived of life, liberty, or property without due process of law. Yet as Chief Justice Charles Evans Hughes had declared in *West Coast Hotel Co. v. Parrish,* the 1937 case that overruled *Adkins* and effectively killed *Lochner,* "The Constitution does not speak of freedom of contract,"[43] and therefore the Supreme Court would neither recognize it nor protect it. Well, the Constitution does not speak of privacy either, and according to both *Parrish* and Footnote Four, that textual absence was a big problem for Douglas and his *Griswold* opinion.

Nor did Douglas do himself any favors when it came to the craft-ing of his legal arguments. On the one hand, he began his opinion by repudiating the liberty of contract line of cases. "Overtones of some arguments suggest that *Lochner v. New York* should be our guide. But we decline that invitation,"[44] he wrote. Yet just two paragraphs later, Douglas proceeded to follow *Lochner* anyway when he cited two prec-edents from the 1920s, *Meyer v. Nebraska* and *Pierce v. Society of Sisters,* in which the Supreme Court relied directly on *Lochner*'s expansive protection of liberty in order to reach its respective holdings. In *Meyer,* for instance, Justice James C. McReynolds nullified Nebraska's ban on teaching young students in a foreign language on the grounds that it interfered with the economic liberty of a Bible teacher who worked at a private school. "Without doubt," McReynolds wrote, citing *Lochner,* the liberty protected by the Fourteenth Amendment "denotes not

merely freedom from bodily restraint, but also the right of the individual to contract, to engage in any of the common occupations of life . . .
and generally to enjoy those privileges long recognized at common
law as essential to the orderly pursuit of happiness by free men."[45] Two
years later, in *Pierce*, McReynolds extended that libertarian principle
to overturn Oregon's Compulsory Education Act, which had forbidden parents from educating their children in private schools. "The
child is not the mere creature of the state,"[46] McReynolds declared.
Whether Justice Douglas wanted to admit it or not, *Lochner*'s DNA is
plainly evident in his *Griswold* opinion.

"I LIKE MY PRIVACY AS
WELL AS THE NEXT ONE"

For Justice Hugo Black, enough was enough. *Griswold* was a *Lochner*-ian
ruling, and Black had no qualms about denouncing it as such. An ardent
New Dealer when he joined the Supreme Court in 1938, the former Alabama senator was outraged by the reappearance of those old legal arguments on behalf of new unwritten rights. "I like my privacy as well as the
next one," Black declared in his *Griswold* dissent, "but I am nevertheless
compelled to admit that government has a right to invade it unless prohibited by some specific constitutional provision."[47]

That remark captures Black's entire jurisprudence in a nutshell.
Nobody's idea of a judicial pacifist, Black would only countenance
judicial review in those cases where he thought the law at issue con-
flicted with an express guarantee of the Constitution. "When judges
have a constitutional question in a case before them, and the public
interest calls for its decision," he would announce, "refusal to carry
out their duty to decide would not, I think, be the exercise of an en-
viable 'self-restraint.' Instead I would consider it to be an evasion of
responsibility."[48]

In fact, when it came to the protections spelled out in the Bill of Rights, Black took a nearly absolutist position in favor of judicial intervention. In his famous 1947 dissent in *Adamson v. California,* for instance, Black argued that not only should the Fifth Amendment's safeguard against self-incrimination be strongly defended against the actions of a state government, the entire Bill of Rights should be applied to the states and aggressively enforced by the federal courts. As for the First Amendment, Black took an even harder stance. "Courts must never allow this protection to be diluted or weakened in any way," he maintained. The First Amendment means exactly what it says, and that meaning must be protected by the courts, "without deviation, without exception, without any ifs, buts, or whereases."[49]

But when it came to the judicial enforcement of unenumerated rights, Black drew a bright line in the opposite direction and simply refused to cross it. "I cannot accept a due process clause interpretation which permits life-appointed judges to write their own economic and political views into our Constitution,"[50] he argued, thereby linking the Court's ruling in *Griswold* to its previous decision in *Lochner.* Indeed, Black's *Griswold* dissent took direct aim at Douglas's use of the libertarian precedents set in *Meyer* and *Pierce,* "both decided in opinions by Mr. Justice McReynolds," Black noted, "which elaborated the same natural law due process philosophy found in *Lochner v. New York.*" That approach, he told his colleagues, "is no less dangerous when used to enforce this Court's views about personal rights than those about economic rights."[51]

Much like Learned Hand and Felix Frankfurter, Hugo Black never forgot his outrage over the Supreme Court's earlier use of the Fourteenth Amendment to attack Progressive and New Deal era legislation. "There is a tendency now among some," Black observed in 1968, "to look to the judiciary to make all the major policy decisions of our society under the guise of determining constitutionality. . . . To the people who have such faith in our nine justices, I say that I have known a different court from the one today. What has occurred may occur again."[52]

Unhappily for these old-line Progressives, however, the call for judicial deference fell on increasingly deaf liberal ears as the twentieth century entered its seventh decade. But there was at least one person paying careful attention to what they had to say. At Yale Law School, a young professor named Robert Bork began dusting off the Progressive case for judicial restraint and refurbishing it into an intellectual weapon he might wield on behalf of conservative legal goals.

MAJORITIES RULE

Here's a surprising fact about Robert Bork: The famous arch-conservative initially welcomed the Supreme Court's decision legalizing birth control in *Griswold v. Connecticut*. Born in Pittsburgh, Pennsylvania, in 1927, Bork received an undergraduate education at the University of Chicago and then stuck around on campus to attend law school, graduating with a law degree in 1953. At that time, the University of Chicago was first solidifying its reputation as a bastion of free-market thought, thanks in large part to the work of economics professor and future Nobel Prize winner Milton Friedman, who championed minimal government interference in all aspects of economic (and private) life and famously blamed federal policies rather than capitalist excesses for causing the Great Depression.[53] Bork's encounter with those ideas initially made him into something of a libertarian, and he began applying the insights of free-market economics to the field of antitrust law when he took up his professorship at Yale Law School in 1962.

The academic world of Yale introduced a decisive new influence on Bork's thinking, that of his law school colleague Alexander Bickel. A former law clerk to Justice Felix Frankfurter, Bickel was a brilliant and persuasive advocate of Progressive-style judicial restraint. In his 1962 book *The Least Dangerous Branch,* for instance, Bickel described judicial review as a "counter-majoritarian force in our system" and therefore a "deviant institution" that required stringent justification before use. "When the Supreme Court declares unconstitutional a legislative act or the action of an elected executive," he wrote, "it thwarts the will of representatives of the actual people of the here and now."[54] As a result, Bickel advocated a very modest role for the courts, urging judges to practice "the passive virtues"[55] and to avoid disruptive confrontations with the elected branches of government whenever it was remotely possible to do so.

"I taught a seminar with Professor Bickel starting in about 1963 or 1964," Bork would later recall. "We taught a seminar called Constitutional Theory. I was then all in favor of *Griswold v. Connecticut.*" As Bork then saw it, if the courts would only ground their reasoning in the principles of individual autonomy that served as the foundation for the Bill of Rights, new rights such as privacy might be properly recognized and defended by the judiciary. "I did that for about 6 or 7 years," Bork remembered, "and Bickel fought me every step of the way; said it was not possible. At the end of 6 or 7 years, I decided he was right."[56] That decision transformed Bork's career and changed the future of American law.

Bork went public with his case against *Griswold* in a 1971 article for the *Indiana Law Review* titled "Neutral Principles and Some First Amendment Problems." It remains one of the most influential and frequently cited law review articles to appear in the last four decades. It also set the tone for all subsequent conservative attacks on liberal judicial activism. The "proper role of the Supreme Court under the Constitution" is the central question of American jurisprudence, Bork observed. "It arises when any court either exercises or declines to exercise the power to invalidate any act of another branch of government.

The Supreme Court is a major power center, and we must ask when its power should be used and when it should be withheld."[57]

In Bork's view, the Court's power plainly should have been withheld in *Griswold*. "Every clash between a minority claiming freedom and a majority claiming power to regulate involves a choice between the gratifications of the two groups,"[58] he wrote, echoing Oliver Wendell Holmes's observation that all laws are "necessarily a means by which a body, having the power, put burdens which are disagreeable to them on the shoulders of somebody else."[59] But unless the Constitution provides clear and specific guidance on how to settle each particular dispute, Bork went on, "courts must accept any value choice the legislature makes." To hold otherwise would be to place the subjective views of the judge on a higher plane than the wishes of the people as expressed via their elected representatives. "The issue of the community's moral and ethical values, the issue of the degree of pain an activity causes, are matters concluded by the passage and enforcement of the laws in question," Bork maintained. "The judiciary has no role to play other than that of applying the statutes in a fair and impartial manner."[60]

Taking another page from the Progressive playbook, Bork faulted the Supreme Court for reading the tea leaves of the Due Process Clause in the hopes of divining whether or not a particular species of liberty deserves special protection from the edicts of the majority. What makes "sexual gratification more worthy than economic gratification?" he asked. Absent a clear answer drawn from an unequivocal constitutional provision, "the only course for a principled Court is to let the majority have its way."[61]

Bork also connected the dots between *Lochner* and *Griswold*, arguing that both cases relied on the same flawed reading of the Due Process Clause as a protector of substantive liberty against the will of the majority. "Substantive due process, revived by the *Griswold* case, is and always has been an improper doctrine," Bork declared. "This means that *Griswold*'s antecedents were also wrongly decided," he went on, pointing not only to *Lochner,* but also to *Meyer,* where the Court voided a state ban on teaching foreign languages to children, and *Pierce,* where the Court overturned a state law prohibiting private schools. "With some of these cases I am in political agreement," Bork added, alluding perhaps to his earlier interest in libertarianism, "but there is no justification for the Court's methods." Quoting directly from the majority opinion in *Lochner,* in a passage in which Justice Peckham had asked, "Are we all . . . at the mercy of legislative majorities?" Bork was quick to supply a response: "The correct answer, where the Constitution does not speak, must be 'yes.'"[62]

"AN EXTREME INDIVIDUALISTIC PHILOSOPHY"

While *Griswold* remains controversial, that dispute is nothing compared to the furor still surrounding the Supreme Court's 1973 opinion in *Roe v. Wade.* In *Roe,* a seven-to-two majority extended the right of privacy first recognized in *Griswold* to cover a woman's decision to terminate her pregnancy. Four decades later, the battle over that decision continues to rage, with no end in sight.

The case originated in Texas, where a state law criminalized all abortions except in those instances where the life of the mother was at risk. In his opinion for the Court, Justice Harry Blackmun struck down that prohibition and replaced it with a tripartite system for determining the permissible scope of state regulation. In effect, *Roe* held that a woman may have an abortion for any reason during the first three months of her pregnancy. During the next three months, up to the point of fetal "viability," the state legislature may impose some additional regulations so long as they "are reasonably related to maternal health."[63] Finally, during the final trimester of pregnancy, the state may regulate "and even proscribe" abortions, except when "the preservation of the life or health of the mother"[64] is at stake. "This right of privacy," Blackmun wrote, "whether it be founded in the Fourteenth Amendment's concept of personal liberty and restrictions upon state action, as we feel it to be, or, as the District Court determined, in the Ninth Amendment's reservation of rights to the people, is broad enough to encompass a woman's decision whether or not to terminate her pregnancy."[65]

Writing in dissent, Justice William Rehnquist, who would later serve as chief justice, chastised the majority for distorting the Constitution in order to advance its liberal agenda. "A transaction resulting in an operation such as this is not 'private' in the ordinary usage of that word," Rehnquist observed. The real question was whether or not "the claim of a person to be free from unwanted state regulation of consensual transactions"[66] counts as a form of protected liberty under the Fourteenth Amendment. If it does, Rehnquist continued, then the majority's holding is "closely attuned to the majority opinion of Mr. Justice Peckham" in the *Lochner* case, where a substantive interpretation of the Due Process Clause was similarly deployed on behalf of an unenumerated individual right. The Court's approach in *Roe,* he concluded, "partakes more of judicial legislation"[67] than it does of principled judicial review.

Robert Bork agreed wholeheartedly. *Roe,* he declared, was "the greatest example and symbol of the judicial usurpation of democratic prerogatives in this century," and therefore "should be overturned"[68] as soon as possible. At least in *Griswold,* "spurious as it was," he wrote, the Supreme Court "seemed to confine 'the right of privacy' to areas of life that all Americans would agree should remain private," such as the marital bedroom. *Roe* made no such effort to cabin the impact of its reasoning. Operating under the spell of "an extreme individualistic philosophy," Bork wrote, the Supreme Court was now asserting "that society, acting through government, had very little interest in such matters."[69] As Bork saw it, society, acting through government, had every interest in such matters of morality, and if any member of the public happened to disagree with the current crop of legislation dealing with sexual and reproductive matters, the only recourse was to vote his or her particular moral preferences into law at the next election. As for the judiciary, its only role was to interpret the laws made by the majority, not to make any new laws of its own devising. "Judges who vigorously deny elected representatives the right to base law on morality, simultaneously claim for themselves the right to create constitutional law on the basis of morality, their morality,"[70] he observed.

Justice Oliver Wendell Holmes could not have said it better himself.

FOUR

LIBERTARIANS VS. CONSERVATIVES

I T WAS THE MORNING OF JULY 25, 2005, AND
the *Washington Post* had just detonated a small bombshell. "Supreme
Court nominee John G. Roberts Jr. has repeatedly said he has no
memory of belonging to the Federalist Society," announced reporter
Charles Lane, "but his name appears in the influential, conservative legal
organization's 1997–1998 leadership directory."[1] Five days earlier, President George W. Bush had nominated Roberts to replace retiring Justice
Sandra Day O'Connor, who was stepping down to help care for her husband, John, who was suffering from Alzheimer's disease. Now, thanks to
the *Post,* Roberts was about to face his first hurdle on the path to eventual
confirmation by the U.S. Senate.

Founded in 1982 by a handful of law students at Yale University and the University of Chicago, the Federalist Society for Law and
Public Policy Studies had quickly grown to become the most influential conservative legal organization in American history.[2] Among
the ranks of its current or former members are federal judges, leading

law professors, and high-ranking government officials, including close advisers to some of the most powerful figures in the Republican Party. Founder Steven Calabresi, for instance, who started the original Yale student chapter, later went on to serve as a senior Justice Department official in the Ronald Reagan administration and as a speechwriter for Vice President Dan Quayle. Lee Liberman Otis, who co-founded the original Chicago student chapter, later served as associate counsel to President George H. W. Bush and as an associate deputy attorney general in the Justice Department of George W. Bush. But perhaps the most prominent and influential alumnus of them all is Supreme Court Justice Antonin Scalia, a former faculty adviser at the University of Chicago and still a frequent speaker at Federalist Society events.

That reputation as a bastion of hardcore conservatives was why the *Washington Post* found Roberts's possible membership to be a newsworthy item. Unlike previous Supreme Court nominees such as Robert Bork, who had written widely during his years as a law professor on a range of controversial topics, and had therefore provided plenty of rich material for journalists and critics to mine during his 1987 confirmation fight, Roberts's paper trail was relatively thin by comparison. Indeed, the heaviest baggage Roberts was carrying around[3] consisted of a number of memos written for his old bosses in the Reagan Justice Department spelling out various conservative legal positions. But possible membership in the Federalist Society? That sparked the curiosity of the Washington press corps, who hoped it might help turn up a few clues to Roberts's personal views about the law. Roberts's liberal detractors, meanwhile, hoped his association with the high-profile conservative outfit just might produce the smoking gun needed to thwart his nomination.

"Just because someone belongs to the Federalist Society does not inherently disqualify them," declared Ralph Neas, president of the liberal advocacy group People for the American Way. "But it certainly raises a lot of questions about whether that individual adheres to the judicial philosophy of Clarence Thomas and Antonin Scalia."[4] As Neas and his allies on the left saw it, Thomas and Scalia had been disasters on the bench. Adding another right-wing justice in their vein would compound the catastrophe and should therefore be opposed by any political means necessary. Federalist Society members, meanwhile, fought back against what they saw as a ridiculous witch hunt. "There's no need to distance Roberts from the Federalist Society, for there's nothing disreputable about membership in it," announced one society member in an editorial written for the *New York Post.* "What are we talking about here: the Communist Party? the Ku Klux Klan? No, we're talking about an organization of conservative and libertarian lawyers and legal scholars, begun nearly a quarter of a century ago in response to the overwhelmingly leftist tilt of the nation's law schools, to try to bring some balance and a different perspective to that insular and highly politicized world."[5]

In the end, Roberts survived the scandal. He said he had no memory of ever officially joining the Federalist Society, the White House said it believed him, and the press moved on to fresher controversies once his confirmation hearings got going in the Senate a few months later. What makes the episode worth remembering today is not what it said about Roberts, which was basically nothing, but what it revealed about the fearsome notoriety of both the Federalist Society and the larger conservative legal movement the society had come to represent. Thirty years earlier, in the wake of landmark liberal rulings such as *Roe v. Wade,* the idea of an impending conservative takeover of the Supreme Court would have been waved away with a few polite chuckles. But by 2005, thanks in large part to the intellectual spadework performed by Federalist Society members and fellow travelers, nobody was laughing at the idea of a conservative legal renaissance anymore.

THE BIG TENT

The conservative legal movement occupies one of the biggest tents in modern American politics, with a membership ranging from religious traditionalists to gay-friendly libertarians who really should not be called conservatives at all. Take a glance at a recent federal court docket and you'll see the movement's fingerprints on all sorts of cases, from legal attacks on the regulatory power of the Environmental Protection Agency to efforts to abolish affirmative action to the 2012 lawsuit that nearly toppled Barack Obama's health care law. The movement's origins lie in the political backlash against the Supreme Court's perceived liberal activism during the 1960s and '70s, when it issued landmark decisions on issues ranging from birth control and criminal justice to school busing, voting, and welfare. In the eyes of many conservatives, the Court was not just fulfilling the liberal wish list at that time; it was engaged in the reckless act of inventing new rights previously unheard of in constitutional law, such as the right to an abortion first recognized in *Roe v. Wade.* In the hopes of undoing some of that perceived damage, many of those same conservatives began plotting a legal agenda of their own.

Several organizations soon formed to carry out that mission, including the Pacific Legal Foundation (founded in 1973), the Landmark Legal Foundation (founded in 1977), and the Washington Legal Foundation (also founded in 1977). They filed *amicus* (friend-of-the-court) briefs, challenged various government regulations, and pursued conservative and/or libertarian policy goals—both in and out of court.

A significant early development came with the formation of the Federalist Society in 1982. It was a modest start, to be sure. The society's first public event was a small conference for law students and professors devoted to the subject of federalism, featuring several prominent right-of-center legal scholars, including Yale's Robert Bork, who had been involved with the society's Yale chapter from its inception.

"Law schools and the legal profession are currently strongly dominated by a form of orthodox liberal ideology which advocates a centralized and uniform society," declared that conference's statement of purpose, drafted by society founders Steven Calabresi, Lee Liberman (now Lee Liberman Otis), and David McIntosh. "While some members of the legal community have dissented from these views, no comprehensive conservative critique or agenda has been formulated in this field. This conference will furnish an occasion for such a response to be articulated."[6]

More than three decades later, the Federalist Society still follows that basic blueprint for conservative advocacy. "We're not a position-taking organization," explained society president Eugene Meyer in a 2010 interview. He should know. He has occupied that leadership role since 1983. "We don't lay down the law from the central office."[7] In fact, the Federalist Society takes no official stand on any public-policy issues, including Supreme Court nominations, which it refuses to officially endorse. Instead, the organization seeks to foster an intellectual environment where conservative legal ideas may develop and thrive, essentially creating a far-flung hub where right-of-center law students, lawyers, academics, and activists can gather to share their views and experiences. In large part, the society simply operates as a classic network, connecting the like-minded through student and lawyer chapters that are now present on the campus of every accredited law school in the United States and in more than sixty cities, respectively.

But at the same time, the Federalist Society is no mere social club. From the outset, the society has placed a high premium on intellectual exchange and the nurturing of conservative legal talent, with its various chapters sponsoring numerous debates, panel discussions, and conferences each year, while the national office hosts a massive annual gathering each fall in Washington, D.C., that is itself replete with panels and debates and typically features a conservative federal judge or Supreme Court justice delivering a keynote speech. And while the focus at these events is always on legal topics that matter first and foremost to conservatives, the Federalist Society consistently attracts top-notch participants from across the political spectrum, including many of the academy's most distinguished liberal scholars. And because society membership is as wide ranging as the conservative movement in general, even the most conservative Federalist Society member has been exposed to libertarian legal ideas at one point or another.

Another key milestone in the legal right's modern resurgence came when President Ronald Reagan appointed conservative lawyer and former law professor Edwin Meese III as attorney general in 1985. An aggressive critic of the liberal legal establishment, Meese made judicial restraint, which had been a conservative rallying cry since the advent of the liberal Warren Court, into a central component of Reagan's domestic agenda. "What, then, should a constitutional jurisprudence actually be?" Meese asked in a 1985 speech to the American Bar Association. It should be one rooted in the original intentions of the founders, he said, and it should be one where judges exhibit "a deeply rooted commitment to the idea of democracy."[8] Writing in the *New York Law School Law Review* a decade later, Meese said this approach was meant to undo "more than a quarter century of judicial activism, in which the text of the Constitution, precedent, and certainty were cast aside in favor of wild flings of judicial fancy."[9]

But perhaps the most important factor of all was the intellectual path blazed by Robert Bork. He was there at the outset, mounting the new right's first authoritative counterattack against the Supreme Court's burgeoning jurisprudence in the realms of privacy and abortion, crafting legal arguments that still remain in use today by conservative lawyers and judges. A decade later, Bork, by then an established and respected legal scholar, took an active role in both the fledgling Federalist Society, where his numerous speeches and debates would influence multiple generations of young lawyers (not to mention future judges and politicians), and in the first wave of what conservatives would dub the "Reagan Revolution," formally joining the ranks in 1982 when the president appointed him to the U.S. Court of Appeals for the District of Columbia Circuit, where Bork was finally able to put his own stamp on the law. His failed 1987 nomination to the Supreme Court, meanwhile, galvanized the American right and transformed Bork into something of a martyr figure among conservative legal activists. In short, it's no overstatement to describe him as the conservative legal movement's most significant figure.

Bork's next contribution to the cause came in 1990, when he gave the movement its first great manifesto. Part legal history, part constitutional treatise, and part personal memoir, *The Tempting of America* was a bestseller upon publication and has never gone out of print. It's a fascinating book, weaving Bork's unsuccessful Supreme Court nomination into his larger theme of what he calls the politicization of the law, or the growing desire by many Americans to use the courts to achieve results that should be properly reached via the legislative process. "A judge who announces a decision must be able to demonstrate that he began from recognized legal principles and reasoned in an intellectually coherent and politically neutral way to his result," Bork wrote. "Those who would politicize the law offer the public, and the judiciary, the temptation of results without regard to democratic legitimacy."[10]

At the heart of the problem, as Bork saw it, was the misguided effort to place individual liberty on a consistently higher plane than majority rule. In Bork's view, that approach was totally at odds with the basic American design. The "first principle" of our system is not individualism, Bork argued, it is majoritarianism, a bedrock point that no judge should ever lose sight of. "In wide areas of life," Bork maintained, "majorities are entitled to rule, if they wish, simply because they are majorities."[11]

That approach became widely accepted on the right, as evinced by the conservative response to issues ranging from the regulation of abortion to the scope of the president's executive authority. In such cases, the default conservative position is for the judiciary to defer to the choices made by the elected branches of government.

But at the same time that Bork was setting the intellectual pace on the right, a new breed of libertarian legal thinkers was beginning to craft an ambitious agenda of their own, one that would soon put them on a collision course with the majoritarian jurisprudence championed by Bork. Why the impending conflict? The answer is simple. As the libertarians saw it, Bork was the one making the fundamental error. Individual liberty comes first, the libertarians declared, not majority rule.

"A STANCE OF ACROSS-THE-BOARD LIBERTARIANISM"

One of the first libertarian challenges to the Borkean view came from University of San Diego law professor Bernard Siegan, whose powerful case for libertarian judicial action reverberated throughout the conservative legal world. Siegan became so influential, in fact, that President Reagan even tried to make him a judge on the U.S. Court of Appeals for the Ninth Circuit, although the Senate ultimately rejected Siegan's 1987 nomination—which came on the heels of the Bork debacle—on a party-line vote.

Born in Chicago in 1924, Siegan served in World War II and then went on to complete a law degree at the University of Chicago in 1949. He spent the next two decades practicing real estate law in the greater Chicago area, where he found himself face-to-face with what he saw as a fundamentally unworkable regulatory and bureaucratic regime. He made the leap to the academic world with the 1972 publication of *Land Use without Zoning,* a book-length argument in favor of de-regulation and laissez-faire, using the example of Houston, Texas—a major American city that had developed and thrived despite having no zoning laws on the books—to support his case. Based on the strength of his scholarship, Siegan joined the faculty of the University of San Diego School of Law in 1973, where he would remain for the next thirty years.

At San Diego, Siegan completed work on the volume that would make his name in libertarian and conservative circles. Published in 1980 by the University of Chicago Press, *Economic Liberties and the Constitution* presented a sweeping legal and historical argument: The Supreme Court was wrong to abandon liberty of contract and in fact subverted the Constitution in the fateful year of 1937. "Justices are not intended to be government agents, furthering the interests of the executive or legislative branches in their disputes with citizens," he observed. "A judicial system more concerned to protect the power of the government than the freedom of the individual has lost its mission under the Constitution."[12] Yet thanks to the bifurcated system put in place by Footnote Four of the *Carolene Products* decision, Siegan maintained, the courts now performed exactly that sort of pro-government role when it came to those cases dealing with allegedly "non-fundamental" rights, such as the economic freedom to work in a common occupation. According to Footnote Four, judicial deference should be the rule in all cases dealing with economic regulation. By contrast, if the dispute was over voting rights, the treatment of racial minorities, or the Bill of Rights, Footnote Four openly invited the courts to practice aggressive judging and put the government's actions under the microscope.

In Siegan's view, it was ludicrous for the Supreme Court to en-force this fictitious distinction. At the same moment the Court was busy recognizing and protecting new rights under the Fourteenth

Amendment, he complained, "economic liberties, which significantly touch almost every person's life, have not been accorded appreciable protection."[13] His solution was for the courts to treat all rights equally and for judges to meaningfully scrutinize the government's actions in every case that came before the bench, not just in those areas where the right at issue had been arbitrarily labeled as fundamental. To accomplish this end, Siegan proposed a three-part test for judges to administer when seeking to determine the constitutionality of economic and social legislation. First, the government must shoulder the burden of proof and demonstrate "that the legislation serves important governmental objectives"; second, there must be a close fit between the regulatory means selected and the governmental ends those means are supposed to accomplish; and third, the government must show "that a similar result cannot be achieved by a less drastic means."[14] In other words, his approach "would require the same judicial priority for economic as for other rights."[15]

It was a brazen challenge to the reigning liberal orthodoxy. But it also flew in the face of the judicial restraint championed by conservatives such as Bork. Remember that Bork agreed with the Progressives and saw the Supreme Court's 1905 ruling in favor of economic liberty in *Lochner v. New York,* in which the Court struck down a state law preventing bakery employees from working more than sixty hours per week, as a regrettable example of conservative judicial activism. Siegan took the opposite view, praising the *Lochner* majority for refusing to defer to New York's "speculative conclusions and paternalism."[16] Whereas Bork took his inspiration from the deferential philosophy of Justice Oliver Wendell Holmes, Siegan followed the path of Justice Stephen Field.

The conflict between Siegan's libertarianism and Bork's majoritarianism was perhaps nowhere more apparent than in Siegan's treatment of the Supreme Court's controversial 1965 decision in *Griswold v. Connecticut,* which recognized the privacy rights of married couples to obtain and use birth control devices. *Griswold* was of course the very case that launched Bork on his career as the right's chief advocate of judicial deference and as its leading critic of activist liberal judging. For Siegan, on the other hand, *Griswold* was a defensible ruling that matched up nicely with his larger argument for how the courts should scrutinize the government's actions in each and every case. In fact, Siegan's only real complaint about *Griswold* was that Justice William O. Douglas had followed the "uncharted and circuitous" path of "emanations" and "penumbras" in his majority opinion rather than just using classic Fourteenth Amendment libertarianism to strike down the offending state law. "Applying pre-1937 substantive due process," Siegan explained, the Court might have simply said, "By selling a professional service to married couples, the defendants were exercising liberty of contract. Connecticut's ban was an arbitrary and unjustifiable infringement of this liberty."[17]

That argument proved appealing to libertarians, but Bork rejected it out of hand. Although he did praise Siegan for the clarity of his thinking, Bork still thought Siegan's basic position would grant the judiciary an impermissible license to do mischief. "The logic is impeccable if one accepts *Griswold* and *Roe,* and much else in contemporary jurisprudence, as proper discharges of the judicial function," Bork granted. But if one did not accept the judicial methodology of those cases, as Bork certainly did not, then Siegan's "case for unmentioned economic liberties is, by a parity of reasoning, defeated." The problem, Bork argued, was that Siegan would place the Supreme Court "in a stance of across-the-board libertarianism," when in fact what the Court should be doing is removing itself entirely from these sorts of disputes and letting the democratic process run its course. "There being nothing in the Constitution about maximum hours laws, minimum wage laws, contraception, or abortion," he concluded, "the Court should have said simply that and left the legislative decision where it was."[18]

"YOUR CLASSIC CASE OF MAJORITARIAN TYRANNY"

From the early 1980s forward, libertarians and conservatives would battle repeatedly over the proper role of the courts, facing off in the halls of the academy, in the pages of learned journals, and in countless debates organized by the Federalist Society and other groups. At first, this debate attracted little notice outside of legal and academic circles. But the clash of visions would not remain hidden in the scholarly shadows for long. Indeed, by the early 2000s, the libertarian-conservative divide would come to play a prominent supporting role in the high-profile struggle over gay rights. Here's how it happened.

In 1986 the U.S. Supreme Court considered the constitutionality of a Georgia law criminalizing the act of sodomy, defined by the state as "any sexual act involving the sex organs of one person and the mouth or anus of another."[19] The case originated in 1982, when the police arrived at the home of an Atlanta man named Michael Hardwick in order to serve a warrant. After a roommate let the officers into the residence, they found Hardwick in his bedroom engaged in sexual activity with another man. Both men were then arrested for committing sodomy, although the district attorney later declined to prosecute. Arguing that the existence of the sodomy ban violated his constitutional rights, Hardwick brought suit and took the case all the way up to the Supreme Court.

Writing for a five-to-four majority in *Bowers v. Hardwick,* Justice Byron White upheld the statute. "The issue presented is whether the Federal Constitution confers a fundamental right upon homosexuals to engage in sodomy," White wrote, "and hence invalidates the laws of the many States that still make such conduct illegal, and have done so for a very long time."[20] He added that the case also raised significant questions about the proper role of the judiciary in a democratic society. Although it is true, White observed, that the Supreme Court had previously protected the sexual privacy of married couples to use birth control in the home without state interference in 1965's *Griswold v. Connecticut,* and then later extended that same right to cover the use of contraceptives by unmarried persons in 1972's *Eisenstadt v. Baird,* the Court was unwilling to push the right of sexual privacy any further in order to reach protected status for homosexual conduct.

Because "the Court is most vulnerable and comes nearest to illegitimacy" when granting judicial protection to unenumerated rights "having little or no cognizable roots in the language or design of the Constitution,"[21] White concluded, the justices lacked sufficient cause to sign off on the recognition of gay rights in the present case. As for Hardwick's claim that the state's ban was rooted in a discriminatory bias against gay people, White responded that legislation "is constantly based on notions of morality, and if all laws representing essentially moral choices are to be invalidated under the Due Process Clause, the courts will be very busy indeed."[22] The fatal combination of majority rule and judicial deference therefore spelled doom for the legal challenge to Georgia's sodomy ban. Predictably, Robert Bork was among the many conservatives who cheered the outcome of the case. "Hardwick's suit," he wrote, "rested upon nothing in the Constitution and so was one more sortie in our cultural war."[23]

In the wake of *Bowers,* gay rights advocates redoubled their efforts, and in 2003 a promising new case landed on the Supreme Court docket. At issue in *Lawrence v. Texas* was the Lone Star State's 1973 Homosexual Conduct Law, which singled out same-sex sodomy as a criminal offense. Once again, the case generated enormous interest among activists on both sides of the contentious issue, with more than thirty different organizations filing friend-of-the-court briefs urging the justices to rule for one party or the other. Among those supporting the state of Texas in its fight to maintain criminal sanctions against homosexuality were well-known conservative groups such as the Family Research Council and Concerned Women for America. Siding with petitioners John Geddes Lawrence and Tyron Garner, the two men originally charged with violating the statute, were liberal stalwarts such as the American Civil Liberties Union and the National Organization for Women.

But Lawrence and Garner also received a critical piece of support from an organization whose involvement on their side of the case surprised more than a few observers at the time. That organization was the Cato Institute, a leading Washington think tank whose agenda of limited government and free-market economics is more typically associated with the political right. Founded in 1977, Cato takes its name from *Cato's Letters,* a series of political pamphlets published in early eighteenth-century Britain that influenced many of the leaders of the American Revolution. The institute's principles are unapologetically libertarian, and its mission is to transform public policy by advancing and defending those principles in the public arena. When the Supreme Court finally ruled to invalidate the Texas ban on homosexual conduct, Cato's friend-of-the-court brief on behalf of Lawrence and Garner would be cited twice by the majority and would play a valuable role in shaping the Court's reasoning.

Cato's influence in the realm of legal affairs is due primarily to the vision of a man named Roger Pilon, the director of the institute's Center for Constitutional Studies, which he founded in 1989 and has been running ever since. Sitting in his Washington office on a crisp November afternoon in 2013, Pilon explained to me why the decision to join the fight against Texas's Homosexual Conduct Law was "an easy call for us." In the wake of *Bowers v. Hardwick,* he said, "this was a case that cried out to be addressed. These are people who are harming no one. It's your classic case of majoritarian tyranny."[24]

By the time *Lawrence* arrived in 2003, Pilon was already a seasoned veteran in the long libertarian war against conservative majoritarianism. He got his start in political philosophy, earning a PhD from the University of Chicago in 1979 with a dissertation entitled "A Theory of Rights: Toward Limited Government." Among the members of his dissertation committee was the Nobel Prize–winning libertarian economist Milton Friedman. "Not fully realizing at that time the jurisprudential implications of what I was doing," Pilon explained, "my aim was to show that the natural rights orientation of the Founders, stemming from Locke, was right, whereas the welfare rights orientation of modern liberals was wrong. Clearly, that set me apart from the anti-rights posture many conservatives were taking in reaction to the liberal judicial activism of the time."[25]

Pilon set himself even further apart from those conservatives when his focus shifted to the philosophy of law. "The conservatives reacted to what the Warren and Burger Courts were doing by criticizing the rights revolution. And I thought to myself, this isn't right either, because this country was founded on the notion of natural rights," Pilon recalled. "So while the liberals are wrong in moving in the direction of constitutionally protected welfare rights," he added, "the conservatives were little better in calling on the Court to defer to the political branches that had given us the Leviathan. So I began thinking there's got to be a path between these two extremes."[26]

Pilon began the work of charting that path by taking his case directly to the conservatives in April 1981, addressing the annual national meeting of the Philadelphia Society, which at that time was the country's foremost gathering of right-leaning intellectuals. Among the members of his audience that night was future Attorney General Ed Meese, who had just arrived in Washington to serve as an adviser to

President Ronald Reagan. Meese was there to deliver the event's keynote address. Pilon's speech, entitled "On the Foundations of Justice," began with a reminder to the assembled conservative worthies that by embracing judicial deference, they were essentially surrendering the field when it came to the fight over an entire branch of the government, and thereby undermining the system of checks and balances in the process. "We do not live in a pure democracy but rather in a republic wherein the 'will' of the legislature or of the executive is subject to scrutiny by the 'reason' of the Court," he observed. Turning next to the text of the Constitution, Pilon observed that its broad guarantees of individual rights are not just there for show, but are instead designed "to stand athwart the utilitarian calculus, to brake the democratic, majoritarian engine."[27]

Pilon later described that speech to me as a "gentle"[28] critique of the conservative mainstream, designed to get the libertarian perspective into circulation among the right's top thinkers. But when it came time to deal with the majoritarian arguments put forward by Robert Bork, Pilon pulled no punches. He first grappled with Bork in the pages of *Reason* magazine, the flagship libertarian monthly, where he argued that Bork's calls for a deferential judiciary "would give wide berth to the majority to plan and regulate our lives." Bork's misguided emphasis on democracy over liberty "is our inheritance from the Progressive Era, not from the Founding," Pilon wrote. "At the Founding they got it right. They started with the individual."[29]

Pilon pressed the point with even greater force in a 1991 editorial written for the *Wall Street Journal* titled "Rethinking Judicial Restraint." Bork's case for a deferential judiciary, Pilon argued, was not just wrong as a strategic matter, it was wrong on the fundamentals of constitutional law. "The Founders took every step to protect our liberties, even from the majority—indeed, especially from the majority," Pilon argued. Yet under the Bork approach, he wrote, the judiciary is required to "shirk its duty to secure those rights by deferring to the political branches in the name of 'self government.'" The correct approach, Pilon countered, was for the courts to "hold the acts of the other branches up to the light of strict constitutional scrutiny. There is no place for 'restraint' in this." The time had arrived, Pilon concluded, for conservatives "to rethink 'judicial restraint' and restore the judiciary to its rightful place in a system of separated powers."[30]

"LIBERTARIANS THREW DOWN THE GAUNTLET"

At the same time, Pilon was also working behind the scenes to advance the growing libertarian insurgency. One of his key contributions came in 1983, when he approached his future colleagues at the Cato Institute with the idea for a conference devoted to the topic of "Economic Liberties and the Judiciary." In a lunch meeting with Cato president Ed Crane and *Cato Journal* editor James Dorn, Pilon pitched the idea of bringing together prominent libertarian and conservative experts to draw attention to the widening debate. "On the back of a napkin," Pilon remembered, "I sketched out who should be there and what should be covered, and a year later it was put together and held in a hotel here in Washington."[31]

The result was a seminal event in the evolution of modern legal conservatism. Held in October 1984, the Cato conference attracted a standing-room-only crowd of Washington insiders. Among the invited participants was University of Chicago law professor and rising libertarian star Richard Epstein, who argued that the judiciary should play an active role in defending economic liberty (much as it did in cases such as *Lochner v. New York*), and Antonin Scalia, then a judge on the U.S. Court of Appeals for the District of Columbia Circuit, who advanced the Borkean (and Oliver Wendell Holmesian) view that the courts should defer to the political branches on such matters.

"The Supreme Court decisions rejecting substantive due process in the economic field are clear, unequivocal and current," Scalia declared. He added that "in my view the position the Supreme Court has arrived at is good—or at least that the suggestion that it change its position is even worse." Scalia clarified that he was not personally hostile to the idea of economic liberty—far from it. "Rather, my skepticism arises about misgivings about, first, the effect of such expansion on the behavior of courts in other areas quite separate from economic liberty, and second, the ability of the courts to limit their constitutionalizing to those elements of economic liberty that are sensible." The best course, he concluded, was for the courts to adopt a thoroughgoing posture of judicial restraint. "In the long run, and perhaps even in the short run, the reinforcement of mistaken and unconstitutional perceptions of the role of the courts in our system far outweighs whatever evils may have accrued from undue judicial abstention in the economic field."[32]

Rising in response, Richard Epstein tossed aside his prepared remarks and instead launched an impromptu attack on Scalia's call for judicial deference. "Scalia's position represents the mainstream of American constitutional theory today," he began. "My purpose is to take issue with the conventional wisdom."[33] Under the view endorsed by Scalia, Epstein declared, "it is up to Congress and the states to determine the limitations of their own power—which, of course, totally subverts the original constitutional arrangement of limited government." The Scalia view, Epstein said, ignores the Constitution's "many broad and powerful clauses designed to limit the jurisdiction of both federal and state governments," as well as those clauses "designed to limit what the states and the federal government can do within the scope of their admitted power."[34] Just compare "the original Constitution with the present state of judicial interpretation," he continued, and "the real issue becomes not how to protect the status quo, but what kinds of incremental adjustments should be made in order to shift the balance back toward the original design." Taking the text of the Constitution seriously, Epstein concluded, requires "some movement in the direction of judicial activism"[35] on behalf of economic rights.

This debate brought the libertarian-conservative divide into the spotlight. "That's why the conference was so important as a benchmark," Pilon later explained. "For the first time, libertarians threw down the gauntlet."[36]

Building on the success of that conference, the Cato Institute and its libertarian allies proceeded to turn up the heat on the Bork-Scalia approach. The next major offensive came in 1986 when Cato published a short book by the Harvard political scientist Stephen Macedo carrying the provocative title *The New Right v. The Constitution*. Macedo's target was the majoritarian jurisprudence of Bork and Scalia. "When conservatives like Bork treat rights as islands surrounded by a sea of government powers," Macedo wrote, "they precisely reverse the view of the Founders as enshrined in the Constitution, wherein government powers are limited and specified and rendered as islands surrounded by a sea of individual rights."[37] That philosophical stance would later animate Cato's brief in the *Lawrence* case challenging Texas's ban on homosexual conduct.

Meanwhile, at the University of Chicago, Richard Epstein was putting the finishing touches on the book that would make him one of the premier names in both libertarian and conservative legal scholarship. Published in 1985 by Harvard University Press, *Takings: Private Property and the Power of Eminent Domain* revolutionized both the academic and political debates over property rights and the Constitution. Drawing from law, philosophy, economics, and history, Epstein advanced a sweeping challenge to the constitutional underpinnings of the modern regulatory state. Pointing to the text of the Fifth Amendment, which forces the government to pay just compensation when it takes private property for a public use, Epstein reasoned that any "taking" of an individual's property, whether it is done through physical seizure or government regulation, triggers the just compensation requirement. Furthermore, because "representative government begins with the premise that the state's rights against its citizens are no greater than the sum of the rights of the individuals whom it benefits in any given situation," a forced taking could only be legitimate if it left "individuals with rights more valuable than those they have been deprived of."[38]

In practical terms, *Takings* argued that "the eminent domain clause and parallel clauses in the Constitution render constitutionally infirm or suspect many of the heralded reforms and institutions of the twentieth century: zoning, rent control, workers' compensation laws, transfer payments, progressive taxation."[39] As a corollary, the federal courts were expected to curtail or invalidate such government practices under Epstein's reading of the Constitution.

The anti-majoritarian implications of this approach were not lost on the members of the conservative old guard. Bork himself rejected Epstein's views as "not plausibly related"[40] to the Constitution, while Charles Fried, who served as Ronald Reagan's solicitor general between 1985 and 1989, later complained about Epstein's pernicious influence on many of the young conservative lawyers then working in the Reagan Justice Department. Those lawyers, Fried recalled in his memoir, "many drawn from the ranks of the then-fledgling Federalist Society and often devotees of the extreme libertarian views of Chicago law professor Richard Epstein—had a specific, aggressive, and it seemed to me, quite radical project in mind: to use the Takings Clause of the Fifth Amendment as a severe brake upon federal and state Regulation."[41]

Epstein's radical position soon became so famous—some might say infamous—that it was even used in an attempt to derail a conservative Supreme Court nominee. During Clarence Thomas's 1991

Supreme Court confirmation hearings, before Anita Hill's explosive allegations of sexual harassment claimed the headlines, Senator Joseph Biden of Delaware tried to discredit Thomas by linking him to Epstein, pointing to a speech Thomas had once given to a conservative audience in which the future justice said he found something attractive in Epstein's arguments. Biden even theatrically waved around a copy of *Takings* to make his point, prompting one libertarian publication to quip that Biden's approach was tantamount to asking, "Are you now or have you ever been a libertarian?"[42]

Theatrics aside, Biden was right to worry. As we'll see in the coming chapters, Clarence Thomas would indeed reveal a libertarian streak in several areas of the law.

"JUDICIAL RESPONSIBILITY"

These various libertarian currents came to a head with the establishment of the Cato Institute's Center for Constitutional Studies in January 1989. In his original October 1988 proposal for the center, an eighteen-page, single-spaced document, Roger Pilon placed heavy emphasis on the libertarian vision of an active judiciary committed to protecting a wide range of fundamental rights, an approach that openly challenged the reigning legal orthodoxies on both the left and the right. "This 'third position'— which in truth is the original position of the Founders—calls upon judges to interpret the broad language of the Constitution neither by deferring to legislative majorities nor by consulting contemporary social values," Pilon wrote, "but rather by repairing to the moral, political, and legal theory of natural rights and individual liberty that has stood behind and informed the Constitution from its inception."[43]

Not only would the proposed Center for Constitutional Studies provide a headquarters for the libertarian insurgency in its escalating campaign against the legal establishment, Pilon argued, it would also serve as a sort of shadow university for libertarian legal scholarship, publishing and promoting such work through books, studies, and articles, as well as through conferences, speeches, and other events aimed at reaching a wider audience. "If the price of liberty is indeed eternal vigilance," Pilon wrote, "then one form that vigilance takes, especially in the age of communications, is constant attention to the ideas that support the institutions of liberty,"[44] including the idea of "a return to judicial responsibility."[45] Over the coming decades, Cato's Center for Constitutional Studies would play precisely that role in the growing national debate over the courts. All things considered, it would be difficult to overstate Cato's influence, particularly in terms of pushing the conservative legal movement in a more libertarian direction.

Which brings us back to *Lawrence v. Texas* and the looming Supreme Court battle over gay rights. When Roger Pilon saw that case coming up in late 2002, he knew immediately that it was a perfect fit for Cato's mission. Working in cooperation with Yale law professor William Eskridge, a leading authority in the areas of gay rights, equal protection, and criminal justice, Pilon, plus his Cato colleague Robert A. Levy, sat down to map out a legal strategy for Cato to use when tackling the case. "Bob, Bill, and I got together over the holidays at Bob's place up in Chevy Chase," Maryland, Pilon remembered. "That was the beginning of it."[46] The final brief, written by Eskridge and edited by Pilon and Levy, was then submitted to the Supreme Court several months ahead of the scheduled oral arguments.

The Cato brief raised two principal challenges to the Texas ban on homosexual conduct. First, it framed the case as a conflict between the individual liberty that all Americans should rightfully enjoy and an illegitimate exercise of state power by overreaching Texas officials. "America's founding generation established our government to protect rather than invade fundamental liberties, including personal security, the sanctity of the home, and interpersonal relations," the Cato brief argued. "So long as people are not harming others, they can presumptively engage in the pursuit of their own happiness. . . . A law authorizing the police to intrude into one's intimate consensual relations is at war with this precept and should be invalidated."[47]

Second, drawing heavily from Eskridge's pioneering book *Gaylaw*, the brief surveyed some 200 years of American history to show that while sodomy laws may have been on the books since the nation's founding, those laws were originally directed overwhelmingly at predatory and public acts (not private consensual conduct) and were largely aimed at the protection of children and other vulnerable groups. Regulations aimed specifically at adult homosexual conduct, on the other hand, only began to appear in the mid-twentieth century. In other words, Texas's Homosexual Conduct Law could find no refuge by trying to place itself in a lengthy historical tradition. "Sodomy law's twentieth century intrusion into the private lives and homes of gay people is a regulatory expansion that violates the Constitution,"[48] the brief argued.

That dual emphasis on liberty and history would help shape the Supreme Court's decision.

GAY RIGHTS ON TRIAL

The Supreme Court heard oral argument in *Lawrence v. Texas*, case number 02–102, on the morning of March 26, 2003. Up first at the lectern that day was Washington lawyer Paul M. Smith, representing Lawrence and Garner in their challenge to the Texas statute. "The State of Texas in this case claims the right to criminally punish any unmarried adult couple for engaging in any form of consensual sexual intimacy that the State happens to disapprove of," Smith began, explaining to the Court that this approach violated the fundamental right of all persons under the Fourteenth Amendment "to be free from unwarranted State intrusion into their personal decisions about their preferred forms of sexual expression."[49] Because the state was unable to offer any justification for its restriction except "we want it that way" and "we don't want those people over there to have that same right,"[50] Smith argued, the sodomy law must be struck down as an illegal exercise of government power.

"You can put it that way," responded Justice Antonin Scalia, reacting to Smith's characterization of the state's motives, "you can make it sound very puritanical." But Scalia failed to see why the majority's disapproval of homosexuality did not qualify as a permissible basis for legislation. "These are laws dealing with public morality," Scalia stressed. "They've always been on the book, nobody has ever told them they're unconstitutional simply because there are moral perceptions behind them."[51] As Scalia saw it, the only question that mattered was whether a cognizable constitutional right was at stake. "Any law stops people from doing what they really want to do,"[52] he told Smith, but that fact alone does not make any of those laws unconstitutional. Scalia left no doubt he believed the majority was entitled to write its moral views into law, including when those views made private homosexual conduct a crime.

It was the libertarian-conservative debate in a nutshell. Does the majority have the right to rule in wide areas of life simply because it is the majority? Or does individual liberty come first, a fact that requires the government to provide the courts with a legitimate health or safety rationale in support of every contested regulation?

That philosophical divide would be thrown into even starker relief once Charles A. Rosenthal, the district attorney of Harris County, Texas, rose in defense of his state's Homosexual Conduct Law. "Texas has the right to set moral standards and can set bright line moral standards for its people," Rosenthal told the Court. "And in the setting of those moral standards, I believe that they can say that certain kinds of activity can exist and certain kinds of activity cannot exist."[53]

Justice Stephen Breyer quickly pushed back against Rosenthal's insistence that public morality alone offered a sufficient justification to sustain the law. What about banning other things a majority of the citizenry might find immoral, Breyer asked him. "People felt during World War I that it was immoral to teach German in the public schools," he observed, referring to the Supreme Court's 1923 decision in *Meyer v. Nebraska,* which struck down that state's ban on foreign-language instruction for children (over the dissent of Justice Oliver Wendell Holmes). "Would you say that the State has every right" to pass a law like that? "See, the hard question here," Breyer continued, "is can the State, in fact, pass anything that it wants at all, because they believe it's immoral? If you were going to draw the line somewhere, I guess you might begin to draw it when the person is involved inside his own bedroom and not hurting anybody else."

As Rosenthal began to answer Breyer's questions, however, a seemingly impatient Scalia jumped back in to supply his own answer. "The rational basis is the State thinks it immoral just as the State thinks adultery immoral or bigamy immoral," Scalia declared.

"Or teaching German," Breyer immediately shot back.

"Well," Scalia began to respond, before Chief Justice William Rehnquist promptly silenced them both. "Maybe we should go through counsel, yes,"[54] Rehnquist gruffly commanded. It would not be the last time Breyer and Scalia debated judicial philosophy on the bench—or off.

Rosenthal remained at the lectern for another eight minutes answering the justices' questions, but by that point it was clear to most observers that the damage was done to his side of the case. Texas had seemingly failed to convince a majority of the Court that its law rested on anything more than a moral disapproval of homosexuality, and that justification alone appeared very unlikely to persuade five or more justices to vote in support of the statute.

Exactly three months later, on the morning of June 26, the Supreme Court dispelled any remaining doubts by announcing its decision in the case. Not only was the Texas statute struck down, the Court declared, but the 1986 decision in *Bowers v. Hardwick* was overruled as well.

"Liberty protects the person from unwarranted government intrusions into a dwelling or other private places," began the majority opinion of Justice Anthony Kennedy. Moreover, "liberty presumes an autonomy of self that includes freedom of thought, belief, expression, and certain intimate conduct."[55] In the Court's view, that autonomy clearly included the private, consensual behavior at issue in the case. Having established that the constitutional guarantee of liberty was at stake, Kennedy continued, the burden therefore fell squarely on the state to justify its intrusion. Since Texas had failed to do so, outside of simply pointing to the majority's moral opprobrium toward homosexuality, the law failed to serve a legitimate government purpose and was declared to be null and void. Among the authorities relied on to support this position was the Cato Institute brief, which Kennedy twice cited approvingly, essentially adopting the brief's broad libertarian stance and detailed historical analysis as the Court's own. As for the seventeen-year-old decision in *Bowers v. Hardwick,* Kennedy continued, "its continuance as precedent demeans the lives of homosexual people." That ruling "was not correct when it was decided," he held, "and it is not correct today."[56]

"A COURT THAT IS IMPATIENT OF DEMOCRATIC CHANGE"

Writing in dissent, Justice Antonin Scalia accused his colleagues in the majority of abandoning all pretense of fair and impartial judging.

"Today's opinion is the product of a Court," he wrote, "that has largely signed on to the so-called homosexual agenda." Never mind that most Americans do not subscribe to that agenda, he continued, the Court has forgotten its role as a neutral voice in our democratic system and "taken sides in the culture war."[57]

What's more, Scalia complained, the *Lawrence* majority had just upended the Court's own precedents in order to engage in a bout of libertarian judicial activism. Pointing to the Court's long line of post-New Deal jurisprudence, where in case after case the Supreme Court had said that only "fundamental" rights are entitled to strong judicial protection, Scalia accused the Court of inventing a new fundamental right to homosexual sodomy without having the courage to come right out and say so. Texas's Homosexual Conduct Law "undoubtedly imposes constraints on liberty," Scalia observed. "So do laws prohibiting prostitution, recreational use of heroin, and, for that matter, working more than 60 hours per week in a bakery,"[58] he wrote, thereby linking the rationale in *Lawrence* to the Court's 1905 ruling in *Lochner,* which overruled a maximum hours law for New York bakers. Yet according to the legal regime that reversed *Lochner* and has been in place since the New Deal, Scalia summarized, a mere constraint on liberty was not enough to trigger searching review by the courts. This case called for judicial deference, Scalia maintained, not judicial scrutiny. To qualify as a fundamental right, he continued, pointing to the Court's previous cases, that right must be "deeply rooted in this Nation's history and traditions."[59] The right of homosexuals to commit sodomy, Scalia announced, plainly failed to meet that test. "What Texas has chosen to do is well within the range of traditional democratic action," he concluded, "and its hand should not be stayed through the invention of a brand-new 'constitutional right' by a Court that is impatient of democratic change."[60]

A LIBERTARIAN DECISION?

Scalia had a point. In a long line of cases stretching back to the 1938 ruling in *United States v. Carolene Products Co.,* the Supreme Court has routinely enforced a distinction between "fundamental" rights, such as free speech, which are entitled to searching judicial protection, and other rights, such as economic liberty, which are not. Scalia was also correct when he said that the Court had developed a test over the years to determine whether or not a particular right would be recognized as fundamental, and he was correct yet again in saying that Kennedy's majority opinion in *Lawrence* failed (or refused) to apply that test in order to determine whether or not gay rights should now be counted as fundamental under the Court's precedents.

But was Scalia also correct when he said that Kennedy's approach in *Lawrence* violated the Constitution? The members of the libertarian legal movement thought not, and one of its leading figures promptly stood up to claim *Lawrence* as a victory for their approach to the law. Writing on the website of *National Review,* libertarian Boston University law professor Randy Barnett, who in 2012 would be described as "the intellectual architect"[61] of the legal challenge to President Barack Obama's health care law, made the case that Kennedy's opinion in *Lawrence* was a long-overdue "libertarian revolution" against the misguided judicial deference first imposed on America during the Progressive and New Deal eras.

"If you reread his opinion," Barnett wrote, "you will see that Justice Kennedy never mentions any presumption to be accorded to the Texas legislature. More importantly, he never tries to justify the right to same-sex sexuality as fundamental." Instead, Barnett continued, Kennedy "puts all his energy into demonstrating that same-sex sexual freedom is a legitimate aspect of liberty—unlike, for example, actions that violate the rights of others, which are not liberty but license."

In other words, the Supreme Court had settled a major case by rejecting the sweeping judicial deference championed by the likes of Oliver Wendell Holmes, Felix Frankfurter, and Robert Bork. On top of that, the Court had done so by breathing real life into the promise of liberty guaranteed by the Fourteenth Amendment, the very thing libertarians have been urging since the time of Justice Stephen Field. As for Scalia's *Lawrence* dissent, Barnett wrote, it was "both entirely predictable and remarkably feeble." To say that the majority has the right to rule simply because it is the majority, Barnett argued, is the worst sort of circular logic. "This judgment of morality means nothing more than that a majority of the legislature disapproves of this conduct, which would be true *whenever* a legislature decides to outlaw something," he wrote. "Such a doctrine would amount to granting an unlimited police power to state legislatures."[62] Put differently, the judiciary is supposed to slam the brakes on the tyranny of the majority, not hit the gas.

It was the 1984 Epstein-Scalia debate all over again, except this time Scalia was a justice on the U.S. Supreme Court, and he was fighting a rearguard action to keep the libertarian insurgency at bay. Nor would it be the last time that Scalia and his fellow justices found themselves under fire from the libertarians. Over the coming decade, on issues ranging from property rights to gun control to medical marijuana, the libertarian legal movement would push the Supreme Court repeatedly to endorse its broad constitutional vision of personal and economic freedom. The battle for control of American law was about to heat up.

FIVE

LITIGATING
FOR LIBERTY

A FUNNY THING HAPPENED ONE DAY IN
April 2012. Judge Janice Rogers Brown, an outspoken conservative who sits on the U.S. Court of Appeals for the District of Columbia Circuit, aggressively criticized a federal regulation for
harassing entrepreneurs, ripping off consumers, and enriching a small
group of politically connected insiders. But then, once she got that out of
her system, Judge Brown went ahead and upheld the regulation anyway.

At issue in the case of *Hettinga v. United States* was a federal regulatory scheme first put in place during the New Deal in order to control the price of milk. Under the terms of the Agricultural Marketing
Agreement Act of 1937, minimum milk prices were set throughout
various geographical areas around the country. Most of the dairy industry fell under the direct control of this system, and still remains so
today, though an exemption was originally granted for what's known
in the trade as "producer-handlers," who are basically dairy farmers
who also bottle and distribute their own milk.

In the early 2000s, Sarah Farms, an Arizona-based producer-handler owned and operated by Dutch immigrant Hein Hettinga and his wife, Ellen, made a splash with consumers throughout Southern California when they started selling their milk for a lower price than the federally fixed minimum on the shelves of Costco and other popular retailers. In response, the Hettingas' competitors turned to the government for help. As the *Washington Post* described it, "a coalition of giant milk companies and dairies, along with their congressional allies, decided to crush Hettinga's initiative. For three years, the milk lobby spent millions of dollars on lobbying and campaign contributions and made deals with lawmakers, including incoming Senate Majority Leader Harry M. Reid (D-Nev.)."[1]

The final result of that lobbying was the Milk Regulation Equity Act of 2005, which, among other things, imposed minimum milk pricing on all producer-handlers operating out of Arizona that distribute at least 3,000,000 pounds of fluid milk per month. Not coincidentally, Sarah Farms was the only producer-handler in the entire state that fit that description. The 2005 law also imposed new minimum price rules on all handlers selling prepackaged milk in California—a provision that also applied to just one existing business, the Arizona-based bottling facility GH Dairy, which also happened to be owned and operated by the Hettingas.

So the family brought suit in federal court, charging the U.S. government with singling out their businesses for abuse and violating their rights under the Constitution. In response, the government argued that the new law was rationally related to its interest in regulating the dairy industry, and was therefore entitled to significant deference from the courts. When Judge Brown finally reviewed the government's justifications, however, she rejected them as pure fantasy, likening the 2005 law to forced collectivization and describing it as a naked wealth transfer that came at the expense of both the Hettingas and the milk-drinking public. So what explains Brown's decision to reaffirm the law despite her obvious distaste for it? "Given the long-standing precedents in this area," she complained, "no other result is possible."[2]

Brown was referring to the rational-basis test, the highly deferential approach to economic regulations the courts have been using since the New Deal. In the 1938 case of *United States v. Carolene Products Co.,* for example, the Supreme Court held that "the existence of facts supporting the legislative judgment is to be presumed" in all cases dealing with "regulatory legislation affecting ordinary commercial transactions."[3] Sixteen years later, in the case of *Williamson v. Lee Optical Inc.,* the Court dug in even further, announcing that when it came to the constitutionality of economic regulations, "It is enough that there is an evil at hand for correction, and that it might be thought that the particular legislative measure was a rational way to correct it."[4] In short, so long as lawmakers *might* have had a "rational basis" for their actions, the courts are supposed to let those actions stand.

"The practical effect of rational basis review of economic regulation," Brown complained in her *Hettinga* opinion, "is the absence of any check on the group interests that all too often control the democratic process. It allows the legislature free rein to subjugate the common good and individual liberty to the electoral calculus of politicians, the whims of majorities, or the self-interest of factions." But because she was duty-bound as a federal appellate judge to follow Supreme Court precedent, she continued, her hands were tied. "Rational basis review means property is at the mercy of the pillagers,"[5] Brown concluded.

Her language was certainly provocative, but Brown's analysis had merit. The rational-basis test does indeed stack the deck in favor of lawmakers. That's the whole reason the Supreme Court adopted it in the first place. It evolved directly from the judicial deference long championed by Justice Oliver Wendell Holmes and his Progressive and New Deal allies, best captured by Holmes's oft-quoted maxim that the judiciary had no business interfering with "the right of a majority to embody their opinions in law."[6] For those plaintiffs unfortunate enough to come up against the rational-basis test in court, the odds are purposefully piled up against them. As the Supreme Court once described it, "the burden is on the one attacking the legislative arrangement to negative every conceivable basis which might conceivably support it."[7] In other words, plaintiffs and their lawyers must not only defeat the government's *stated* rationale for the contested regulation, they must also defeat any *hypothetical* rationale that a government lawyer, or even the presiding judge, might "conceivably" imagine in defense of the statute during trial.

To say the least, that is a rocky road to travel on the quest to invalidate a statute. But it is not an impossible road to travel, as has been proved repeatedly in recent years by a small band of libertarian lawyers employed by the Institute for Justice (IJ), an Arlington, Virginia–based outfit that styles itself as "the nation's only libertarian, civil liberties, public interest law firm." Over the past two decades, the Institute for Justice has defeated government regulations in dozens of major cases, including winning the first victory for economic liberty at the federal appellate court level since the New Deal. On top of that, IJ lawyers have won four times at the U.S. Supreme Court, including a 2005 decision invalidating protectionist state laws that banned the direct sale of wine to consumers from out-of-state wineries. And they have triumphed in such cases despite the extraordinary disadvantages they face under the rational-basis test and other widely practiced forms of judicial restraint.

If the libertarian legal movement is waging an insurgency, then the lawyers at the Institute for Justice comprise the elite core of its frontline fighters. Their mission is to defeat the enemy on its own ground and persuade deferential judges to overrule government actions. And

while they don't win every case, they have found more than a few ways
to advance the cause.

"A CLARENCE DARROW TYPE"

The Institute for Justice was founded in Washington, D.C., in 1991 under the leadership of William H. "Chip" Mellor, a veteran litigator with
deep roots in the libertarian and conservative legal movements. Mellor's
interest in politics dates back to his undergraduate years at Ohio State
University in the early 1970s, when he was a student protestor raging
against the Vietnam War. "During that time," he later remembered, he
had "a bit of an epiphany, and that was that both the left and right were
really seeking the same thing, which was to use power in order to force
others to do their bidding." That realization sent him on a quest to find
a better approach to politics, one more attuned to the rights of the individual. Eventually he would discover the works of libertarian writers such
as Milton Friedman and Ayn Rand. "That convinced me that libertarianism had a lot to offer and that the arena in which I thought that was most
potentially effective was the courtroom."

So Mellor enrolled in law school at the University of Denver with
the express purpose of becoming a crusading libertarian lawyer. "I
thought I'd be like a Clarence Darrow type," he recalled, referring to
the famous defense attorney, and "ride into court and advocate on behalf of these wonderful clients and change the world." He graduated in
1977 and quickly discovered that the pressing requirements of private
practice left him little time to fight the good fight. But then a chance
encounter changed everything. On a visit to his old law school campus
that year, Mellor noticed a job listing for the position of law clerk at an
organization called the Mountain States Legal Foundation. That ad
featured one phrase in particular that caught Mellor's eye: "free mar-
kets, private property rights, and individual liberty." "I'd never seen

anything remotely like that *anywhere*," he remembered with a laugh. "So I came up short and said, 'Whoa, I've got to find out more about this.'" He went by the group's office the next day to drop off his résumé in the hope that they might someday need another lawyer; when the spot for a new staff attorney soon opened up, he eagerly signed on.

The conservative legal movement was still in its infancy in 1977, and the Denver-based Mountain States Legal Foundation was one of just a handful of organizations then focused on promoting a right-of-center agenda in court. Founded that year thanks to seed money provided by the beer magnate Joseph Coors, a prominent supporter of conservative causes who also sat on the foundation's original board of directors, Mountain States pursued a now-familiar conservative program, targeting environmental regulations, affirmative action policies, and government infringements on the free enterprise system. Mellor initially found it to be a decent fit for his admittedly non-mainstream views, although by no means a perfect one. "The people who were running it had never heard the term 'libertarian' before," he recalled with a wry smile.

The first signs of real trouble came in the fall of 1982, when Mountain States launched a high-profile lawsuit against the city of Denver over its decision to award a single private company, Mile Hi Cablevision, the exclusive franchise to wire the entire city for cable television. It "sounds very quaint today," Mellor explained, but cable television was a cutting-edge technology in those days, and the city's plans were very ambitious. The real problem, as Mellor saw it, was the granting of the exclusive franchise, which violated the rights of "small guys trying to break into the oligopoly or monopoly situation."

So Mellor and his colleagues filed suit against the city and promptly found themselves on the receiving end of national media attention, a most welcome development. Looking back today, Mellor still thinks it was a great lawsuit, "except for one thing." It "ran up against, and challenged, the interests of the powers-that-be in Colorado, who happened to be very Republican at that time. And Mountain States was very connected to the Republican Party." The decision to pursue the case had sparked heated disagreement within the organization, ultimately leading Joseph Coors to resign from the board of directors. In the end, Mountain States dropped the litigation. "We were right on the issue, but we were wrong on the politics," Mellor said. "And that ultimately led to my leaving Mountain States under less than happy circumstances."

It was a difficult experience for the idealistic young lawyer, but it turned out to be an invaluable one. For one thing, it impressed upon Mellor the fact that libertarianism was not synonymous with the interests of big business, including businesses being run by Republicans. But perhaps more important, it taught him an organizational lesson he would never forget. "Funding must never drive case selection," he explained. "You must have a principled, long-term, philosophically and tactically consistent approach to litigation, rather than an ad hoc, reactive, and defensive one." The Institute for Justice would eventually be founded on those very insights.

THE CENTER FOR APPLIED JURISPRUDENCE

In the meantime, Mellor needed a job, so he moved east to Washington in order to take up a post in Ronald Reagan's Department of Energy, where he would remain until 1986. One day in 1985, Mellor received a surprise phone call from Antony Fisher, a philanthropist and activist heavily involved in the creation of several pioneering free-market think tanks and research outfits, including the Institute of Economic Affairs in London and the Manhattan Institute in New York City. Fisher was calling to gauge Mellor's interest in running the Pacific Research Institute (PRI) in San Francisco, which specialized in economic analyses of public policy issues, particularly in the areas of monetary and environmental policy. "I said to Antony, 'I'm very flattered,'" Mellor recalled, but he told him, "'I've got a dream, and what I intend to do is establish a libertarian public interest [legal] organization.' And he said, 'OK, thanks for your time.'"

But then Fisher called back a week or so later and repeated the offer, with some added incentives to sweeten the proposal. He told Mellor there was room for growth at the Pacific Research Institute, and as long as he kept everything else on track, there was no reason why Mellor could not also begin to develop his dream legal outfit under the PRI wing. That sealed the deal.

According to Mellor, one of the key lessons he took away from his less-than-happy break with the Mountain States Legal Foundation was that while the potential for libertarian public interest law was there, it would only work if it was done right. "And I swore at that moment I was gonna do it the right way sometime, I just had to figure out how." Now settled in at the reins of the Pacific Research Institute, Mellor got serious about solving the how problem. Under the rubric of PRI, Mellor established a Center for Applied Jurisprudence, which would serve as the base of operations for his first foray into libertarian legal planning. The next step was a frank assessment of the strengths and weaknesses of the concept to date. "My belief was that there was no single individual who knew exactly what to do when it came to any one issue, much less than when it came to the strategic approach to litigation I was trying to pursue," he explained. Mellor had his own ideas, of course, "but I believed that there were others out there whose wisdom and expertise we could draw on."

To capture that dispersed knowledge, the center put together three task forces organized around the subjects of economic liberty, property rights, and the First Amendment, three areas that Mellor and his colleagues had already identified as ripe for potential libertarian legal advocacy. Each task force consisted of a dozen or so experts in the field, mostly law professors and economists, including big names such as Milton Friedman, who participated in seminar-type discussions aimed at gleaning their insights. Also present at those seminars was a designated author, charged with synthesizing and applying that information and producing what Mellor called a "strategic litigation blueprint." "The idea there," he explained, "was that it would be best if we had a book, or multiple books, that then could be disseminated to law schools and lawyers and the media and whatnot, to show some substance to this."[8] The final result was three books published by the Pacific Research Institute between 1990 and 1993, each one laying out a proposed line of future legal attack. Those books are *Unfinished Business: A Civil Rights Strategy for America's Third Century,*[9] *Freedom, Technology and the First Amendment,*[10] and *Grand Theft and Petit Larceny: Property Rights in America.*[11] At last, Mellor and his allies were figuring out how to do libertarian public interest law right.

"THE NECESSITY OF JUDICIAL ACTION"

The most influential of those three litigation blueprints was the book *Unfinished Business,* written by Clint Bolick, a former colleague of Mellor's at the Mountain States Legal Foundation and his longtime co-conspirator in the quest to create a libertarian public interest law firm. In 1991, the two men would together found the Institute for Justice. "The judicial nullification of economic liberty stands as one of the most pervasive and debilitating deprivations of civil rights in America today,"[12] Bolick announced in *Unfinished Business,* and it was time to do something about it. Modeling his litigation strategy explicitly on that of the civil rights movement of the 1950s and 1960s, Bolick urged libertarian lawyers to bring a series of test cases, each one matching a sympathetic client with a government regulation that had been pre-selected for destruction. Through painstaking work, the libertarians would then build up a body of favorable legal rulings against government overreach, thereby setting the stage for a future Supreme Court victory in their favor. This systematic approach, Bolick argued, was the best method for grappling with the significant disadvantages they faced under the rational-basis test. On top of that, Bolick counseled, they needed an overarching goal to keep their various efforts on track. "We should establish as our ultimate objective the reversal of *The Slaughter-House Cases,* much as the NAACP did when it set as its long-range goal the toppling of *Plessy v. Ferguson.*"[13] Why *Slaughter-House*? Because, he explained, that was the case where the Supreme Court first unmoored the Fourteenth Amendment from its free labor origins. The libertarians would strike at the root of the problem and restore the Fourteenth Amendment as a shield for economic liberty.

A self-described "really nerdy kid," Clint Bolick initially wanted to pursue a career in Republican politics until he "fell in love" with constitutional law after reading about the civil rights movement during his senior year in college. "Seeing cases like *Brown v. Board of Education* made me realize that one can achieve pretty radical change in the courts without having to compromise on principles," he later explained. "You either win or you lose, and if you win you can fundamentally change the world." That led him to law school at the University of California, Davis, where his political views took on an increasingly libertarian cast. After graduating in 1982, Bolick signed on as an attorney at the Mountain States Legal Foundation, where he began working with his future IJ co-founder Chip Mellor.

Like Mellor, Bolick also left Mountain States in the wake of the Denver cable case and moved east to Washington, where he accepted a position in the Reagan administration's Equal Employment Opportunity Commission (EEOC), the federal agency charged with enforcing federal anti-discrimination laws. Heading up the EEOC at that time was a young and virtually unknown lawyer named Clarence Thomas.

"It really wasn't until I worked at the EEOC with Clarence Thomas that I began to think of economic liberty as a civil rights issue," Bolick later remembered. The two men became fast friends, and spent many hours together talking about law and history. A frequent topic in those days was the original meaning of the Fourteenth Amendment. "In Clarence Thomas I found a real kindred spirit on this issue," Bolick said. "He felt that the whole concept of civil rights had been mis-defined over the years, that when you look at it from a historical standpoint, the Civil Rights Act of 1866 was all about economic liberties. And that was a very exciting concept for me."[14]

Another key influence on Bolick's thinking at that time came from reading the work of George Mason University economist Walter Williams, whose 1982 book *The State against Blacks* argued that government restrictions on economic liberty were particularly harmful to African Americans and other disadvantaged groups.[15] A child of Philadelphia's Richard Allen housing projects, where his neighbors included a young Bill Cosby, Williams combined scholarly analysis with his own first-hand insights into the economic obstacles facing black Americans. "There are many laws in the United States that systematically discriminate against the employment and advancement of people who are outsiders, latecomers and poor in resources,"[16] Williams argued, pointing to various licensing restrictions placed on occupations such as electrician, plumber, and taxi cab driver. Those regulations may not explicitly mention race, Williams observed, but "they are discriminatory in the sense that they deny full opportunity for the most disadvantaged Americans, among whom blacks are disproportionately represented."[17] Williams wanted to see those regulatory obstacles struck from the books, and Bolick became determined to see that result achieved through litigation.

Armed with such ideas, and with Clarence Thomas serving as both boss and mentor at the EEOC, Bolick began putting the whole thing together into a coherent legal philosophy, ultimately writing a book on the subject called *Changing Course: Civil Rights at the Crossroads,* which appeared in 1988. If *Unfinished Business* was IJ's original strategic litigation blueprint for advancing economic liberty, then *Changing Course* was the first draft of that strategy. "The civil rights movement should seek to reverse *The Slaughter-House Cases,* which upheld the power of government to create monopolies and impede entrepreneurial opportunities,"[18] Bolick wrote in *Changing Course.* But in order for that to happen, he continued, the doctrine of judicial deference must be rejected. "What the advocates of judicial abstinence overlook is the crucial role assigned by the Constitution to the judiciary in the protection of civil rights, without which the state will be free—as in the Jim Crow era—to subvert civil rights virtually unchecked."[19] In short, Bolick argued, the libertarian legal movement must embrace "the necessity of judicial action."[20]

Three years later, with Mellor at the helm and Bolick serving as second-in-command, the Institute for Justice opened its doors and began putting that libertarian strategy into practice.

"SYMPATHETIC CLIENTS, OUTRAGEOUS FACTS, EVIL VILLAINS"

You know an IJ case when you see one. "We start with the principle we seek to vindicate," Chip Mellor explained, "and the issue that enables us to do it. And then we look for sympathetic clients, outrageous facts, evil villains." Take the principle of economic liberty, which IJ lawyers seek to vindicate by overturning economic regulations in court. The typical IJ client in such cases is a fledgling entrepreneur or small-business owner battling a government agency over some sort of preposterous red-tape requirement. But the real issue at stake, IJ's lawyers always tell the presiding judge, is the right to earn an honest living, a fundamental civil right that is eminently worthy of judicial respect and protection.

For instance, in the first case IJ filed back in 1991, *Taalib-Din Abdul Uqdah v. District of Columbia,* the Institute represented the owner of an African hair-braiding salon, Cornrows & Co., who had run afoul of the District's requirement that he obtain a government-issued cosmetology license. That requirement made no sense, Mr. Uqdah tried explaining to city officials, because the lengthy (and costly) licensing process never once touched on even the rudiments of hair braiding or related techniques, and focused instead on things like chemical treatments and the execution of out-of-date hair styles that had been popular when the regulation first went into effect in the 1930s, such as "finger waves" and "pin curls." In other words, the regulation had nothing to do with his business and did nothing to protect the health, welfare, or safety of anybody involved in the process of traditional African hair braiding. All it did was interfere with his ability to earn a living and pay his employees.

IJ agreed with that assessment, and on November 1, 1991, the Institute filed suit on Uqdah's behalf in the U.S. District Court for the District of Columbia. In the meantime, the D.C. City Council, spurred to action by the unwelcome media attention generated by the case, started rethinking its whole approach to cosmetology licensing. A little more than a year after the lawsuit was filed, the City Council voted to repeal the regulation. Thanks to the Institute for Justice, Cornrows & Co. was back in business.

It was a genuine libertarian victory over arbitrary government, and IJ's lawyers were thrilled to score their first win right out of the gate. But it was a legislative fix, not a judicial one, and IJ's long-term agenda centered on securing greater judicial protection for economic liberty. So the hunt for the next test case continued. "All along the issue of occupational licensing was at the heart of our economic liberty work," Mellor explained. "And so we were always looking for different occupations that were suffering from unreasonable licensing laws where there wasn't a fit between any arguable legitimate public health and safety rationale and the means by which the government is seeking to achieve that."

That search ultimately led Mellor and his colleagues to the state of Tennessee, where, according to a law called the Funeral Directors and Embalmers Act, only state-licensed funeral directors were permitted to sell coffins to paying customers. And that government license did not come cheap. Would-be license holders had two options: either complete one year of classroom work and a one-year apprenticeship under a licensed funeral director, or forgo the classroom entirely in favor of a two-year apprenticeship. In either case, the training process required many hours of labor and study, including the embalming of twenty-five human bodies. "In order to sell a box, you had to be a fully licensed funeral director," Mellor recalled, laughing in disbelief. "Once I saw that, it just jumped out."

Mellor had no problem with the idea of requiring actual funeral directors to carry a license—after all, their work did involve legitimate public health issues such as handling human remains and embalming dead bodies. But this statute went far beyond that and applied to any retail entrepreneur who simply wanted to sell caskets for a living, and who never once came in contact with a dead body as part of her job. Meanwhile, as Mellor discovered, established funeral directors throughout the state were marking up the price of coffins by as much as 600 percent, yet thanks to the burdensome licensing requirements, upstart competitors were effectively barred from coming in to offer a better price. And while state officials claimed the law was there to protect the health and safety of the public, Mellor learned that Tennessee placed no regulations of any kind on the design or manufacture of caskets. Indeed, it was perfectly legal in Tennessee to build your own casket for burial (with or without a sealed lid) or to be buried without a casket. "You start looking into it," he said, and "it was just the perfect no-fit between any legitimate health and safety reason and all these burdens they are putting on."[21]

So in September 1999 IJ filed suit in federal district court on behalf of several local entrepreneurs looking to break into the coffin business, including the case's lead client, the Reverend Nathaniel Craigmiles of Chattanooga, who had cofounded an operation called Craigmiles Wilson Casket Supply in order to offer his parishioners and their families a more affordable alternative. Eleven months later, IJ won the first round in the case. Despite the pro-government deference mandated by the rational-basis test, the federal district court struck down the regulation.

Tennessee promptly appealed the loss, and on December 6, 2002, the U.S. Court of Appeals for the Sixth Circuit came down with its decision on the matter in *Craigmiles v. Giles*. Once again, IJ was victorious. Having reviewed the evidence before him, wrote Judge Danny Boggs for a unanimous three-judge panel of the Sixth Circuit, he saw no reason to defer to the state's assertion that it had a rational basis for enacting the licensing law. "Tennessee's justifications," Boggs declared, "come close to striking us with the force of a five-week-old, unrefrigerated dead fish."[22]

Not since the New Deal had a federal appellate court (the highest level short of the U.S. Supreme Court) struck down an economic regulation for violating the economic liberties secured by the Fourteenth Amendment. And it had done so in spite of the extraordinary judicial deference it was required to extend to lawmakers under the rational-basis test. "This measure," the Sixth Circuit announced, "is not animated by a legitimate governmental purpose and cannot survive even rational basis review."[23]

IJ had just scored a landmark victory, but there was no time to
rest on its laurels. Indeed, the game was now afoot. In Oklahoma, a
similar IJ lawsuit was then underway against that state's nearly identical casket-sale licensing regulation. But in an unwelcome twist, the
U.S. Court of Appeals for the Tenth Circuit voted in August 2004 to
uphold the Oklahoma statute in the case of *Powers v. Harris*. To add
insult to injury, Mellor was blindsided by that outcome. "During the
oral argument it went so well in our favor, in terms of just the dynamic
in the courtroom and everything," he recalled, "that the attorney for
the state of Oklahoma came up afterwards and all but admitted defeat." As Mellor later acknowledged, he felt great when he stepped out
of the courtroom that day. "And then not only did we lose, we lost
three-zip."[24]

In retrospect, that feeling of optimism makes sense. In its ruling,
the Tenth Circuit essentially agreed with IJ's main argument and conceded the state's failure to provide any sort of rational public health
or safety justification for its licensing law. But then the Tenth Circuit
turned the tables and said the government had yet another arrow in
its quiver of conceivable justifications: the economic protection of the
state's funeral industry from unwelcome competition. "While base-
ball may be the national pastime of the citizenry, dishing out special
economic benefits to certain in-state industries remains the favored
pastime of state and local governments,"[25] the Tenth Circuit observed.
And under the judicial deference demanded by the rational-basis test,
the court held, those lawmakers are fully entitled to dish out the goods.
"As a creature of politics, the definition of the public good changes
with the political winds," the Tenth Circuit wrote. "There simply is no
constitutional or Platonic form against which we can (or could) judge
the wisdom of economic regulation."[26] Put differently, it remained illegal in Oklahoma to sell a box without a government-issued license.

No lawyer likes to lose a big case, and this was no exception. But Mellor and his colleagues did identify one potential upside to the Tenth Circuit's ruling. As Clint Bolick had argued in *Unfinished Business,* from the perspective of a public-interest litigator, every losing case is also a potential winner, since that loss may still be appealed to a higher court, and perhaps even reach the U.S. Supreme Court. So the loss in *Powers v. Harris* still fit within the organization's long-term litigation strategy. What's more, IJ's loss at the Tenth Circuit had created what's known as a "circuit split," meaning the Tenth Circuit and the Sixth Circuit had now issued clashing opinions on the same legal issue, a fractured state of affairs that normally prompts the Supreme Court to step in to settle the controversy.

Thanks to IJ's litigation, the stage was now at least partially set for a showdown before the highest court in the land. The Tenth Circuit's ruling "creates a split on the basic question of whether pure economic protectionism is a legitimate state interest under the rational basis test," IJ told the Supreme Court in a November 2004 petition seeking review of the case. "If permitted to stand, the Tenth Circuit's decision would drain rational basis review of all content and would convert the right to earn a living—which this Court has consistently recognized since its earliest days—into a mere privilege."[27]

Unhappily for IJ, however, the justices declined to take the case. As is customary, the Court gave no explanation for its rejection of the appeal, though the most likely reason is the Court's deeply ingrained habit of judicial restraint. The justices did not wish to enter the thicket.

The Institute for Justice lost that battle, but the larger campaign is far from over. In a span of just five years, IJ's lawyers secured not only a landmark victory for economic liberty at the Sixth Circuit, they presented the Supreme Court with a clear circuit split on the same issue. Those libertarian precedents remain on the books, ready to be used by a future Supreme Court that is willing to grapple with the issue of economic liberty and the Fourteenth Amendment.

"TAKEN FOR A PUBLIC USE"

The rational-basis test has been a thorn in the libertarian side since the New Deal. It has been a pain in property-rights cases for nearly as long.

According to Footnote Four of the famous 1938 *Carolene Products* decision, while the Supreme Court would henceforth presume the constitutionality of economic regulations and grant significant deference to the lawmaking bodies that passed them, "more exacting judicial scrutiny" would still be appropriate in other types of cases. For instance, "when legislation appears on its face to be within a specific prohibition of the Constitution, such as those of the first ten amendments,"[28] the Court would carefully examine the government's actions to make sure no part of the Bill of Rights had been violated.

Or at least that's what the Supreme Court said. What the Court has done is something different. Consider the issue of eminent domain. According to the Fifth Amendment, "private property [shall not] be taken for public use without just compensation." Also known as the Takings Clause, this provision authorizes the government to wield the power of eminent domain in limited circumstances. In the classic example, the government turns to eminent domain when it needs to acquire privately owned land in order to build a road or a bridge—two undeniable instances of use by the public—and then compensates the former landowner at fair market value from the public treasury.

Yet in the 1954 case of *Berman v. Parker,* the Supreme Court ignored its own *Carolene Products* framework and quietly introduced rational-basis-style deference into its treatment of the Takings Clause, despite the fact that the clause is clearly a part of the Bill of Rights. At issue in *Berman* was a so-called slum clearance measure from Washington, D.C. Essentially, government officials had determined that a poor neighborhood in southwest Washington was beyond repair, and they therefore wanted to seize all privately held property in the area, raze it, and start over from scratch—an approach also known as "urban renewal." Among the properties targeted for condemnation was a department store, whose owner loudly objected to the government's plans to bulldoze his non-blighted, non-slum property.

Writing for a unanimous Supreme Court, Justice William O. Douglas took the government's side. According to Douglas, the judiciary had no business second-guessing whether or not a particular exercise of the eminent domain power counted as a valid public use. That determination rested solely with the legislature. "When the legislature has spoken," Douglas wrote, "the public interest has been declared in terms well nigh conclusive."[29] Indeed, he declared, so long as just compensation has been paid, "the rights of these property owners are satisfied."[30] Although the public use requirement is a "specific prohibition of the Constitution," the *Berman* Court ignored Footnote Four and failed to provide "more exacting judicial scrutiny" on its behalf.

Unsurprisingly, the lawyers at the Institute for Justice have a fundamental disagreement with this deferential approach, and from day one they were on the lookout for a property rights case strong enough to challenge the status quo. They hit the jackpot in 1994 when they took on the matter of *Casino Reinvestment Development Authority v. Coking.* The case originated in Atlantic City, New Jersey, where local authorities sought to condemn the home of an elderly widow named Vera Coking, who lived just off the city's famous beachfront boardwalk, in order to turn her land into a limousine parking lot for the neighboring Trump Plaza, the high-rise hotel and casino owned by real estate tycoon Donald Trump. As Coking saw it, there was nothing remotely public-minded about the government's demolishing her home of more than thirty years in order to provide extra parking spots for Trump's customers. The lawyers at the Institute for Justice could not have agreed more, so they took up Coking's case, fought it out in court, and ultimately prevailed, allowing her to remain in her home.

It was a flagrant example of eminent domain abuse, and it was also precisely the sort of David against Goliath story that journalists love to cover. As a result, IJ also won a resounding victory in the court of public opinion, earning sympathetic coverage from outlets ranging from *The Economist,* which called it a battle between those who value "thrusting, self-promoting moguls" and those who value "small businesses, families and property rights,"[31] to the *New York Times,* which described IJ's courtroom triumph with the words "today, the little guys won."[32]

But that publicity also had far-reaching consequences that extended well beyond the Atlantic City boardwalk. Some 250 miles to the north, in the modest city of New London, Connecticut, a small band of property owners were fighting their own uphill battle to save their homes and neighborhood from the forces of eminent domain. Once those folks learned about IJ's victory over Trump, they knew right where to turn for the legal help they so desperately needed.

THE LITTLE PINK HOUSE

The saga officially began on February 3, 1998, when the pharmaceutical company Pfizer announced its plans to build a giant new research and development facility in New London, Connecticut. As part of the deal, city officials agreed to refurbish the surrounding area, including the adjacent neighborhood of Fort Trumbull, a ninety-acre working-class enclave. The idea was for New London to buy out existing property owners and then turn their land over to a private developer who would construct a new luxury hotel, apartment buildings, office towers, and other upscale amenities to complement the new Pfizer facility. This redevelopment scheme was supposed to lure new businesses to the area, create new jobs, and broaden the tax base.

The driving force behind this massive project was the New London Development Corporation (NLDC), a quasi-public entity endowed by the city with tremendous governmental powers, ultimately including the authority to seize private property on the city's behalf via eminent domain. Heading up the NLDC at this time was a woman named Claire Gaudiani, who also served as the president of nearby Connecticut College. As it happened, Gaudiani had a number of close ties to Pfizer's local power brokers, a friendly arrangement that helped smooth the eventual real estate deal. For one thing, her husband was a Pfizer employee who worked under company executive George Milne Jr., president of Pfizer's central research division. For another, Milne sat on the board of trustees at Connecticut College. Based on that relationship, Milne accepted Gaudiani's offer to join the NLDC board in 1997. Within a year, Milne was pushing Pfizer to partner with the NLDC and build its new research and development facility in New London.

Among the local residents who took a dimmer view of the city's plans was Susette Kelo, a registered nurse and divorced mother of three. In August 1997, Kelo had purchased a run-down house in Fort Trumbull, which she picked for its stunning views of the nearby Thames River, and had immediately gone to work fixing it up. As she would tell the press time and again as the conflict unfolded, she loved her "little pink house" and did not want to see it bulldozed by the city for the benefit of Pfizer and other private interests. Her principled opposition would eventually form the backbone of a local property rights movement that in turn sparked the high-profile lawsuit against the redevelopment scheme.[33]

ENTER THE BULL

Senior Attorney Scott Bullock has been a fixture at the Institute for Justice from day one. A self-described libertarian since high school, as an undergraduate at Grove City College in western Pennsylvania Bullock studied Austrian economics, a branch of the field closely associated with such free-market thinkers as Friedrich Hayek and Ludwig von Mises. At the same time, he later explained, "I always had an interest in legal issues and in particular in the Constitution, and I saw constitutional law as a way of combining the principles of liberty with the ability to do something about it."[34] That growing interest led him to enroll in law school at the University of Pittsburgh in 1988, though it was during his summer breaks that he really laid the foundation for his future legal career. During his first summer off from law school, Bullock served as the inaugural intern at the Cato Institute's new Center for Constitutional Studies. The next year, Bullock spent the summer working for Clint Bolick, who had since left the Reagan administration in order to practice law at the Landmark Legal Foundation's Center for Civil Rights. One day over lunch, Bolick told him about his and Chip Mellor's plans to open an explicitly libertarian public interest law firm and said Bullock should come work for them once he had his law degree in hand. On the spot, Bullock made up his mind to do precisely that.

Now fast-forward to May 2000. Bullock was working at his desk one day when he came upon a letter mailed to the Institute for Justice by a man named Peter Kreckovic of New London, Connecticut. Kreckovic turned out to be a local artist working with Susette Kelo and several of her neighbors in their fight against New London's proposed use of eminent domain against their properties. After that group learned about IJ's role in the Trump fight, Kreckovic was deputized to draft a letter to the organization asking for its help.

"I read the letter and saw that it was exactly the type of situation we were working against," Bullock later recalled. So he got on the telephone to Kreckovic to get more information. "That led to me traveling to New London and going to the little pink house and meeting Susette and the other property owners and some of the local activists and going on from there."

At that point, Kelo and her neighbors had already been fighting New London and the NLDC for more than two years, but a major new battlefront was about to open up. Although nobody realized it at the time, Kreckovic's letter had just launched a five-year courtroom odyssey that ultimately took Kelo, Bullock, and their allies from the Superior Court of New London, where they won a partial victory after a seven-day bench trial in 2002, to the Connecticut Supreme Court, where the property owners lost on all counts in 2004, and finally to the highest court in the land in 2005, where the justices of the U.S. Supreme Court would consider the following question: "What protection does the Fifth Amendment's public use requirement provide for individuals whose property is being condemned, not to eliminate slums or blight, but for the sole purpose of 'economic development' that will perhaps increase tax revenues and improve the local economy?"[35]

THE "THEME OF JUDICIAL DEFERENCE"

According to city officials in New London, they needed to seize the properties owned by Susette Kelo and her neighbors in order to bring about a sweeping plan for the "revitalization" of the ninety-acre Fort Trumbull neighborhood that was designed to piggyback on the new Pfizer facility. That redevelopment would ultimately benefit the rest of the city, those officials claimed, through the creation of new jobs and increased tax revenues. As the city saw it, those results obviously qualified this taking of private property as a legitimate public use.

The Connecticut Supreme Court agreed. Pointing to what it called the U.S. Supreme Court's "theme of judicial deference to the legislative public use determination," the Connecticut high court's March 2004 decision applied that same approving standard to New London's planned condemnations in Fort Trumbull. According to the Connecticut Supreme Court, so long as "the appropriate legislative authority rationally has determined" that a proposed economic development project will create jobs, increase taxes, or otherwise benefit the city, it constitutes "a valid public use for the exercise of the eminent domain power under either the state or federal constitution."[36]

That "theme of judicial deference" included not only the Supreme Court's 1954 ruling in *Berman v. Parker,* it also included a more recent opinion, the Court's 1984 ruling in *Hawaii Housing Authority v. Midkiff.* In that case, the Court had cited *Berman* extensively while upholding Hawaii's seizure of private property for the purposes of breaking up what it called a land oligopoly, a situation where nearly half of the island's lands were in the possession of seventy-two private owners. "When the legislature's purpose is legitimate and its means are not irrational," the Court declared in *Midkiff,* borrowing language from the rational-basis test, "our cases make clear that empirical debates over the wisdom of takings—no less than debates over the wisdom of other kinds of socioeconomic legislation—are not to be carried out in the federal courts."[37] Translation: The Supreme Court would practice judicial deference in public use cases.

Bullock and his IJ colleagues had no illusions about the difficult task they faced under those two sweeping precedents. Indeed, as a law student, Bullock had been taught that the public use provision of the Takings Clause was effectively meaningless thanks to the Supreme Court. "The professor's attitude was, 'this used to be a controversy but now basically anything goes. Let's turn to other issues,'" he recalled with a grim laugh. On top of that, the author of the majority opinion in *Midkiff* was none other than Justice Sandra Day O'Connor, a moderate conservative who was still sitting on the Court. To say the least, O'Connor was not going to be interested in overruling her own previous decision. Yet in order to win the case, the Bullock team was going to need her support.

"We knew it was going to be hard to cobble together five votes" to overturn *Berman* and *Midkiff,* Bullock explained. So IJ decided not to ask. "That was something that we said was an option,"[38] but they basically left it at that in their briefing. Instead, IJ argued that *Kelo* was distinguishable from *Berman* and *Midkiff* because in those earlier cases the government had used eminent domain to remove two immediate public problems: namely, blight and oligopoly. In *Kelo,* on the other hand, no comparable social ills were in need of correction. In fact, far from being blighted, Fort Trumbull was a respectable working-class neighborhood full of residents who loved their well-tended homes and had no desire to move out. One of IJ's clients in the case, a woman named Wilhelmina Dery, still lived in the very same Fort Trumbull house where she was born in 1918. She had never lived anywhere else.

"To petitioners, like most Americans, their homes are their castles," IJ told the Supreme Court in its main brief. "In this case, they face the loss of the homes and neighbors they cherish through the use of eminent domain not for a traditional public use, such as a road or public building, nor even for the removal of blight." Instead, the city of New London seeks "to take Petitioners' 15 homes to turn them over to other private parties in the hope that the City may benefit from whatever trickle-down effects those new businesses produce."[39] Yes, *Berman* and *Midkiff* granted the government broad powers to take private property, IJ acknowledged. But those precedents did not authorize anything as far reaching as what New London wanted to do here. To uphold the city's actions, IJ maintained, would require "a dramatic departure from this Court's jurisprudence."[40]

Meanwhile, as Bullock and his colleagues were putting the finishing touches on their legal arguments, IJ was assembling an impressive cast of bipartisan allies to lobby the Supreme Court with friend-of-the-court briefs filed on Susette Kelo's behalf. Among those who joined the property rights side were parties ranging from the libertarian Cato Institute to the famous urban theorist Jane Jacobs, author of *The Death and Life of Great American Cities*. But perhaps the most notable support of all came from the NAACP, which told the Supreme Court that "Elimination of the requirement that any taking be for a true public use will disproportionately harm racial and ethnic minorities, the elderly, and the economically underprivileged." To rule in New London's favor, the NAACP said in its brief, "would virtually eliminate judicial review and fail to protect the rights of already disadvantaged groups from majoritarian pressures."[41] With the NAACP now officially allied with the libertarians, IJ co-founder Clint Bolick's original civil rights strategy had come full circle.

EMINENT DOMAIN ON TRIAL

When the Supreme Court assembled to hear oral argument in *Kelo v. City of New London* on the morning of February 22, 2005, it did so with two empty seats on the bench. Chief Justice William Rehnquist was at home that day, battling the thyroid cancer that would claim his life seven months later. Justice John Paul Stevens, meanwhile, was stranded at the airport in Florida, his flight back to Washington delayed due to bad weather. That left Justice Sandra Day O'Connor, the most senior justice in attendance, to call the proceedings to order.

"We will now hear argument in the case of *Kelo v. City of New London*," she announced at 10:12 a.m. "Mr. Bullock."

"Justice O'Connor, and may it please the Court," Bullock began, employing the traditional opening used by all parties who appear before the Supreme Court. "This case is about whether there are any limits on government's eminent domain power under the public use requirement of the Fifth Amendment. Every home, church or corner store would produce more tax revenue and jobs if it were a Costco, a shopping mall or a private office. But if that's the justification for the use of eminent domain," he stressed, "then any city can take property anywhere within its borders for any private use that might make more money than what is there now."[42]

It was IJ's entire case in miniature. New London wanted to bull-doze a working-class neighborhood and replace it with various upscale businesses operated on a for-profit basis. That was not a legitimate public use under the Constitution, IJ said; it was public power un-leashed on behalf of private gain.

But the Court's liberal justices did not quite see it that way. "Mr. Bullock, you are leaving out that New London was in a depressed eco-nomic condition," interjected Justice Ruth Bader Ginsburg as Bullock was wrapping up his opening statement. "The critical fact on the city side, at least, is that this was a depressed community and they wanted to build it up, get more jobs." Bullock responded that while New Lon-don may have been experiencing some economic troubles, the Con-necticut law at issue actually allowed any city in the state to employ eminent domain for any economic development purposes at any time, not just in those cases where the municipality was facing some specific financial hardship. "Every city has problems. Every city would like to have more revenue," he argued. "But that cannot be a justification for the use of eminent domain."[43]

Meanwhile, Justice Stephen Breyer was wondering whether the Supreme Court had any business reviewing the city's determination of what counted as a legitimate public use in the first place. "There is no taking for private use that you could imagine in reality that wouldn't also have a public benefit of some kind, whether it's increasing jobs or increasing taxes, et cetera. That's a fact of the world. And so given that fact of the world," Breyer said, "virtually every taking is alright, as long as there is some public benefit, which there always is, and it's up to the legislature."

That statement frustrated Bullock, and he did his best not to show it. Under Breyer's logic, he thought, the public use requirement might as well be erased from the Constitution. "Your Honor, we think that cuts way too broadly," he responded. "Because then every property, every home, every business can then be taken for any private use."

But Breyer refused to budge. "No," he snapped back in response. "It could only be taken if there is a public use and there almost always is."[44]

The next line of attack came from Justice David Souter, who wanted to know what was wrong with a city's acquiring private property for the purposes of redevelopment. Assume that instead of using eminent domain, Souter said, the city just used money from its tax coffers to buy up the land and then sold it to a developer. "Would you say just within the general understanding of proper governmental purposes that the city was acting in a way that had no legitimate public purpose?"

Bullock agreed that Souter's hypothetical would be legitimate. So then "why isn't there a public purpose here?"[45] Souter asked. Because the Takings Clause of the Fifth Amendment imposed additional restrictions on government power, Bullock answered.

Justice Antonin Scalia then entered the fray with a question that reshuffled the entire debate. "Mr. Bullock, do you equate purpose with use?" he asked. "Does the public use requirement mean nothing more than that it have a public purpose?"

"No, Your Honor," Bullock replied.

"But if that is your answer," Souter promptly piped back up, "then the slum clearance cases have got to go the other way."[46]

Bullock had just entered a minefield, and he knew it. In its 1954 decision in *Berman v. Parker,* the so-called slum clearance case from

Washington, D.C., the Supreme Court had granted Congress wide latitude in determining what counted as a public use under the Fifth Amendment, and in the course of doing so, the Court had used the phrase "public purpose" as if it were synonymous with the phrase "public use." "The legislature, not the judiciary, is the main guardian of the public needs to be served by social legislation," Justice William O. Douglas had written in *Berman*. "The role of the judiciary in determining whether that power is being exercised for a public purpose is an extremely narrow one."[47]

To make matters worse for Bullock, in its 1984 opinion in *Hawaii Housing Authority v. Midkiff*, the Supreme Court had quoted extensively from *Berman* and also adopted that case's "public purpose" formulation in an opinion written by Justice Sandra Day O'Connor, who was now sitting just a few feet in front of him. Bullock therefore needed to distinguish *Kelo* from *Berman* and explain why the slum clearance case could stay on the books even if his clients won the case.

The difference, Bullock explained, hewing closely to the arguments laid out in IJ's brief, is that in *Berman,* "the public purpose, if you want to call it that, was served once the blight was removed." By the same token, in *Midkiff,* "the public purpose was served once the oligopoly was broken up."[48] In both cases, "the public purpose was direct and immediate."

By contrast, he told the justices, in this case "the only public benefits that come about, if they come about at all, are completely dependent upon private parties actually making a profit."[49] It was trickle-down economics, he said. There was nothing direct or immediate about it.

At this point, Justice Anthony Kennedy began signaling his own thinking on the matter—and it did not look good to the Bullock team. "Precisely the description you gave applied to the railroads in the west," Kennedy told Bullock.

But that's a different issue, Bullock tried to explain before Kennedy cut him off. "The argument is, and I don't know of any reason to doubt it," Kennedy said, that buying up needed land "by voluntary acquisition and sale doesn't work. . . . There isn't another practical way to do it."

That proved to be almost too much for Bullock to swallow. "Your Honor," he carefully responded, "there are many ways to do economic development without condemnation. It happens every single day in this country."[50]

Unfortunately for Bullock, the die appeared to be cast. "The most frustrating justice for us was Kennedy," he later acknowledged. "I felt like I was just not making any progress with him during the argument, and he just did not seem to be really troubled by this."[51] That lack of progress was especially notable in light of Kennedy's previous jurisprudence. In a 1993 opinion, for instance, Kennedy had declared, "individual freedom finds tangible expression in property rights."[52] Yet during the *Kelo* arguments, Kennedy appeared totally unmoved by any such libertarian concerns. It was a distressing omen for the Bullock team.

"I WOULD NOT DRAW A LINE"

Next up at the lectern was Wesley W. Horton, a veteran Connecticut litigator hired by the city to argue on its behalf. He came out swinging in favor of judicial restraint. "Justice O'Connor, and may it please the Court," Horton began. "The principal purpose of the takings clause is to provide for just compensation."

"But it has to be for a valid public use," O'Connor immediately shot back.

"I completely agree with that," Horton rallied. "But the primary purpose of the takings clause is not to regulate legislative determinations of that."[53]

Horton had opened his remarks by paraphrasing the conclusion of *Berman,* in which Justice Douglas maintained that so long as just compensation was paid, the rights of the department store owner under the Takings Clause were fully vindicated. Yet O'Connor refused to let Horton's gloss on *Berman* go unchallenged. Was she now having second thoughts about the sweeping judicial deference she had endorsed in her *Midkiff* opinion? The packed courtroom was about to find out.

But first Justice Scalia wanted to know just how much power the government was claiming for itself in this case. "What difference does it make, that New London was in an economic depression?" Scalia asked. "Would it not be fully as much, under your theory of a public use, for a city to say, yes, we are not doing badly, but we could do better. Let's attract some high-tech industry here. You can't possibly draw a line between depressed cities and undepressed cities, can you?"

Horton conceded, "I would not draw a line."

Scalia kept at it. "You wouldn't. And you wouldn't ask us to do it either." Then Scalia moved in for the kill. Under your theory of the case, he asked Horton, "you could take [private property] from A and give it to B if B is richer, and would pay higher municipal taxes, couldn't you?"

"Yes, Your Honor,"[54] Horton replied calmly. The city could do that under New London's theory. Bullock was shocked by Horton's admission. "That's what we were saying,"[55] he later recalled. New London had just admitted the principal theme of IJ's case.

Nor was Bullock the only person in the courtroom to be surprised by Horton's answer. "For example," O'Connor quickly interjected on top of Scalia's questioning, "Motel 6 and the city thinks, well, if we had a Ritz-Carlton, we would have higher taxes. Now, is that okay?"

"Yes, Your Honor, that would be okay,"[56] Horton promptly responded.

Once again, Bullock was shocked. And this time so was O'Connor. "When you're that close to them you can really see the looks on their faces," Bullock recalled. And from where he was sitting, he watched a visibly flabbergasted O'Connor take a moment to digest Horton's answer. "I could tell that she was shocked that he would just concede that up front and go on with it. That was really encouraging for having her vote, especially given the fact that she had written the *Midkiff* opinion."[57]

Horton's frank endorsement of government power appeared to trouble even some of the Court's more liberal justices, who up until that point had seemed fully in favor of the city's position. "Could the courts, under this clause, at least review what you've said for reasonableness?" Breyer asked him several minutes later. "I mean, look at the reasonableness of a claim that this is for—basically for a public use. . . . Is that a possible kind of review that you might find appropriate here?"

But Horton refused to give an inch. "No, Your Honor, if what you're defining as reasonableness is being higher than rational basis."[58] This case called for judicial deference to lawmakers, Horton maintained. End of story.

As Horton's time at the lectern began winding down, Bullock started gathering his own thoughts in preparation for his final rebuttal, which would last approximately three minutes. He knew immediately that he should refocus the Court's attention on O'Connor's troubling exchange with the Connecticut lawyer. "I think the key to understanding their argument," Bullock told the justices in summary, "is the answer to the question of, can you take a Motel 6 and give it to a fancier hotel? Their answer is yes. And that's what's really at stake here."[59]

"OUR LONGSTANDING POLICY OF DEFERENCE"

The Supreme Court normally takes at least several months to issue a ruling in a big case, particularly when the outcome is closely divided. The

Bullock team waited a full three months for the opinion in *Kelo*, and when it finally arrived on the morning of June 23, 2005, the second-to-last day of the 2004–2005 term, it came as a supreme disappointment to the libertarians. "We were hopeful but we knew it was going to be very close,"[60] Bullock recalled. Close it was. By a vote of five to four, the Supreme Court upheld New London's use of eminent domain for the purposes of economic development. And just as Bullock had feared, Kennedy joined the Court's liberals—Stevens, Breyer, Ginsburg, and Souter—in voting to allow the forced condemnations to proceed.

Ironically, Stevens, who had missed the oral argument due to his weather-delayed flight, wrote the majority opinion. "The disposition of this case," he declared, "turns on the question of whether the City's development plan serves a 'public purpose.' Without exception, our cases have defined that concept broadly, reflecting our longstanding policy of deference to legislative judgments in this field."[61] Referring repeatedly to the Court's unwillingness to "second-guess" the city's determinations, Stevens maintained that it was up to the legislature, not the judiciary, to decide, "what public needs justify the use of the takings power."[62]

Bullock had also been right about O'Connor. Writing in dissent, she accused her colleagues in the majority of abdicating their constitutional responsibility to safeguard every word of the Constitution. The result of today's decision, she wrote, in an opinion joined by Chief Justice Rehnquist and Justices Scalia and Clarence Thomas, "is to wash out any distinction between private and public use of property—and thereby effectively delete the words 'for public use' from the Takings Clause of the Fifth Amendment."[63]

As he often does, Justice Thomas also filed a solo dissent in which he laid out an even stronger critique of the majority opinion than the one offered by his fellow dissenters. He pulled no punches here. Poor and minority neighborhoods will bear the brunt of this decision,

Thomas declared, echoing the arguments made in the NAACP brief, both because those neighborhoods are the most likely to be targeted by the government for "renewal" and because the people who live in them lack the political clout to stop it. "If ever there were justification for intrusive judicial review of constitutional provisions that protect 'discrete and insular minorities,'" Thomas wrote, quoting from Footnote Four of the *Carolene Products* opinion, "surely that principle would apply with great force to the powerless groups and individuals the Public Use Clause protects. The deferential standard this Court has adopted for the Public Use Clause is therefore deeply perverse."[64] Thomas left no doubt that if it were up to him, both *Kelo* and *Berman* would have come out the other way.

"I'M SORRY"

As news of the opinion spread, the outcry against the Court's ruling was fast and furious. Democratic Representative Maxine Waters of California, for instance, an outspoken liberal, called *Kelo* "the most un-American thing that can be done." Her Republican colleague Tom DeLay of Texas, normally an ideological opponent, offered a similar critique. "The Supreme Court voted last week to undo private property rights and to empower governments to kick people out of their homes and give them to someone else because they feel like it,"[65] DeLay fumed. National polls would later echo that initial negative reaction. According to a 2008 Associated Press/National Constitution Center poll, for instance, 87 percent of Americans said they were opposed to the government's having "the power to take people's private property in the interests of redeveloping an area."[66]

"It really was devastating to come that close and to not prevail," IJ president Chip Mellor later said, but he was also determined to capitalize on the public outrage. "So I came in the next day and said we are going to get space at the National Press Club and we are going to hold a news conference launching a national initiative to secure greater constitutional protection in all fifty states. And we did."[67] To date, that post-*Kelo* campaign has helped spark legislative reform in more than forty states. At the same time, IJ has continued to press its property rights arguments in state courts under the respective state constitutions. Among the fruits of that litigation strategy was a unanimous 2006 ruling by the Ohio Supreme Court that explicitly repudiated *Kelo* and declared the seizure of private property for the purpose of economic development to be unconstitutional in the Buckeye State.[68]

On the national level, meanwhile, *Kelo* quickly became a new talking point in the debate over the courts, even emerging as a new litmus test for judicial candidates. Since 2005, every Supreme Court nominee has faced sharp questioning about the case from Senate Republicans, who also typically use the opportunity to call for *Kelo*'s reversal. During Sonia Sotomayor's 2009 confirmation hearings, for instance, Republican Charles Grassley of Iowa asked her repeatedly if she agreed with the outcome in *Kelo,* causing the future justice to visibly wilt under the pressure. "I can only talk about what the—the Court said in the context of that particular case and to explain that it is the context of the Court's holding," Sotomayor told him in frustration. The best she could manage, she said, was that as a legal precedent "it's entitled to *stare decisis* effect and deference."[69] Not exactly reassuring to *Kelo*'s many critics.

Back in New London, meanwhile, the situation went from bad to worse. Despite prevailing at the Supreme Court, the development project that was supposed to entice Pfizer and provide "appreciable benefits to the community"[70] (in the approving words of Justice Stevens's majority opinion) was never built, and in November 2009 Pfizer announced that it was closing shop and pulling out of New London entirely. As for Fort Trumbull, the razed neighborhood was never redeveloped and continues to stand empty today. In fact, in the aftermath of Hurricane Irene in 2011, New London officials encouraged city residents to use Fort Trumbull as a dumpsite for storm debris.

But that's not the worst of it. As *Hartford Courant* reporter Jeff Benedict revealed in September 2011, Connecticut Supreme Court Justice Richard N. Palmer, one of the four justices who voted against the property owners and thus directly precipitated their appeal to the U.S. Supreme Court, personally apologized to Susette Kelo at a May 2010 event at the New Haven Lawn Club. "Justice Palmer turned to Susette, took her hand and offered a heartfelt apology," Benedict reported. "Tears trickled down her red cheeks. It was the first time in the 12-year saga that anyone had uttered the words 'I'm sorry.'"[71]

A LIBERTARIAN LESSON

Today, *Kelo* serves as a rallying cry for the libertarian legal movement, an object lesson for judges, lawyers, and politicians about the dangers of judicial deference. And that lesson has not been lost on the American right. Indeed, conservatives now overwhelmingly oppose *Kelo* and favor its repeal in a future case. When it comes to the judicial protection of property rights, the conservative legal movement has gone libertarian.

SIX

GUNS, LAWYERS, AND BUTCHERS

T'S HARD TO IMAGINE A GREATER VICTORY FOR the conservative legal movement than *District of Columbia v. Heller*, the 2008 ruling in which the Supreme Court struck down Washington, D.C.'s handgun ban. Not only did the Court, for the first time in its history, recognize the Second Amendment as securing an individual right to keep and bear arms, it did so in the language of "originalism"—the school of thought, increasingly popular among conservatives, that says the Constitution must be interpreted according to its original meaning at the time it was adopted.

It was therefore surprising when a leading conservative jurist, Judge J. Harvie Wilkinson III of the U.S. Court of Appeals for the Fourth Circuit, once rumored to be on George W. Bush's short list of potential Supreme Court nominees, denounced the *Heller* opinion as a shameless piece of right-wing judicial activism. *Heller*, Wilkinson wrote in the *Virginia Law Review*, "encourages Americans to do what conservative jurists warned for years they should not do: bypass the ballot and seek to press their political agenda in the courts." *Heller* may be "a triumph for conservative lawyers," Wilkinson granted. "But it also represents a failure—the Court's failure to adhere to a conservative judicial methodology in reaching its decision."[1] Wilkinson even compared Justice Antonin Scalia's majority opinion in *Heller* to the Supreme Court's abortion-affirming opinion in *Roe v. Wade*, which is not exactly the nicest thing you can say to a guy like Scalia.

But Wilkinson did have a point. Scalia's ruling in *Heller* marched the justices of the U.S. Supreme Court straight into the political thicket of gun control, overturning the regulatory consensus that had been reached by the local officials directly accountable to Washington's residents. It was nobody's idea of judicial deference.

Wilkinson also had a point about methodology. *D.C. v. Heller* was not a conservative case—it was a libertarian case. The original lawsuit that sparked the ruling was conceived, bankrolled, and executed entirely by a small team of libertarian lawyers closely associated with two of the libertarian legal movement's principal organizations, the Institute for Justice and the Cato Institute. *Heller* was a triumph of libertarian legal methodology, and a repudiation of the deferential conservative alternative.

Furthermore, the conservative National Rifle Association (NRA), which tends to get credit for the ruling in many mainstream accounts, actually had nothing to do with launching the case, and in fact initially opposed the lawsuit and even tried to derail it for being too risky and aggressive. It was the libertarians who pushed forward, in the face of both liberal and conservative opposition, convincing the Supreme Court to strike down a major gun control law while simultaneously issuing a sweeping and historic affirmation of the Second Amendment's place in America's constitutional order.

With *D.C. v. Heller,* the libertarian legal movement fully emerged as an independent force to be reckoned with.

TWO LIBERTARIANS WALK INTO A BAR

It was June 2002 and a pair of young lawyers from the Institute for Justice, Clark Neily and Steve Simpson, were drinking beer and talking guns at a Northern Virginia bar called Carpool. "We got to talking about the *Emerson* decision and what significance it might have for the future of the Second Amendment,"[2] Neily recalled. *Emerson* refers to *United States v. Emerson,* a surprising 2001 opinion by the U.S. Court of Appeals for the Fifth Circuit in which that court, in a break with several other federal circuits, held that the Second Amendment secured an individual—rather than a collective—right to keep and bear arms.

The clash over interpretation stemmed from the text of the amendment itself. "A well regulated Militia, being necessary to the security of a free State," the Second Amendment reads, "the right of the people to keep and bear Arms, shall not be infringed." Does that language protect an individual liberty, just as its neighboring amendments in the Bill of Rights secure individual liberties? Or does the prefatory clause, "a well regulated militia, being necessary to the security of a free State," limit the scope of "the right of the people," and effectively protect only a collective right to keep and bear arms that is tied to service in a state militia?

This is no mere squabble over linguistics. If the Second Amendment protects only a collective right tied to militia service, that means the right to own a gun for hunting or sport shooting is not protected by the amendment, nor is the right to own a gun for the purpose of self-defense. In other words, the collective-right interpretation opens the door to a vast range of gun control measures, including prohibition. By contrast, the individual-right interpretation places a constitutional check on many such regulations and basically invites judicial review of all gun control laws. The legal debate over the meaning of the Second Amendment therefore has profound real-world implications for the hot-button debate over guns in America.

For much of the twentieth century, the collective-right view proved dominant in elite legal circles. But that began to change in the last thirty years, first as conservative and libertarian scholars began researching more deeply into the amendment's text and history, and then as prominent liberal academics followed suit. A major turning point occurred in 1989 when University of Texas law professor Sanford Levinson, a leading liberal scholar, published an essay in the prestigious *Yale Law Journal* titled "The Embarrassing Second Amendment." The embarrassment, Levinson argued, came from the legal left's refusal to take the Second Amendment seriously. "I cannot help but suspect that the best explanation for the absence of the Second Amendment from the legal consciousness of the elite bar," he wrote, "is derived from a mixture of sheer opposition to the idea of private ownership of guns and the perhaps subconscious fear that altogether plausible, perhaps even 'winning,' interpretations of the Second Amendment would present real hurdles to those of us supporting prohibitory regulation."[3]

Eleven years later, Harvard law professor Laurence Tribe, a respected scholar and teacher whose former students include a young Barack Obama, amended the new third edition of his legal treatise *American Constitutional Law* to officially endorse the individual-right interpretation of the Second Amendment. This was a marked change from the two previous editions, where Tribe had accepted the collective-right view. "My conclusion came as something of a surprise to me, and an unwelcome surprise," Tribe admitted to the *New York Times* after the third edition came out. "I have always supported as a matter of policy very comprehensive gun control."[4]

One year later, the Fifth Circuit came down with its *Emerson* decision, drawing heavily on this growing scholarly consensus to conclude that the Second Amendment does indeed protect an individual right and must therefore be recognized as a full-throated member of the Bill of Rights.

That ruling, Clark Neily explained, was "the catalyst for bringing what became the *Heller* case." As he and Steve Simpson sat drinking their Yuenglings and talking guns that night at happy hour, they both agreed that "the issue was very likely on a short track to the Supreme Court." For one thing, the federal circuits were now split on a major constitutional question. For another, Neily explained, "*Emerson* basically inspired criminal defense attorneys all over the country to begin asserting Second Amendment defenses to gun charges in cases where they probably wouldn't have done so otherwise. So you have this tidal wave of Second Amendment litigation, mostly on the criminal side."[5] Neily and Simpson both felt that the last thing they wanted to see was a criminal gun defendant reach the Supreme Court before "a carefully constructed civil rights test case." At that point in the conversation, Neily said, "the light went on and we looked at each other and said, 'Well, jeez, we should do it.'" And so they did.

As senior attorneys at the Institute for Justice, the two men already carried heavy caseloads. But that was no deterrent in the face of potentially making legal history. However, because the Institute for Justice does not litigate gun rights cases, this lawsuit would have to be launched on their own time. Their boss, Chip Mellor, signed off on Neily's pursuing the case, but because Simpson had only recently joined the firm, Mellor preferred to keep him working exclusively on IJ litigation. So Neily got to work. His first, and perhaps most consequential, step was to enlist the perfect ally to help him transform a barroom brainstorming session into a landmark Supreme Court decision.

Robert A. Levy spent twenty-five successful years in business before deciding to devote his time to constitutional scholarship and libertarian legal advocacy. To that end, the forty-nine-year-old tech entrepreneur entered law school at George Mason University in 1991.

After graduation he went on to clerk for Judge Royce Lamberth of the U.S. District Court in Washington, D.C., clerked once more for Judge Douglas Ginsburg of the U.S. Court of Appeals for the District of Columbia Circuit, and from 1997 to 2004 served as an adjunct law professor at Georgetown. These days, Levy serves as chairman of the board of the Cato Institute. Back in 2002, he was a senior fellow at Cato's Center for Constitutional Studies.

Neily and Levy first met when they clerked together for Judge Lamberth on the D.C. District Court, and in fact it was Levy, who also sits on the board of the Institute for Justice, who originally introduced Neily to his future bosses at IJ. "I ran the idea for a Second Amendment case by Bob," Neily explained, "and Bob said, 'I think it's a great idea. Let me know what you need from me. We should do it.'" A self-made millionaire, Levy would fund the litigation all the way through to the U.S. Supreme Court.

"SYMPATHETIC CLIENTS, OUTRAGEOUS FACTS, EVIL VILLAINS"

Although it was not technically an Institute for Justice case, the lawsuit that became *District of Columbia v. Heller* has all the hallmarks of the IJ approach. As IJ co-founder Chip Mellor likes to say, every Institute for Justice case features "sympathetic clients, outrageous facts, evil villains."[6] Thanks to careful early planning by Neily and Levy, this case would have all three elements in spades. "Anytime you are trying to chart new territory in Supreme Court jurisprudence," Neily said, "you want to look for the most egregious law you can find. And it turned out D.C. actually had the most sweeping ban on gun ownership in the history of the United States." In addition to imposing a total ban on handguns, D.C. also required that all shotguns and rifles be legally registered and kept inoperable while inside the home, meaning that the guns must be unloaded and also either disassembled or kept under a trigger lock. "And there was no exception for self-defense," Neily emphasized. Put differently, if you lived in a dangerous neighborhood and were forced one day to load your rifle and use it in self-defense against a violent intruder inside your residence, you faced the risk of criminal prosecution for violating D.C.'s gun laws. "What you were really allowed to own was a club that looked like a gun or rifle but you could never put a round in the chamber," Neily said.

That took care of the outrageous facts and the evil villains. Now they needed to find the sympathetic plaintiffs. "We spent the spring and most of the summer of 2002 getting the word out that we were putting together a Second Amendment challenge and we were looking for plaintiffs," Neily explained. With the help of another Cato Institute staffer and fellow lawyer, Gene Healy, they ultimately interviewed some three dozen potential candidates before winnowing the list down to the six individuals who would appear on the original legal complaint.

Among those six was Dick Heller, a white D.C. special police officer contracted by a private firm to provide armed security at the Thurgood Marshall Federal Judicial Center in Washington. A gun rights advocate, Heller found it preposterous that the District trusted him with a weapon at work but then refused to allow him to defend himself with an operable gun at home. Another early plaintiff was Tom Palmer, an openly gay man and a colleague of Levy's at the Cato Institute. Years earlier in California, Palmer had nearly been killed by a mob of homophobic skinheads. The gang only dispersed when he produced a handgun from his backpack and threatened to shoot.

But the original lead plaintiff in the case was an African American woman named Shelly Parker. A self-appointed community activist, Parker had made enemies among the local drug dealers by repeatedly confronting them and threatening to call the police when she saw them at work in her neighborhood. Those bold actions resulted in several threats on her life, including one night when a local thug tried to kick his way into her apartment, screaming, "Bitch, I'll kill you!" After that, Parker wanted to keep a gun at home for self-defense.

"Those were the kinds of plaintiffs that we put together for the challenge," Neily explained, "and we absolutely made clear that those were the kind of people that we were asserting a Second Amendment right to own a gun for." What's more, "we essentially put the onus on the people who disputed that right to explain what the Tom Palmers and Shelly Parkers of the world are supposed to do if they ever face those circumstances again in a place like the District of Columbia."

THE NRA COMES CALLING

Founded in 1871, the National Rifle Association is America's oldest and most famous organization devoted to promoting and defending gun ownership. It therefore came as no surprise when the NRA took an interest in the Levy team once the news of their impending Second Amendment lawsuit began filtering through the conservative and libertarian legal network. What is surprising is the form that interest took.

In August 2002 Levy received a phone call from Nelson Lund, who then held the NRA-endowed Patrick Henry Professorship of Constitutional Law and the Second Amendment at George Mason University Law School. Lund asked him for a meeting. So Levy and Neily sat down at the Cato Institute with Lund and a second NRA-affiliated lawyer, former Reagan Justice Department official Charles Cooper. Those two men brought a message from the NRA: Drop the case. "They felt the NRA had an incremental litigation strategy that was still the best way to proceed," Neily recalled, "and they really didn't think that we should proceed with our lawsuit. We had a cordial but frank exchange of views on that. We didn't agree." A major sticking point centered on the post-*Emerson* legal landscape. Levy and

Neily emphasized the flood of recent criminal litigation surrounding the Second Amendment and wanted to know if the NRA had "a plan for preventing a criminal from getting to the Supreme Court first and asserting a Second Amendment defense to some gun charge, because that of course would be a much less desirable setting," Neily explained. "And they didn't have a plan, they just sort of assured us that that wasn't going to happen." The Levy team made clear that they were committed to going forward with the case, and that they would be doing so on their own terms, not on the NRA's.

In the meantime, Neily had become "bogged down"[7] in several cases at the Institute for Justice, prompting Levy to propose adding one more lawyer to the team who would be responsible for taking the lead in court. That lawyer was Alan Gura, a rising young litigator and former Institute for Justice clerk. "I probably identified as a libertarian by the time that I went to work at the Institute for Justice as a second year law student at Georgetown," Gura recalled. "It was a revelation to work with those attorneys and to learn about some of these issues. It really spoke to me."[8]

The Levy team offered Gura what Neily jokingly referred to as "a very discount rate," though it was understood that if the case did reach the Supreme Court, it would be Gura's case to argue. He happily signed on. A little more than a month later, in February 2003, the three lawyers filed their initial complaint at the D.C. District Court, listing Shelly Parker as the lead plaintiff and Dick Heller, Tom Palmer, and three others as co-plaintiffs. The groundbreaking Second Amendment case of *Parker v. District of Columbia* was now officially underway.

THE NRA FIRES BACK

The Levy team got their second unpleasant surprise from the NRA a few weeks later when the organization funded its own legal challenge to the D.C. gun laws, a case known as *Seegars v. Ashcroft*. As the case name suggests, the NRA-backed suit was filed not only against the District of Columbia, but also against the Department of Justice (DOJ), since DOJ lawyers (who then reported to Attorney General John Ashcroft) technically enforce local laws in the District. "We thought that was a major tactical blunder," Neily said. Essentially, the NRA-backed suit "made this really inexplicable decision to go to court against the junior varsity and the varsity, represented by the DOJ lawyers."

Indeed, it turned out to be a fatal mistake for the NRA side, and nearly proved fatal to the Levy team as well. That's because as the two cases moved forward in court, the DOJ lawyers came up with the idea of resisting the NRA-backed suit on the grounds of a legal doctrine known as "standing." Basically, because D.C. officials had not technically denied anyone a gun license, the NRA-backed plaintiffs had suffered no concrete injury and therefore had no standing to bring suit. The federal court accepted that argument and threw out the NRA-funded challenge. D.C.'s lawyers, by contrast, had not thought to mount that particular defense on their own.

In the meantime, however, injury was added to insult when the *Seegars* team moved to have its case consolidated with the *Parker* case, a move the Levy team saw as tantamount to a hostile takeover attempt by the NRA. If successful, consolidation would have forced the two sides to cooperate and work as a single team—a surefire recipe for internal conflict and perhaps even the implosion of the case. "They tried to take their highly defective case and glom it on to our very clean, rifle-shot case," Neily complained, the frustration still evident in his voice. That was the final straw. "Derail, undermine, sandbag, I think all of those are fair," he said. "I think they were absolutely trying to sandbag the case."[9] Fortunately for the Levy team, the federal court refused the motion to consolidate the two cases.

Alan Gura was equally frustrated by the NRA's attempts to muscle in on the libertarians. "The NRA is an organization that, whatever it thinks about the Second Amendment—and I think they are sincere, they do actually care about the Second Amendment as they conceive it—holds the Second Amendment as a secondary concern," he said. "The organization's primary concern is to maintain and promote itself, to maintain its brand, and to make sure that when people think 'guns' they think 'NRA.' And they are very successful at that."[10] For its part, the NRA has consistently maintained that its only concern was putting together the best possible case against the D.C. gun laws.

To make matters worse for the libertarians, the DOJ's standing argument had by then worked its way into the *Parker* case, prompting the U.S. Court of Appeals for the District of Columbia Circuit to give the boot to five of the Levy team's six plaintiffs, including original lead plaintiff Shelly Parker. Only Dick Heller, the D.C. special police officer, was found to have legal standing to challenge D.C.'s gun laws. Why? Because Heller, following the sage advice of his friend and fellow gun rights enthusiast Dane von Breichenruchardt, had gone down to city hall for the sole purpose of receiving a slip of paper officially denying him a gun license. "He filled out a completely meaningless piece of paper," Neily later marveled. "But the D.C. Circuit found that futile act was sufficient to confer standing on Dick Heller but none of the other plaintiffs."[11] *Parker v. District of Columbia* would therefore become *Heller v. District of Columbia*. And the legal battle was about to hit the big time.

"THE RIGHT OF THE PEOPLE"

The District of Columbia advanced two principal arguments in defense of its handgun ban and related gun control provisions. First, it said the

Second Amendment only protected a right that was directly related to militia service. In essence, it was the collective-right interpretation. As evidence, D.C. pointed to the wording of the amendment, with its references to the militia and the bearing of arms, both of which are military concepts. Taken as a whole, the District of Columbia argued, the text and history of the Second Amendment precludes the constitutional recognition of a private right to own guns for non–militia-related purposes. Second, D.C. maintained that under any reading of the Second Amendment, its laws still passed muster because they were reasonable regulations enacted by duly elected officials responding to local conditions. Because the city faced high rates of gun violence, the government's lawyers maintained, it had perfectly rational reasons to outlaw handguns and impose other restrictions. In short, D.C.'s gun control judgments were entitled to significant deference by the courts.

The Levy team made precisely the opposite arguments, stressing that the text and history of the Second Amendment pointed overwhelmingly toward the existence of an individual "right of the people" to keep and bear arms for purposes of self-defense. Nor did the libertarians find anything reasonable about D.C.'s total ban on handguns and its effectively total ban on all operable long guns within the home.

To the dismay of District of Columbia officials, the D.C. Circuit sided with the legal challengers, ruling on March 9, 2007, that "the Second Amendment protects a right of individuals for private use." As for the government's reasonableness claim, the D.C. Circuit rejected that argument as "frivolous."[12] It was a definitive win for the Levy team and for the gun rights community at large.

The next move now rested in the hands of the District. If it appealed the loss, the U.S. Supreme Court was virtually guaranteed to take the case. "We spent several months wondering whether the D.C. government would go for review in the Supreme Court," Neily recalled. "We were walking on eggshells for most of that summer of

2007 waiting to see what they would do."[13] Unlike most lawyers who win a major victory in federal appeals court, Neily, Levy, and Gura wanted the losing side to file an appeal. Indeed, from the moment the case was first conceived at that June 2002 happy hour, the whole point had been to reach the Supreme Court. They had no interest in stopping short of total victory.

On September 4, the District of Columbia granted the libertarians their wish by asking the Supreme Court to take the case. The Levy team promptly responded, seconding the District's request. Both sides had now asked the Supreme Court to step in and definitively settle the question of whether or not the Second Amendment secured a personal right to keep and bear arms. On November 20, the Court accepted this dual invitation and agreed to hear arguments the following year in *District of Columbia v. Heller.*

"A LIBERTARIAN IDEAL"

"We will hear argument today in case 07–290, *District of Columbia v. Heller,*" declared Chief Justice John Roberts on the morning of March 18, 2008. The great constitutional showdown over the meaning of the Second Amendment had begun.

Up first at the lectern was Walter Dellinger, an experienced litigator and former acting solicitor general under President Bill Clinton, hired by the District of Columbia to argue its case. "Good morning, Mr. Chief Justice, and may it please the Court," Dellinger began. "In the debates over the Second Amendment, every person who used the phrase 'bear arms' used it to refer to the use of arms in connection with militia service and when Madison introduced the amendment in the first Congress, he exactly equated the phrase 'bearing arms' with, quote, 'rendering military service.'" The text and history of the amendment, Dellinger emphasized to the Court, were solidly on his side.

But the chief justice immediately pushed back. "If you're right, Mr. Dellinger, it's certainly an odd way in the Second Amendment to phrase the operative provision," Roberts responded. "If it is limited to State militias, why would they say 'the right of the people'? In other words, why wouldn't they say 'state militias have the right to keep arms'?"[14]

Justice Antonin Scalia soon joined in. "Why isn't it perfectly plausible, indeed reasonable," Scalia said, "to assume that since the framers knew that the way militias were destroyed by tyrants in the past was not by passing a law against militias, but by taking away the people's weapons—that was the way militias were destroyed. The two clauses go together beautifully: Since we need a militia, the right of the people to keep and bear arms shall not be infringed."[15]

But Dellinger refused to accept those interpretations. "Even if the language of keeping and bearing arms were ambiguous," he maintained, "the amendment's first clause confirms that the right is militia-related."[16] As for the Levy team's assertion of a personal right to own a gun for self-defense, he later added, "that is a libertarian ideal. It's not the text of the Second Amendment, which is expressly about the security of the State; it's about well-regulated militias, not unregulated individual license."[17]

In the meantime, Justice Anthony Kennedy, widely seen as holding the decisive fifth vote in the case, offered his own interpretation of the Second Amendment, and it came as music to the ears of the Levy team. "In effect," Kennedy said, "the amendment says we reaffirm the right to have a militia, we've established it, but in addition, there is a right to bear arms."[18] A few minutes later, Kennedy followed up with a related argument, one that also rejected Dellinger's view that the Second Amendment was exclusively militia based. "It had nothing to do with the concern of the remote settler to defend himself and his family against hostile Indian tribes and outlaws, wolves and bears and grizzlies and things like that?"[19] Kennedy asked.

"Alan and I basically exchanged glances without turning our heads when Kennedy asked that question," Clark Neily recalled, "because we both knew that we had won the case." As the libertarian lawyers immediately understood, Kennedy "had just shown his hand."[20]

Dellinger also seemed to realize he wasn't making much progress with the Court's conservatives, so he soon switched to his second line of argument. "I think you ought to consider the effect on the 42 states," he said, that "have adopted a reasonableness standard that has allowed them to sustain sensible regulation of dangerous weapons."

But once again, the chief justice launched an immediate counterattack. "What is reasonable about a total ban on possession?" he asked the attorney.

"What is reasonable about a total ban on possession," Dellinger fought back, "is that it's a ban only on the possession of one kind of weapon, of handguns, that's been considered especially—especially dangerous."

"So if you have a law that prohibits the possession of books, it's all right if you allow the possession of newspapers?"[21] Roberts retorted. Dellinger had once again failed to gain traction with the Court's conservative justices.

"SOME VERY INTRICATE STANDARD"

Up next at the lectern was Solicitor General Paul Clement, who was granted fifteen minutes of argument time by the Supreme Court to explain the George W. Bush administration's views on this pressing constitutional question. The members of the Levy team were none too pleased by what Clement had to say.

"The Bush administration filed this incredibly waffling, on the whole very harmful brief written by then Solicitor General Paul Clement in which they actually urged the Supreme Court to reverse the

D.C. Circuit, take that win off the board, and send it back to the district court," Neily complained. "Very disappointing from an administration that claimed to believe in the Second Amendment."[22] Neily had good reason to feel disappointed. In May 2001, Bush's attorney general, John Ashcroft, had thrilled the gun rights community when he detailed his views on the Second Amendment in a letter to the NRA's executive director. "While I cannot comment on any pending litigation," Ashcroft wrote, "let me state unequivocally my view that the text and the original intent of the Second Amendment clearly protect the right of individuals to keep and bear firearms."[23] That letter went out on government stationery bearing the official seal of the U.S. Department of Justice. Yet when the moment finally arrived to champion that view before the Supreme Court in *Heller,* the administration switched gears and adopted a tone of cautious moderation. The libertarians were simply too bold for the White House.

The main point of contention centered on the degree of judicial review that Second Amendment cases should trigger. In its 2007 ruling against the District's gun laws, the D.C. Circuit seemed to endorse "strict scrutiny," the most meaningful form of inquiry used by the courts to determine whether a regulation should be struck down. Clement, by contrast, was pushing for an "intermediate level of review,"[24] and urging the Supreme Court to send *Heller* back down to the lower courts for reconsideration under that more lenient standard.

But Clement ran into trouble right away with the Court's conservatives. Justice Scalia, for example, failed to see why the Second Amendment was entitled to anything less than strict scrutiny. "We certainly apply it to freedom of speech, don't we?"[25] he asked Clement. Why should the Second Amendment receive any less respect than the First Amendment?

Chief Justice Roberts raised a more fundamental objection. "I'm not sure why we have to articulate some very intricate standard,"

Roberts said. "I mean, these standards that apply in the First Amendment just kind of developed over the years as sort of baggage that the First Amendment picked up. But I don't know why when we are starting afresh, we would try to articulate a whole standard that would apply in every case?"[26] The solicitor general had failed to persuade the Court to adopt his intermediate approach in Second Amendment cases.

"THERE IS A ROLE FOR JUDICIAL REVIEW"

When they arrived at the Supreme Court that morning, the three libertarian lawyers were feeling extremely confident. Nothing they heard during the ninety-seven-minute oral argument would shake that feeling. "To the contrary," Clark Neily later said, the oral argument only reaffirmed their conviction in the strength and rightness of their case. "We had had five or six moot courts at that point with some of the top Second Amendment litigators in the country," he recalled. "I don't think there was a single question that came up during the oral argument that we hadn't been over in those moot courts and worked out very meticulously what the best answer would be."[27]

Standing at the lectern, Alan Gura faced the first of those questions courtesy of Justice Stephen Breyer. "Assume," Breyer told him, "that there is an individual right, but the purpose of that right is to maintain a citizen army; call it a militia." Under that assumption, Breyer asked, "Why isn't a ban on handguns, while allowing the use of rifles and muskets, a reasonable or a proportionate response on behalf of the District of Columbia?"

"It's unreasonable," Gura responded, "and it actually fails any standard of review that might be offered under such a construction of individual rights because proficiency with handguns . . . proficiency in use and familiarity with the handgun at issue would be one that would further a militia purpose."[28]

The next line of questioning came from Justice John Paul Stevens, who asked Gura if "to understand the amendment, you must pay some attention to the militia requirement?"

"Yes, Your Honor," he answered. "We must."

But before Gura could explain further, the chief justice cut him off. "So a conscientious objector who likes to hunt deer for food, you would say, has no rights under the Second Amendment," Roberts interjected. "He is not going to be part of the militia. He is not going to be part of the common defense, but he still wants to bear arms. You would say that he doesn't have any rights under this amendment?"

"No, Your Honor," Gura quickly responded. The militia clause "informs a purpose," he explained. "It gives us some guideposts as to how we look at the Second Amendment, but it's not the exclusive purpose of the Second Amendment."[29] Indeed, Gura would argue, the personal right of self-defense was at the core of the amendment.

Justice Kennedy soon entered the fray, posing the same question he had asked earlier. "I want to know whether or not, in your view, the operative clause of the amendment protects, or was designed to protect in an earlier time, the settler in the wilderness and his right to have a gun against some conceivable Federal enactment which would prohibit him from having any guns?"

"Oh, yes. Yes, Justice Kennedy,"[30] Gura happily replied. Once again, Kennedy had shown his hand.

Justice Stevens, meanwhile, began challenging Gura on his interpretation of Second Amendment history. As Stevens saw it, the amendment was clearly *not* intended to protect a personal right to gun ownership, a theme Stevens would later develop in his lengthy dissenting opinion. "You say that the right of self-defense was at the heart of the Second Amendment, in your view," he said. Yet "some provisions suggested that and were not accepted by the authors of the Second Amendment."

"Which provisions were those, Justice Stevens?" Gura asked.

"Pennsylvania," the justice responded.

"Pennsylvania's provision was certainly influential," Gura answered. Indeed it was. The primary voices raised in favor of adding the Bill of Rights to the new Constitution were those of the Anti-Federalists, the group that attacked the Constitution for granting too much power to the central government, and for providing too few protections for individual rights.[31] Pennsylvania was an Anti-Federalist stronghold. "Remember, Madison was trying to mollify the Anti-Federalists' concerns," Gura explained. "The Second Amendment is clearly addressed to Pennsylvania and New Hampshire and New York and all these other States that were demanding a right to keep and bear arms, and there was always understood to be an individual right because that is the way in which the right was violated by the British in the war of revolution that occurred not too long ago."[32] The original meaning of the Second Amendment, Gura stressed, was on his side.

Gura faced his final challenge that morning from Justice Breyer, who circled back to the question of whether D.C.'s gun laws should count as reasonable regulations. "Do you want thousands of judges all over the United States to be deciding that kind of question rather than the city councils and the legislatures that have decided it in the context of passing laws?" Breyer asked, a sharp note creeping into his voice.

But Gura refused to accept Breyer's deferential premise. "When a fundamental right is at stake," the libertarian responded, "there is a role for judicial review."[33]

"SHALL NOT BE INFRINGED"

And so there was. On June 26, 2008, the last day of the Supreme Court's 2007–2008 term, the Supreme Court invalidated D.C.'s handgun ban, as well as its prohibition on keeping operable long guns within the home.

"There seems to us no doubt, on the basis of both text and history," declared the majority opinion of Justice Antonin Scalia, "that the Second Amendment conferred an individual right to keep and bear arms."[34]

Pointing to numerous founding-era sources for support, Scalia argued that while the Second Amendment's militia clause "announces the purpose for which the right was codified," it "does not suggest that preserving the militia was the only reason Americans valued the ancient right; most undoubtedly thought it even more important for self-defense and hunting."[35] Indeed, Scalia argued, the right of self-defense is "inherent"[36] in the Second Amendment, and was understood to be so by those who drafted the amendment and those who ratified it.

But that right is not unlimited, Scalia added. "Nothing in our opinion should be taken to cast doubt on longstanding prohibitions on the possession of firearms by felons and the mentally ill, or laws forbidding the carrying of firearms in sensitive places such as schools and government buildings, or laws imposing conditions and qualifications on the commercial sale of arms,"[37] he wrote.

"Undoubtedly," Scalia concluded, "some think the Second Amendment is outmoded" in our modern world, "where well-trained police forces provide personal security, and where gun violence is a serious problem. That," he continued, "is perhaps debatable, but what is not debatable is that it is not the role of this Court to pronounce the Second Amendment extinct."[38]

Writing in dissent, Justice John Paul Stevens took issue with Scalia on every point. "The 'right to keep and bear arms' protects only a right to possess and use firearms in connection with service in a state-organized militia,"[39] Stevens maintained. It had nothing to do with personal uses such as hunting or self-defense.

Stevens also faulted Scalia for his lack of judicial restraint. "Until today, it has been understood that legislatures may regulate the civilian use and misuse of firearms so long as they do not interfere with the preservation of a well-regulated militia," he wrote. "The Court's announcement of a new constitutional right to own and use firearms for private purposes upsets that settled understanding," he complained, and "will surely give rise to a far more active judicial role in making vitally important national policy decisions."[40]

In a footnote to that passage, Stevens pressed the point further, contrasting Scalia's approach in *Heller* with the approach of New Deal era Justice Felix Frankfurter, who famously counseled the Supreme Court against entering the "political thicket"[41] of legislative redistricting. Frankfurter was "by any measure a true judicial conservative," Stevens wrote, and Scalia ought to follow his example. "Adherence to a policy of judicial restraint would be far wiser than the bold decision announced today,"[42] Stevens declared.

"FILE IT!"

In the three-month waiting period that fell between the oral argument and the opinion announcement in *D.C. v. Heller,* the three libertarian lawyers went their separate working ways. Levy returned to his job at the Cato Institute, Neily refocused his efforts at the Institute for Justice, and Alan Gura got to work on a new case. That new case of Gura's would soon be known as *McDonald v. City of Chicago,* and in 2010 it would become his second gun rights victory before the U.S. Supreme Court.

"As we advanced through the D.C. circuit and on to the Supreme Court," Gura recalled, "my thoughts turned to the next step because we felt there was a very good chance the Supreme Court would uphold the D.C. Circuit's opinion, which meant that the Fourteenth Amendment issue would be instantly ripe."[43]

That Fourteenth Amendment issue was a legal doctrine known as "incorporation." Over the past century, the Supreme Court has gradually applied, or incorporated, most of the provisions in the Bill of

Rights against state and local governments. In the 1925 case of *Gitlow v. United States,* for instance, the Court first held that "freedom of speech and of the press—which are protected by the First Amendment from abridgment by Congress—are among the fundamental personal rights and 'liberties' protected by the due process clause of the Fourteenth Amendment from impairment by the States."[44] The rest of the Bill of Rights gradually followed suit in later cases, though the right to keep and bear arms remained a notably unincorporated exception. Because *Heller* dealt exclusively with the Second Amendment's role in the District of Columbia, which is a federal enclave, the question of state incorporation was not raised by the litigation. But with the Court now seemingly poised to recognize the Second Amendment as securing an individual right, Gura knew the time for a new incorporation case had arrived.

He began by selecting the local gun law he would seek to invalidate. "Everyone identified Chicago as the logical place," Gura recalled, because that city's handgun ban was virtually identical to the ban being challenged in *Heller.* "And if a handgun ban is unconstitutional," Gura explained, "then that's a very clean case. The only thing you have to discuss really is the Fourteenth Amendment."

The next task was finding sympathetic clients willing to put their names to the legal challenge. By this point, Gura had formed a new relationship with a gun rights outfit called the Second Amendment Foundation (SAF), who expressed an eagerness to help fund and organize his next case. "They are a terrific client," Gura stressed. "I can't say enough positive things about them." With the help of SAF, plus one other group, the Illinois State Rifle Association, Gura soon located four individuals ready and willing to challenge the Chicago handgun ban and several related gun control laws. His lead plaintiff would be seventy-six-year-old Otis McDonald, an African American grandfather, retired maintenance engineer, and lifelong Democrat.

Like Shelly Parker in the District of Columbia, McDonald also had a habit of standing up to local drug dealers and therefore wanted to keep a handgun in his South Side Chicago home for self-defense. While the Supreme Court was still deliberating *Heller,* Gura flew to Chicago to meet with McDonald and his other future clients. "We had a good discussion and laid out the plan," Gura said, "and decided to move forward such that the day that the *Heller* decision was announced we were able to immediately file our case in Chicago."

When *Heller* finally arrived on June 26, Gura was sitting in the courtroom next to Clark Neily, savoring their historic victory. But he was also preparing to spring into action. "On the way out of the building I stopped by the Public Information Office and we picked up copies of the slip opinion that the Court distributes," Gura recalled. "And I skimmed it very rapidly to see what if anything the Supreme Court had said about the question of incorporation and the Fourteenth Amendment."[45]

Gura soon found what he was looking for. In Footnote 23 of the *Heller* decision, Justice Scalia addressed the relevance of an 1876 opinion known as *United States v. Cruikshank.* At issue were the arrests of three Louisiana men for participating in a notorious event known as the Colfax massacre, in which a white supremacist mob in Louisiana murdered dozens of African Americans in what historian Eric Foner has called "the bloodiest single act of carnage in all of Reconstruction."[46] Federal authorities levied multiple charges against the defendants, including conspiring to violate the First and Second Amendment rights of their victims. But the Supreme Court threw out those convictions. Among other reasons, the Court held that the First and Second Amendments applied only against the actions of the federal government.

"With respect to *Cruikshank*'s continuing validity on incorporation, a question not presented by this case," Scalia wrote in Footnote

23 of *Heller,* "we note that *Cruikshank* also said that the First Amendment did not apply against the States and did not engage in the sort of Fourteenth Amendment inquiry required by our later cases."[47] The implication was clear. Because *Cruikshank* "did not engage" in the Fourteenth Amendment jurisprudence now "required" by the Supreme Court, it was effectively a dead letter in First Amendment cases. It took no leap of imagination to see the same reasoning apply in the Second Amendment context. Footnote 23 "suggested very much that this is an open question and one that would need to be resolved," Gura said. "There was nothing in the opinion obviously that precluded the Chicago litigation and in fact there was what appeared to be an invitation for it and a suggestion that it needed to be done. So I immediately called my co-counsel in Chicago, David Sigale, and said, 'File it!'"[48]

Remarkably, that phone call was when Clark Neily first learned about Gura's sequel to *Heller.* "I have to say that it was something of a surprise to me when Alan brought the case," Neily later recalled with a laugh. "I have a very vivid recollection of walking down the steps of the Supreme Court on the day the *Heller* decision was handed down and looking back over my shoulder at Alan who was on his cell phone. I have to commend him for his entrepreneurial spirit."[49]

A TALE OF TWO ORIGINALISMS

Since joining the Supreme Court in 1986, Justice Antonin Scalia has emerged as the Court's foremost advocate of "originalism," the legal approach that says the Constitution must be read according to its original meaning at the time it was adopted. As Scalia argued in his 1997 book, *A Matter of Interpretation,* "if the people come to believe that the Constitution is *not* a text like other texts; that it means, not what it says or what it was understood to mean, but what it *should* mean, . . . well, then, they will look for qualifications other than impartiality, judgment, and lawyerly acumen in those whom they select to interpret it. More specifically," he stressed, "they will look for judges who agree with *them* as to what the evolving standards have evolved to; who agree with them as to what the Constitution *ought* to be."[50]

To Scalia's evident satisfaction, the legal debate in *District of Columbia v. Heller* focused overwhelmingly on the original meaning of the Second Amendment. Indeed, not only did Scalia's majority opinion make copious use of historical materials; Justice Stevens's dissent also delved into some of that history. The Court's decision in *Heller,* Scalia told the journalist Marcia Coyle, was a "vindication of originalism."[51]

Alan Gura's follow-up to *Heller, McDonald v. Chicago,* would also center on the original meaning of a constitutional provision. Except this time around, Scalia would prove decidedly uninterested in conducting a careful historical examination. In fact, during the March 2010 oral argument in *McDonald,* Scalia actually mocked Gura's emphasis on originalism, a notorious event that continues to rankle every libertarian lawyer I have spoken with about the case.

What explains Scalia's rapid downshift from originalism in *Heller* to something less than originalism in *Chicago?* The answer lies in the Supreme Court's long and complicated relationship with the Fourteenth Amendment.

BACK TO *SLAUGHTER-HOUSE*

As the Supreme Court began selectively incorporating the Bill of Rights against the states in the early decades of the twentieth century, it did so via the mechanism of substantive due process. Essentially, the Court read the Fourteenth Amendment's guarantee that no state shall deprive any person of life, liberty, or property without due process of law to include most of the rights spelled out in the Bill of Rights. Yet if there is one thing today's legal conservatives do not like, that thing is substantive due process. For starters, it's the legal approach responsible for *Roe v. Wade,* where the Court located the unenumerated right to an abortion in the Due Process Clause of the Fourteenth Amendment. Many conservatives argue that the phrase "due process," by definition, applies solely to procedural safeguards, and that the courts have no business enforcing any substantive rights via the Due Process Clause. One such conservative is Antonin Scalia, who has lashed out repeatedly against substantive due process over the years, denouncing it as a "judicial usurpation"[52] and as an excuse "to render democratically adopted texts mere springboards for judicial lawmaking."[53]

So Gura offered Scalia and his fellow conservatives an alternative in *McDonald v. Chicago:* incorporation via the Fourteenth Amendment's Privileges or Immunities Clause, which reads, "No State shall make or enforce any law which shall abridge the privileges or immunities of citizens of the United States." As Gura argued in the lengthy brief he submitted to the Supreme Court, the Privileges or Immunities Clause's text, original meaning, and history, including the stated goals of its framers and ratifiers, show that it was designed to secure individual rights, including the right of armed self-defense, against abusive state and local governments.

The problem is that the Supreme Court rendered the clause a nullity with its 1873 decision in *The Slaughter-House Cases,* which upheld a Louisiana law granting a slaughterhouse monopoly to a private corporation over the objections of local butchers. Writing for the five-to-four majority in that case, Justice Samuel F. Miller said the Privileges or Immunities Clause imposed no substantive restrictions on the authority of the states, and in fact protected only a meager selection of national rights (such as the right to access federal waterways). Writing in dissent, Justice Stephen Field attacked Miller's decision for eviscerating the Privileges or Immunities Clause and for violating the free labor rights of the butchers.

For decades, libertarian legal activists have been championing Field's dissent and gunning for *Slaughter-House*'s demise. Institute for Justice co-founder Clint Bolick, for example, first called for the case to be overruled in his 1988 book *Changing Course,* and then repeated the call to arms in 1990's *Unfinished Business,* which the Institute for Justice soon adopted as its "strategic litigation blueprint." In fact, according to Gura, "the first time I really dealt with *The Slaughter-House Cases* and the Privileges or Immunities Clause was at the Institute for Justice when I was interning there as a law student." His reaction, he said, was "that it was an abomination and a complete farce of a decision."[54] Now, more than a decade later, Gura finally had the opportunity to do something about it. In *McDonald,* Gura would argue that the text and original meaning of the Constitution required the Supreme Court to strike down *Slaughter-House* and apply the Second Amendment to the states via the Privileges or Immunities Clause. If successful, this approach would advance the twin libertarian goals of expanding gun rights and securing economic liberties.

CONSERVATIVES VS. LIBERTARIANS

To put it mildly, many conservatives were not thrilled about Gura's quest to overrule *Slaughter-House.* In fact, many of those conservatives thought the case was correctly decided back in 1873. Foremost among them was Robert Bork. "What is striking about the *Slaughter-House Cases* is not the caution displayed by the majority but rather the radical position of the four dissenters," Bork argued in his book *The Tempting of America.* Miller's majority opinion followed a "sound judicial instinct," Bork maintained, and should be applauded as "a narrow victory for judicial moderation." As for the Privileges or Immunities Clause, Bork added, its original meaning "is largely unknown." In fact, he went on, "It is quite possible that the words meant very little to those who adopted them."[55] (As we saw in the first chapter of this book, the historical evidence proves Bork wrong on that count.) In essence, Bork approached *Slaughter-House* the same way he approached substantive due process. He wanted the courts to steer clear of recognizing fundamental rights under the Fourteenth Amendment.

Antonin Scalia adopted a similar position in his 1984 Cato Institute debate with libertarian law professor Richard Epstein. According to then-Judge Scalia, if the courts went back to protecting economic liberties under the Fourteenth Amendment, that would only encourage liberal judges to perform greater feats of liberal judicial activism. "In the long run, and perhaps even in the short run," Scalia declared, "the reinforcement of mistaken and unconstitutional perceptions of the role of the courts in our system far outweighs whatever evils may have accrued from undue judicial abstention in the economic field."[56] Scalia's answer was for the courts to double-down on judicial deference.

With *McDonald v. Chicago* working its way to the Supreme Court, Alan Gura was on a collision course with the Bork-Scalia brand of conservatism. And once again, Gura's old antagonists at the National Rifle Association would be there to throw a monkey wrench into his plans.

HISTORY MATTERS

Because *Slaughter-House* is a Supreme Court decision, the lower courts are duty-bound to follow it in appropriate cases. Only the Supreme Court may overturn one of its own precedents. So as Gura began litigating *McDonald v. Chicago,* he kept his Privileges or Immunities Clause argument in reserve and made the Due Process Clause his primary method for urging the courts to incorporate the Second Amendment. But he always knew both arguments would come in handy once he reached the Supreme Court. "It seems very strange to think that having issued *Heller,* which

is all about history, the Court would then come back immediately there-
after and on the Fourteenth Amendment speak only about its precedent
and not try to understand what the text of the Fourteenth Amendment
means, and what the framers thought they were doing when they ratified
it," Gura said. "There was no way to get around it."

After losing at the U.S. Court of Appeals for the Seventh Circuit
on June 2, 2009, Gura finally had the opportunity to put both clauses
into play. On June 9, he asked the Supreme Court to invalidate Chicago's handgun ban by applying the Second Amendment to the states via
either the Privileges or Immunities Clause or the Due Process Clause
of the Fourteenth Amendment; or if it so chose, the Court could rely
on both.

McDonald was not the only Chicago gun case to arrive on the
docket, however. The Supreme Court had also received a petition in the
case of *National Rifle Association v. Chicago*. Like Gura, the NRA also
filed suit in the wake of *Heller*, challenging the gun laws in both Chicago and its nearby suburb of Oak Park. But Gura beat the NRA to the
punch when the Court granted review in his case alone. That forced
the NRA to find a new angle in order to keep itself in the running.

That angle turned out to be Gura's emphasis on the Privileges
or Immunities Clause and his attempt to have *Slaughter-House* overruled. "They made common cause here with some of their socially
conservative friends who don't like the Privileges or Immunities argument for other reasons," Gura said. "These are the people who support
presidential candidates that think contraception is the business of the
White House. And so they made this unholy alliance with the NRA
and we saw efforts from some of the social conservative people to actually attack our historical originalist argument."[57]

The most prominent attack came in the form of an *amicus* brief
filed by several leading right-wing groups, including the American Civil
Rights Union and the Family Research Council. Ostensibly filed "in

support" of Gura and his clients, in reality the brief urged the Supreme Court to reject Gura's *Slaughter-House* argument and instead leave that 1873 decision on the books. Overruling *Slaughter-House,* the conservative brief stated, "would render the Privileges or Immunities Clause a *tabula rasa,* which this Court in the future could interpret to mean anything this Court chooses, making that clause a cornucopia of various rights devoid of any textual support in the Constitution, with profound implications for both social and economic policy issues in this country, as future Members of this Court could constitutionalize their personal preferences, foreclosing political solutions on these matters."[58]

In a companion editorial written for the *Washington Times,* one of the brief's co-authors, Ken Klukowski of the American Civil Rights Union, writing jointly with Ken Blackwell of the Family Research Council, presented a few more objections to Gura's legal strategy. Striking down *Slaughter-House* "could completely change American culture," the two conservatives claimed, "with the court having a new basis upon which to declare constitutional rights to abortion, same-sex marriage, obscene material or a child's 'right' to a public-school education over his parents' objections. It's because of these social issues, in particular, that the Family Research Council has weighed in on this case."[59]

"All I can say about that," Gura later told me, "is that approach elevates other social conservative concerns above the Second Amendment right that we were trying to vindicate, as well as above the level of freedom that the Fourteenth Amendment guarantees. It also proved that they have no particular interest in reviving the Fourteenth Amendment's guarantee of economic liberty, the main obvious consequence of restoring the amendment's original meaning."[60]

In the meantime, the NRA made a brazen attempt to insert itself in the case, asking the Supreme Court on January 5, 2010, to grant the NRA's lawyer, former Solicitor General Paul Clement, ten minutes of oral argument time, to be subtracted from the thirty minutes originally allotted to Gura. Why? Because the Gura team "in their opening brief have concentrated their argument on a Privileges or Immunities Clause theory that would require overruling at least three of this Court's precedents." The NRA, by contrast, painted itself as the champion of substantive due process, a legal theory the NRA said it wanted to see "adequately presented" during oral argument. To that end, the NRA "respectfully"[61] nominated itself to advocate on behalf of the Due Process Clause, plainly suggesting that Gura would fail to do the job.

Gura was infuriated by this maneuver and immediately filed a brief opposing the NRA's motion. We "argued the Due Process Clause issues in the court below, briefed the issues in this Court, and will be fully prepared to address these issues before this Court at oral argument," he told the Supreme Court. "Any argument on this topic by NRA would at best be redundant."[62]

But despite Gura's objections, the Supreme Court granted the NRA's request. Paul Clement, who had recently infuriated gun rights activists during *Heller* by advocating for "intermediate" scrutiny in Second Amendment cases, would now enjoy ten minutes of oral argument time in *McDonald,* and those ten minutes would come at Gura's direct expense. With that, the longstanding conflict between libertarians and conservatives was finally laid bare for the entire legal world to see. "It's regrettable that the bible thumpers and holy rollers who are so afraid of freedom went out of their way to attack us on the Privileges or Immunities issue, and the NRA being the opportunistic people that they are, were all too happy to join in that chorus. But such is life," Gura later said. "I think the big lesson of *McDonald* is that conservatives and libertarians are not always on the same side."[63]

"EVEN I HAVE ACQUIESCED"

On March 18, 2008, Alan Gura had made his first ever appearance before the U.S. Supreme Court to argue *District of Columbia v. Heller*. Two years later, on March 2, 2010, he was back before the Court in the hopes of extending *Heller*'s Second Amendment victory to the states.

"We will hear argument first this morning in Case 08–1521, *McDonald v. City of Chicago*," declared Chief Justice John Roberts. "Mr. Gura."

"Mr. Chief Justice, and may it please the Court," Gura began. "Although Chicago's ordinances cannot survive the faithful application of due process doctrines, there is an even simpler, more essential reason for reversing the lower court's judgment," he said. That reason is the "plain text" of the Privileges or Immunities Clause, "as understood by the people that ratified it."

"Of course," the chief justice responded, "this argument is contrary to *The Slaughter-House Cases*, which have been the law for 140 years. It might be simpler," Roberts granted, "but it's a big—it's a heavy burden for you to carry to suggest that we ought to overrule that decision."

Gura was ready with a response. "Your Honor," he said, "*The Slaughter-House Cases* should not have any *stare decisis* effect before the Court. The Court has always found that when a case is extremely wrong, when there is great consensus that it was simply not decided correctly, especially in a constitutional matter, it has less force."[64]

That argument did not sit well with Justice Antonin Scalia, and he wasted no time letting Gura know it. "Mr. Gura," Scalia began, an impatient tone creeping into his voice, "do you think it is at all easier to bring the Second Amendment under the Privileges and Immunities Clause than it is to bring it under our established law of substantive due process?"

It is easier, Gura answered, "in terms, perhaps, of—of the text and history of the original public understanding of . . ."

But Scalia promptly cut him off. "No, no. I'm not talking about whether *The Slaughter-House Cases* were right or wrong." Unless you are "bucking for a—a place on some law school faculty," Scalia quipped, prompting laughter in the courtroom, "why are you asking us to overrule 150, 140 years of prior law?"

"I have left law school some time ago," Gura carefully responded, "and this is not an attempt to—to return."

But Scalia continued to mock the libertarian lawyer. "What you argue is the darling of the professoriate, for sure, but it's also contrary to 140 years of our jurisprudence," Scalia said. "Why do you undertake that burden instead of just arguing substantive due process, which as much as I think it's wrong, I have—even I have acquiesced in it?"

It was a stunning declaration. Scalia, the Supreme Court's leading proponent of originalism, had just responded to Gura's arguments about the original meaning of the Fourteenth Amendment with contempt and dismissal. Unlike in *Heller*, where constitutional history was at the heart of Scalia's majority opinion, in *McDonald* the conservative justice waved away his previous commitment to originalism and instead announced his intention to acquiesce to substantive due process, an approach he himself admitted to be "wrong."

"Justice Scalia," Gura again responded carefully, "we would be extremely happy if the Court reversed the lower court based on the substantive due process theory that we argued in the Seventh Circuit."[65]

"PRINCIPLED JUDICIAL APPLICATION"

In spite of that contentious exchange with Scalia, the morning's oral argument left little doubt that Gura was going to win the case. None of the five conservative justices who had recently recognized an individual right in *Heller* raised any meaningful objections to incorporating that right via substantive due process, and in fact they seemed to welcome that result.

Or at least four of them did. Justice Clarence Thomas did not ask a single question during oral argument that morning, a peculiar habit of silence he has maintained since 2006, which was the last year he asked a question in court. But Thomas's views on the Fourteenth Amendment would not remain hidden for long.

On June 28, 2010, the Supreme Court announced its decision in *McDonald v. Chicago.* As expected, the Court incorporated the Second Amendment against the states and invalidated Chicago's handgun ban and related gun control provisions. But there was a twist. Only four justices—Roberts, Scalia, Kennedy, and Alito—had voted for incorporation via the Due Process Clause. Thomas had filed a separate concurring opinion in which he joined the Court in its outcome but reasoned his own way to the conclusion. Acting alone, Thomas sided with the libertarians and voted for Second Amendment incorporation via the Privileges or Immunities Clause.

"I believe the original meaning of the Fourteenth Amendment offers a superior alternative," Thomas wrote, "and that a return to that meaning would allow this Court to enforce the rights the Fourteenth Amendment is designed to protect with greater clarity and predictability than the substantive due process framework has so far managed."[66] In other words, while the Second Amendment now applied against all fifty states, a majority of the Supreme Court could not agree on precisely what part of the Fourteenth Amendment made it applicable.

In his fifty-six-page opinion, Thomas offered an originalist tour de force on behalf of his preferred solution. "The record makes plain," he maintained, surveying sources ranging from the congressional debates of 1866 to the writings of leading abolitionists like Frederick Douglass[67] to contemporaneous accounts of Southern officials forcibly disarming the freedmen under the Black Codes, "that the Framers of the Privileges or Immunities Clause and the ratifying-era public understood—just as the Framers of the Second Amendment did—that the right to keep and bear arms was essential to the preservation of liberty."[68]

As for the conservative fear that reviving the Privileges or Immunities Clause would unleash a "cornucopia" of judicial activism, Thomas was untroubled. "Ironically, the same objection applies to the Court's substantive due process jurisprudence," he retorted. "But I see no reason to assume that such hazards apply to the Privileges or Immunities Clause. The mere fact that the Clause does not expressly list the rights it protects does not render it incapable of principled judicial application."[69]

A LIBERTARIAN VICTORY?

McDonald v. Chicago was a profound victory for gun rights, as the Supreme Court finally granted the Second Amendment its full due as a member of the Bill of Rights applicable to all fifty states. But it was not the sweeping libertarian victory Alan Gura had fought for. After all, the Privileges or Immunities Clause was not restored, nor was *Slaughter-House* wiped from the books. Yet Gura told me he has no regrets about the case, and in fact believes his controversial strategy was fully vindicated by the final outcome. For one thing, as Justice Thomas proved in his concurrence, there simply were not five votes to incorporate the Second Amendment on due process grounds alone. But just as important, Gura stressed, is the fact that *McDonald* is "the first time in history that the Privileges or Immunities Clause was consequential to a decision in this way. It's the first time that the anti-*Slaughter-House* position was influential in determining the outcome of the case." That lesson will not be lost on future generations of lawyers, Gura maintained. "Students will have to read *McDonald* in law school. They'll have to read Thomas' opinion."[70]

Alan Gura is not the first libertarian lawyer to look to the future and settle in for the long haul. In his 1990 book *Unfinished Business*, Institute for Justice co-founder Clint Bolick (who counts his old EEOC boss Clarence Thomas as a friend and mentor) urged the fledgling libertarian legal movement to remember that meaningful change does not come quickly in our constitutional system. "It took the NAACP nearly half a century to dismantle separate but equal," Bolick wrote. "It may take a long time to dismantle *Slaughter-House*."[71]

Judging by that timeline, the libertarians are just getting warmed up.

SEVEN

OBAMACARE
ON TRIAL

THE DATE WAS NOVEMBER 29, 2004, AND
Randy Barnett, a libertarian lawyer and Boston University law
professor, was defending the use of medical marijuana before the
U.S. Supreme Court. His case, *Gonzales v. Raich*, centered on a clash between California's Compassionate Use Act, a 1996 voter initiative legalizing the use of medical marijuana within state borders, and the federal
Controlled Substances Act, which outlawed the use of marijuana for any
purpose anywhere in the United States. The question before the Court
that day was whether the federal ban exceeded the bounds of the Commerce Clause, the constitutional provision authorizing Congress to "regulate commerce . . . among the several states."

Standing at the lectern, Barnett told the justices that his lead client, a critically ill cancer patient named Angel Raich, was not engaged
in interstate commerce because the medical marijuana she had legally
used under California law had been grown and consumed entirely
within the confines of that state. "The class of activities involved in

this case are non-economic and wholly intrastate,"[1] he declared in his opening remarks. Because the Commerce Clause was not an unlimited grant of federal power, Barnett maintained, the Controlled Substances Act should not effectively trump California's efforts to legalize medical marijuana. If the Supreme Court was serious about holding Congress to its constitutional limits, Barnett argued, then the federal ban on marijuana must be overruled as applied to Angel Raich. She was no criminal, and the federal government should not be permitted to treat her as such.

Unfortunately for Barnett, a majority of the Supreme Court thought differently. By a vote of six to three, with both conservative Justice Antonin Scalia and moderate conservative Anthony Kennedy voting in favor of the federal government, the Supreme Court upheld the restriction. "Well-settled law controls our answer," declared the majority opinion of Justice John Paul Stevens. "The [Controlled Substances Act] is a valid exercise of federal power, even as applied to the troubling facts of this case."[2]

Barnett's opponent that morning in *Raich* was Solicitor General Paul Clement, an official in the George W. Bush administration. Clement told the Court that under existing precedent, including the landmark New Deal case of *Wickard v. Filburn,* the federal government enjoyed vast regulatory powers via the Commerce Clause and, moreover, the Supreme Court was in no position to second-guess the government's legislative judgments in this realm. His arguments carried the day and scored a win for judicial deference.

It was a painful defeat for the libertarian legal movement, whose members saw the ruling as a potential deathblow for the cause of limited government. Barnett was so dejected at the time, he later admitted, he thought that, "there would never be another Commerce Clause case."[3] And at least one member of the Supreme Court appeared to share his despondency. "If Congress can regulate this under the Commerce Clause," fumed the dissenting opinion of Justice Clarence Thomas, "then it can regulate anything—and the Federal Government is no longer one of limited and enumerated powers."[4] It was a classic dissent by Thomas: forcefully argued, replete with historical evidence, and cast alone. Contrary to his (false) reputation as Scalia's ideological twin, Thomas routinely breaks with his fellow conservatives in order to advance his own distinctive brand of libertarian-flecked jurisprudence.

But as it turned out, *Gonzales v. Raich* was not the last Commerce Clause case. Just seven years later, in fact, Barnett and Clement were back before the Supreme Court to present new arguments about the proper scope of federal authority in *National Federation of Independent Business v. Sebelius*. Except this time, the two former adversaries were fighting on the same side—and the stakes could not have been higher. Indeed, the dispute this time around was over nothing less than the constitutionality of President Barack Obama's signature legislative achievement, the sweeping health care overhaul known as the Patient Protection and Affordable Care Act of 2010, or ACA for short.

At issue was a lawsuit originally filed by Florida and twelve other states on the very day the president signed the health care reform bill into law. Although the suit challenged several components of the legislation, its main target was the controversial "requirement to maintain minimum essential coverage." Also known as the individual mandate, this provision was designed to force all Americans to obtain medical coverage meeting minimum standards set by the government. To justify the health insurance mandate, the act cited Congress's powers to regulate interstate commerce. By the time the legal challenge reached the Supreme Court, a total of twenty-six states had joined it, along with the National Federation of Independent Business (whose legal team included Barnett) and several individuals.

Facing the Supreme Court in March 2012, Paul Clement, who was now serving as the attorney for those twenty-six states, relied in part on libertarian legal theories developed and popularized by his old foe Randy Barnett, telling the justices that Congress did *not* possess the power under the Commerce Clause to force every American to buy health insurance. "The mandate represents an unprecedented effort by Congress to compel individuals to enter commerce in order to better regulate commerce,"[5] he declared.

It was a tectonic shift on the American right. In less than a decade, Barnett had gone from being a libertarian outsider to a highly influential conservative insider. Where he had once squared off against the combined forces of the Bush administration, Barnett was now providing intellectual ammunition for elite Republican lawyers to use in the national battle over health care reform. What's more, the conservative rank and file joined those elites in abandoning any lingering fealty to the idea of judicial deference—they too wanted to see the health care law struck down by the Supreme Court. Libertarian legal thinking had entered the conservative mainstream, and the future of Obama's presidency hung in the balance.

"ARE YOU SERIOUS?"

While it might seem inevitable in hindsight that the Supreme Court would weigh in on the constitutional merits of the individual mandate, that outcome was far from preordained. "When the idea for the challenge was created," observed Orin Kerr, a conservative George Washington University law professor and former clerk to Justice Anthony Kennedy, "it was understood to be a long shot."[6] The legal challengers faced all sorts of obstacles along the way, including the daunting task of persuading federal courts to plunge into the highly political thicket of health care reform.

"We were confident that if we got one ruling against [the ACA], it would go to the Supreme Court,"[7] said Ilya Shapiro, a libertarian lawyer and senior fellow at the Cato Institute's Center for Constitutional Studies, who wrote multiple *amicus* briefs supporting the challenge and provided early legal advice to Florida and the other state challengers.

Some of the Affordable Care Act's supporters didn't think Shapiro and his allies would score even that one victory. Back in October 2009, a reporter asked Democratic House Speaker Nancy Pelosi, "Where specifically does the Constitution grant Congress the authority to enact an individual health insurance mandate?" Her reply: "Are you serious?" Nadeam Elshami, Pelosi's communications director, later amplified the response, telling CNS News, "You can put this on the record: That is not a serious question."[8]

It seemed serious enough to me as I sat in the Supreme Court on March 27, 2012, watching one justice after another grill Obama's solicitor general, Donald Verrilli, about the individual mandate's constitutional defects. And Verrilli was not only taking heat from the Court's most conservative members; he also faced extremely tough questioning from Justice Kennedy, the right-leaning moderate who often casts the decisive fifth vote in tight cases. "I understand we must presume laws are constitutional, but, even so, when you are changing the relation of the individual to the government in this, what we can stipulate is, I think, a unique way," Kennedy asked Verrilli as a hushed courtroom looked on, "do you not have a heavy burden of justification to show authorization under the Constitution?"[9]

Suddenly, the legal challenge didn't seem like such a long shot anymore. How did the challengers narrow the odds to a razor-thin margin? By constructing a potent, case-specific legal strategy on a foundation of painstaking libertarian legal scholarship built over the course of three decades.

"COMMERCE . . . AMONG
THE SEVERAL STATES"

On its face, the Commerce Clause seems like a straightforward proposition. Article One, Section Eight of the U.S. Constitution grants Congress the power "to regulate commerce with foreign nations, and among the several states, and with the Indian tribes." The framers and ratifiers of the Constitution understood that middle part, "among the several states," to mean that Congress may regulate commerce that crosses state lines but not the economic activity that occurs within each state.

In *Federalist* 42, James Madison explained that without the Commerce Clause, Congress would be powerless to clear away the tariffs, monopolies, and other interstate trade barriers erected by various state governments under the Articles of Confederation. "A very material object of this power," he wrote, "was the relief of the States which import and export through other states from the improper contributions levied on them."[10] Madison and the other framers believed that if the new United States was going to make it, the federal government needed to secure what today we might call a domestic free trade zone.

Compared to the decentralized Articles of Confederation, the Commerce Clause was a very significant grant of power to the new federal government—but it was not a blank check. As Alexander Hamilton, normally a champion of broad federal authority, explained in *Federalist* 17, the Commerce Clause did not extend congressional power to "the supervision of agriculture and of other concerns of a similar nature, all those things, in short, which are proper to be provided for by local legislation."[11] The Commerce Clause gave Congress no power to touch intrastate economic activity. Indeed, the framers understood "commerce" to refer to the trade or exchange of goods, including transportation, not to commercial endeavors such as farming or manufacturing.

That original understanding held sway for a century and a half, until the Supreme Court dramatically expanded the federal government's powers under the Commerce Clause in a series of New Deal cases, culminating in the 1942 ruling in *Wickard v. Filburn*. At issue in *Wickard* was Congress's attempt, via the Agricultural Adjustment Act of 1938, to inflate crop prices by limiting the amount farmers were permitted to grow. Among those farmers was Roscoe Filburn of Montgomery County, Ohio, who violated the law by planting twice the amount of wheat allowed by his quota. In his defense, Filburn noted that he did not send that extra wheat off to the market. Instead he consumed it entirely on his own farm, either by feeding it to his animals or turning it into flour for use in his kitchen. Yet according to the Supreme Court, those actions still counted as "commerce . . . among the several states." Filburn's extra wheat may not have crossed any state lines, Justice Robert Jackson wrote for the majority, but he and other similarly disobedient farmers nevertheless exerted a "substantial economic effect"[12] on the interstate wheat market by growing what they otherwise might have bought.

Wickard opened the door to a wide variety of government actions that would have previously been seen as unconstitutional under the Commerce Clause, including federal penalties for local crimes like loan sharking and federal wage controls for state and municipal employees. In the 2005 *Raich* case, the Supreme Court arguably went further than *Wickard* did by upholding the federal ban on marijuana even as applied to local medical use that was permitted under state law. Taken together, *Wickard* and *Raich* meant that Congress possessed vast powers to regulate the American economy, including purely local activities that in the aggregate can be said to affect interstate commerce. Congress relied on the language of these rulings in drafting the Patient Protection and Affordable Care Act. As Section 1501 of the law puts it, the individual mandate "is commercial and economic in nature, and substantially affects interstate commerce."[13]

But there was a catch. As the libertarian and conservative law-yers who crafted the legal challenge to the health care law would later emphasize, *Wickard* and *Raich* were not the only Commerce Clause precedents that mattered.

"WE START WITH FIRST PRINCIPLES"

On November 8, 1994, the Supreme Court heard oral argument in the case of *United States v. Lopez*. At issue was whether the Commerce Clause allowed Congress to forbid the possession of a gun within 1,000 feet of a school. Unlike the federal price-rigging scheme upheld in *Wickard,* the Gun-Free School Zones Act challenged in *Lopez* had no direct connection to economic activity, whether local or national. Instead the government claimed that gun violence, taken in the aggregate, undermined the na-tion's educational system, which in turn substantially affected the U.S. economy.

The case originated in 1992 when a twelfth grader in Texas was arrested for bringing a gun to school and subsequently charged with violating the Gun-Free School Zones Act. In response, the young man's lawyer raised the surprising argument that the case should be dropped because Congress lacked the power to regulate what went on in and around a public school. To say the least, that sort of thinking had gone out of fashion after *Wickard* in the 1940s. But in another surprise twist, the U.S. Court of Appeals for the Fifth Circuit accepted the argument, finding the Gun-Free School Zones Act to be an illegiti-mate exercise of congressional authority.

"When we saw that case coming up from the Fifth Circuit, you can imagine how excited we were," recalled Roger Pilon, the founder and director of the Cato Institute's Center for Constitutional Studies. This was not your run-of-the-mill gun case, he realized, it was an op-portunity to advance the libertarian agenda by curbing federal power.

For years, Pilon and his colleagues had been advocating the revival of a legal principle known as the "doctrine of enumerated powers." Put simply, it's the idea that the government may only exercise those powers specifically granted to it by the text of the Constitution. And even then, the government must not stray too far from the text.

"Because we were pushing [that doctrine] we were on the lookout" for promising cases, Pilon explained. And when he saw *Lopez,* "I thought, 'My God, this is the kind of case we've been looking for!'"[14] To help shape the terms of the looming debate, Pilon quickly commissioned a paper by University of Tennessee law professor Glenn Harlan Reynolds, who, with additional input from Pilon, marshaled a range of legal and historical evidence to explain why "*Lopez* is not about gun control or even about federal-state relations but about whether the Court is ready to hold Congress to its constitutional limits."[15]

The evidence cited in that paper included a groundbreaking 1987 *Virginia Law Review* article by the libertarian legal scholar Richard Epstein, then a law professor at the University of Chicago. "The expansive construction of the clause accepted by the New Deal Supreme Court is wrong, and clearly so,"[16] Epstein concluded in "The Proper Scope of the Commerce Power." Based on a careful analysis of numerous founding-era sources, including the text and structure of the Constitution, Epstein's argument rang out like a constitutional call to arms. When *Lopez* hit the Supreme Court docket in 1994, Pilon and his colleagues at Cato were ready to heed that call.

"Six weeks before oral argument in the case," Pilon explained, "we sent copies [of the study] to each justice and to each of their clerks."[17] It did the trick. Not only did many of the justices voice skepticism about the government's claims during oral argument, several justices even adopted the Cato study's main points as their own. "Is the simple possession of something at or near a school 'commerce' at all?" Justice

Sandra Day O'Connor asked Solicitor General Drew Days. "Is it?" When Days responded that he thought it was, O'Connor shot back, "I would have thought that it wasn't, and I would have thought that it, moreover, is not interstate."[18]

Five months later, the Court nullified the law. It was the first time since the New Deal that a federal regulation had been struck down for exceeding the scope of the Commerce Clause. "We start with first principles," Chief Justice William Rehnquist wrote for the majority. "To uphold the Government's contentions here, we would have to pile inference upon inference in a manner that would bid fair to convert congressional authority under the Commerce Clause to a general police power of the sort retained by the States. . . . This we are unwilling to do."[19]

Five years later, in *United States v. Morrison,* the Court extended this line of reasoning to void a provision of the Violence Against Women Act that created a federal cause of action for victims of gender-motivated crimes. The government's argument in that case was essentially the same as its argument in *Lopez:* that violence against women ultimately has an adverse effect on the national economy. In both cases, the Court ruled that the Commerce Clause is not broad enough to reach such non-economic local activity.

But then *Raich* came along in 2005, apparently slamming the brakes on the Supreme Court's burgeoning "federalism revolution." To the dismay of the libertarians, moreover, *Raich* arguably took *Wickard*'s "substantial economic effects" logic a step further by applying it to someone who was not even a commercial farmer. Was the Commerce Clause now truly dead and buried? Not necessarily. One big question remained unanswered in the wake of *Raich.* Namely, did the limits on congressional power articulated in *Lopez* and *Morrison* still retain any force? The libertarian lawyer Randy Barnett soon came to think that they did.

"UNPRECEDENTED AND
UNCONSTITUTIONAL"

Nowadays, Randy Barnett is best known as a constitutional scholar, a reputation he solidified in 2004 with the publication of his acclaimed treatise *Restoring the Lost Constitution,* which offers a definitive statement of the libertarian legal philosophy. But his relationship with America's founding document was not always so friendly. In fact, Barnett once thought the Constitution was not worth the paper it was drafted on. "My view as a law student was, 'If the Supreme Court is not going to take the text of the Constitution seriously, then why should I?'" he recalled with a laugh in 2012. "So I was going to do something like be a contracts professor where texts are treated with a lot more respect."[20]

After serving a stint in the prosecutor's office in Cook County, Illinois, Barnett did precisely that, settling down to teach contracts law at Boston University. But things began to change for him shortly after he received a surprise invitation to speak on a panel about the First Amendment at the Federalist Society's 1986 National Student Symposium, held that year at Stanford Law School. "It was a distinguished group of speakers and, as a relatively unknown contracts professor, I sorely wanted to accept," Barnett later wrote, though at first he declined the offer. "I just do not do constitutional law," he told the sponsors. But eventually he came around and began to prepare his remarks. Because he "wrongly thought [the Federalist Society] was a monolithically conservative group," Barnett was not exactly optimistic about the reception his decidedly libertarian views would receive. Furthermore, he was planning to argue that while the First Amendment did not specifically mention the right to freedom of association, that unenumerated right was nonetheless entitled to constitutional protection. How would he justify that position to the conservative crowd? "In my speech, my answer was to read the text of the Ninth

Amendment," which declares, "'The enumeration in the Constitution of certain rights shall not be construed to deny or disparage others retained by the People.'"

To his surprise, that rhetorical flourish proved to be a major crowd-pleaser. "A roaring cheer came up from the students," Barnett remembered. "I was startled to discover that, contrary to their detractors, the Federalist Society was indeed a robust coalition of both conservative and libertarian students with a diversity of views among them."[21] Buoyed by the response, Barnett decided to give the Constitution a second look, starting with a deep dive into the text and history of the Ninth Amendment. Within a few years, Barnett had established himself as a leading academic authority on the topic.

That reputation soon led him to the Commerce Clause, the area of constitutional law for which he is perhaps best known today. "I was at Boston University and I got a call from one of the lawyers for the Oakland Cannabis Buyers' Cooperative," Barnett recalled. The Oakland Cannabis Buyers' Cooperative (OCBC) was one of the many outfits in California working to facilitate the legal distribution of medical marijuana under the 1996 Compassionate Use Act. Facing federal drug charges, OCBC was then fighting for its survival in court. "They were going around the country trying to find someone who knew something about the Ninth Amendment," Barnett explained. "The principal part of their case was a Commerce Clause challenge. It was only the trial judge that said you should brief the Ninth Amendment. So I got into the Commerce Clause then."

Barnett's own medical marijuana case, *Gonzales v. Raich,* grew directly out of that experience. "We brought the *Raich* case because we wanted facts that would better fit with a Commerce Clause challenge," he said. "In OCBC you have money and marijuana changing hands, which is economic activity. In fact, it's commerce." By contrast, his clients, a brain cancer patient named Angel Raich and

a victim of chronic back pain named Diane Monson, had not purchased anything. Their physician-prescribed marijuana was entirely
homegrown, cultivated either by themselves or by their caretakers.
"We wanted a case in which there was no money and marijuana
changing hands so there wasn't even economic activity," Barnett
explained.

When *Raich* ultimately came down against him, Barnett recalled,
he decided, "there would never be another Commerce Clause case"
because the Court's interpretation seemed as expansive as it could possibly get. But Congress and the White House surprised him in 2009
when they settled on the idea of forcing every American to buy health
insurance as the centerpiece of the Patient Protection and Affordable
Care Act. "It turns out they found something new that they hadn't
ever done before," he said. "And the very fact that it's new means it's
subject to question. If they were just sticking with it, just trying to
regulate interstate activity the way they were before, we wouldn't be
able to stop them."[22]

In both *Lopez* and *Morrison,* Congress had sought to regulate
non-economic activities by citing their aggregate impact on interstate
commerce. But the Supreme Court refused to "pile inference upon
inference," following the hypothesized chain of effects from gun possession or rape to "commerce . . . among the several states." As the
Court held in *Morrison,* "thus far in our Nation's history our cases
have upheld Commerce Clause regulation of intrastate activity only
where that activity is economic in nature."[23] *Raich* continued this
trend, with the Court deeming the act of growing your own marijuana
to be economic.

Now consider the individual mandate. The failure to buy health
insurance is not even an activity, Barnett came to think, let alone
an economic one. Because the Supreme Court has never said Congress may regulate *inactivity,* Barnett and his allies would argue, the

individual mandate violated the Court's precedents (as well as the long-lost original meaning of the Commerce Clause). For federal judges who were interested in placing some limits on congressional power but who nevertheless felt themselves bound by the Supreme Court's expansive New Deal interpretation of the Commerce Clause, the distinction between activity and inactivity might just prove to be an attractive legal argument.

Barnett, along with two co-authors, Nathaniel Stewart and Todd Gaziano, spelled out this argument in a seminal 2009 Heritage Foundation paper titled "Why the Personal Mandate to Buy Health Insurance Is Unprecedented and Unconstitutional."[24] Heritage, a prominent conservative think tank in Washington, unveiled the paper at a December 9, 2009, event featuring a debate between Barnett and other legal experts on the mandate's constitutionality. Also present was Republican Senator Orrin Hatch of Utah, who delivered a well-received keynote speech. Later that month, Hatch and other Senate Republicans raised a point of constitutional order against the Affordable Care Act, which was still being debated in Congress. Those Republicans cited Barnett's Heritage paper and also had it entered into the *Congressional Record*. From that point forward, the GOP would attack the ACA on constitutional grounds.

Barnett formally joined the legal challenge roughly a year later, when the National Federation of Independent Business (which had joined Florida's suit) retained him as counsel. Until that point, he said, "I was attempting to influence the discourse solely from the outside of the case, through blogging and writing."[25] It worked. If you read Barnett's 2009 Heritage paper and related writings today, you will find virtually every major argument that was deployed against the individual mandate through every stage of litigation, from Florida's original March 2010 lawsuit to the March 2012 oral arguments at the Supreme Court. In other words, a libertarian lawyer helped spark the biggest challenge to federal power since the New Deal. What's more, the conservative legal establishment welcomed him with open arms.

SETTING THE STAGE

The challenge kicked off officially on March 23, 2010, when Florida, joined by twelve other states, and Virginia, acting alone, filed separate federal lawsuits charging the ACA with exceeding congressional authority and undermining the principles of federalism. As the Florida complaint put it, "The Constitution nowhere authorizes the United States to mandate, either directly or under threat of penalty, that all citizens and legal residents have qualifying healthcare coverage."[26] Several other challenges soon followed, including suits by the Thomas More Law Center, a public-interest law firm focusing on religious freedom, and Liberty University, the conservative Christian college founded by the late Jerry Falwell.

But it was the Florida-led challenge that won big enough to reach the Supreme Court. Its first victory came on January 31, 2011, in a ruling by U.S. District Judge Roger Vinson. "Congress must operate within the bounds established by the Constitution," Vinson declared, striking down the individual mandate for exceeding those bounds. Furthermore, Vinson ruled, because the ACA did not include a so-called severability clause, which would have specified what happens to the rest of the law when a single provision is struck down, "the entire Act must be declared void."[27]

A little over six months later, on August 11, the U.S. Court of Appeals for the Eleventh Circuit partially affirmed Vinson's ruling, voting to strike down the individual mandate but allowing the rest of the ACA to stand. "We have not found any generally applicable, judicially enforceable limiting principle that would permit us to uphold the mandate without obliterating the boundaries inherent in the system of enumerated congressional powers,"[28] the Eleventh Circuit declared.

It was a major blow to the Obama administration, which just two months earlier had won a resounding victory for the health care law at the U.S. Court of Appeals for the Sixth Circuit. In that earlier case, conservative Judge Jeffrey Sutton, a George W. Bush appointee and former clerk to Justice Antonin Scalia, had surprised many observers by voting with the majority to uphold the ACA. One reason he did so, Sutton explained, was because of judicial restraint. "Time will assuredly bring to light the policy strengths and weaknesses of using the individual mandate as part of this national legislation," Sutton wrote, "allowing the peoples' political representatives, rather than their judges, to have the primary say over its utility."[29]

Because the Sixth and Eleventh Circuits were now in open disagreement, the Supreme Court was virtually guaranteed to step in and resolve the split. In the meantime, the Fourth Circuit voted to uphold the law on September 8 and the D.C. Circuit did likewise on November 8. Six days after the D.C. Circuit's ruling, the Supreme Court made the announcement everyone was waiting for: The Court would hear oral arguments the following year to determine the constitutionality of the Affordable Care Act.

THE STAKES

Oral arguments were scheduled to run for a modern record of five and a half hours (later expanded to six hours) spread out over the course of three days: March 26, 27, and 28, 2012. In addition to the constitutionality of the individual mandate, the Court would consider three other issues.

The first was whether the legal challenge to the ACA must be dismissed under the terms of the Anti-Injunction Act, an 1867 statute that says, "no suit for the purpose of restraining the assessment or collection of any tax shall be maintained in any court."[30] In other words, a tax cannot be challenged in court until it has been assessed and paid. Did the "shared responsibility payment" imposed on people who disobey the individual mandate count as a tax, even though Congress specifically called it a penalty? If so, the legal challenge to the ACA would have to wait until 2015, when the mandate was scheduled to take effect. The Court set aside ninety minutes for this question on March 26.

The second additional question concerned the issue of severability. In his January 2011 ruling, Judge Vinson held that because the ACA lacked a severability clause, the whole law must fall if the mandate is ruled unconstitutional. The Supreme Court reserved ninety minutes on March 28 to hear arguments for and against that proposition. Later that same day, the Court would hear one final question: Does the ACA's expansion of Medicaid, the joint federal-state health care program for the poor, represent an unconstitutionally coercive use of Congress's spending power? One hour was set aside for that.

But the main event was scheduled for the morning of March 27, when the Supreme Court would devote two full hours to the constitutionality of the ACA's controversial centerpiece: the individual mandate.

JUDICIAL MODESTY

To prevail, the Obama administration needed to persuade at least one of the Supreme Court's five right-leaning justices to uphold the ACA. Conventional wisdom quickly settled on the most likely candidate. "The fate of health care reform is where it was yesterday," announced *Slate* reporter Dave Weigel, "in the hands of Supreme Court Justice Anthony Kennedy."[31] *Time* magazine made the same confident prediction, adorning its June 18, 2012, issue with a close-up of Kennedy's face under the blaring headline, "From Gay Marriage to Obamacare, Justice Anthony Kennedy Is the Decider."[32]

Kennedy, a perennial swing vote on the Court, was indeed a potential ally for the federal government. But the Obama administration had an equally plausible ally in the form of Chief Justice John Roberts—a fact many observers failed to grasp at the time. The evidence, however, was right there in his record. For example, in the 2010 case *United States v. Comstock,* which posed the question of whether the Necessary and Proper Clause allowed federal officials to order the indefinite civil commitment of "sexually dangerous" persons who had already finished serving their prison sentences, Roberts sided with the Court's liberals, endorsing a broad understanding of federal power. The health care case presented the chief justice with a similar opportunity.

Then there's the issue of judicial restraint. During his 2005 Senate confirmation hearings, Roberts repeatedly stressed his belief that the Supreme Court should practice "judicial modesty," a respect for precedent and consensus he extended even to the abortion-legalizing *Roe v. Wade,* a case Roberts conceded to be "the settled law of the land."[33] He made a related point about *Kelo v. City of New London,* the 2005 opinion affirming the use of eminent domain to broaden the local tax base. Responding to a statement by Republican Senator Sam Brownback of Kansas, who described *Kelo* as a disastrous ruling that "really shocked the system" and inspired "great criticism,"[34] Roberts pointed to the existence of post-*Kelo* legislation aimed at protecting property rights as "a very appropriate approach to consider." In other words, Roberts explained, the Supreme Court's ruling "leaves the ball in the court of the legislature, and I think it's reflective of what is often the case and people sometimes lose sight of, that this body [Congress] and legislative bodies in the States are protectors of people's rights as well."[35]

It was a subtle nod to judicial restraint—the idea that people should seek relief at the ballot box, not at the courthouse—and there's no doubt the savvy chief justice-to-be knew exactly what he was saying. For well over a century, prominent legal figures ranging from

Oliver Wendell Holmes to Learned Hand to Robert Bork had made that very same argument. Roberts was signaling his own support for the same deferential philosophy.

To be sure, Roberts has also revealed a willingness to wield judicial power on other occasions. In the Supreme Court's 2010 ruling in *Citizens United v. Federal Election Commission,* for instance, Roberts joined the conservative majority in nullifying portions of several campaign finance regulations and overruling one of the Supreme Court's previous campaign finance decisions. Not exactly a deferential maneuver. Yet even then, Roberts still made a point of reiterating his commitment to modesty, writing a separate concurring opinion in *Citizens United* "to address the important principles of judicial restraint and *stare decisis* implicated in this case."[36] Those principles remain core judicial values, Roberts stressed, but "there is a difference between judicial restraint and judicial abdication."[37] For instance, "if adherence to a precedent actually impedes the stable and orderly adjudication of future cases"—when, for example, "the precedent's validity is so hotly contested that it cannot reliably function as a basis for decision in future cases"[38]—the Supreme Court is justified in taking action.

Which version of John Roberts would emerge in the health care case? Would it be the champion of judicial modesty, or the critic of judicial abdication? In an August 2011 column for Reason.com, I offered my own prediction: "Roberts may very well uphold the health care law as an act of judicial restraint."[39]

DAY ONE: "A CAREFULLY MADE REPRESENTATION"

"We will hear argument this morning in case 11–398, *Department of Health and Human Services v. Florida.*"[40] So declared Chief Justice

Roberts on the morning of March 26, 2012. The three-day legal marathon to determine the constitutionality of Obamacare was officially underway.

The focus of the first day's arguments was the Anti-Injunction Act, which says one cannot challenge a federal tax in court until that tax has been assessed and paid. If the Supreme Court was looking for a chance to dodge the bullet, this was it. By declaring the ACA to have imposed a tax, the Court could dismiss the entire case on jurisdictional grounds and avoid a bitter constitutional showdown. Yet none of the justices revealed the slightest interest in that approach during their questioning. The Supreme Court was clearly ready to rule on the fate of the individual mandate, the subject of the next day's oral arguments.

In that sense, day one was simply a warm-up for day two, the main event. But it was not without its moments of high drama, particularly during two rounds of questioning that previewed the legal fireworks to come. The first such exchange occurred at the one-minute mark of Solicitor General Donald Verrilli's time at the lectern.

"General Verrilli, today you're arguing that the penalty is not a tax," said Justice Samuel Alito. "Tomorrow you're gonna be back and you'll be arguing that the penalty is a tax. Has the Court ever held that something that is a tax for purposes of the taxing power under the Constitution is not a tax under the Anti-Injunction Act?"

"No, Justice Alito,"[41] Verrilli was forced to admit. The Court had never done so. Alito had just honed in on what appeared to be a glaring inconsistency in the government's posture. In its briefs, the Obama administration had justified the individual mandate under both the Commerce Clause and the so-called taxing power, the constitutional provision authorizing Congress "to lay and collect taxes." Yet here was the solicitor general telling the Supreme Court that the Anti-Injunction Act did *not* bar the litigation from proceeding because the individual mandate did *not* impose a tax. As Alito pointed out, this was indeed a curious position to take. Is it a tax or isn't it a tax?

Several minutes later, Justice Sonia Sotomayor returned to that seeming inconsistency in the government's case. "Could we address, General, the question of whether there are any collateral consequences for the failure to buy—to not buy health insurance? Is the only consequence the payment of the penalty?" According to the National Federation of Independent Business, she went on, if an individual is on probation and "they don't buy health insurance, they'd be disobeying the law and could be subject to having their supervised release revoked."

"That is not a correct reading of the statute," Verrilli responded. "The only consequence that ensues is the tax penalty. And the—we have made a representation, and it was a carefully made representation, in our brief that it is the interpretation of the agencies charged with interpreting this statute, the Treasury Department, the Department of Health and Human Services, that there is no other consequence apart from the tax penalty."[42] In other words, perhaps the mandate requiring the purchase of health insurance was not a mandate requiring the purchase of health insurance after all. Verrilli would return to this argument on day two.

DAY TWO: "ALL BETS ARE OFF"

"People say I'm a libertarian," Justice Anthony Kennedy told the *New York Times* in 2005. "I don't really know what that means."[43] Most libertarians would tend to agree with him. In 2004, when the libertarian lawyer Randy Barnett stood before the Supreme Court to explain why his client Angel Raich was not engaged in interstate commerce because her medical marijuana had been cultivated and consumed entirely within the state of California, Kennedy did not buy it. Several months later,

Kennedy joined Justice John Paul Stevens's majority opinion upholding the federal ban on marijuana as a valid exercise of congressional power under the Commerce Clause.[44]

But Kennedy seemed to have a different take on the reach of federal power when Solicitor General Verrilli made his case for the individual mandate on the second day of oral arguments over the ACA. Kennedy not only suggested that Verrilli had "a heavy burden of justification" but also described a mandated purchase as so "different from what we have in previous cases" that it "changes the relationship of the federal government to the individual in a very fundamental way."[45]

At another point, however, Kennedy seemed inclined to accept the government's argument that all of us will at some point receive health care, so it is reasonable to regulate the manner in which we pay for it. In an exchange that occurred toward the end of that day's oral arguments, he referred to an uninsured young person as "uniquely proximately very close to affecting the rates of insurance and the costs of providing medical care in a way that is not true in other industries." Then again, Kennedy prefaced that statement with yet another reference to the government's failure to articulate any limits on its own power. "The government tells us that's because the insurance market is unique," he said. "And in the next case, it'll say the next market is unique."[46]

Would Kennedy's willingness to accept the government's description of the health care market outweigh his obvious discomfort with the government's potentially unlimited assertion of congressional power? The nation would soon learn the answer.

In the meantime, Verrilli was enduring a grueling attack from Chief Justice Roberts, who wasted no time tearing apart the government's Commerce Clause argument, which rested on the idea that because we will all require health care at some point, the government may stipulate how we pay for it in order to prevent the uninsured from imposing a burden on others in the marketplace. "Once we say that there is a market and Congress can require people to participate in it, as some would say, or as you would say," Roberts told the solicitor general, "it seems to me that we can't say there are limitations on what Congress can do under its commerce power." In fact, Roberts continued, "given the significant deference that we accord to Congress in this area, all bets are off."[47]

Justice Antonin Scalia voiced similar misgivings. "Why do you define the market that broadly?" he asked the solicitor general. "Everybody has to buy food sooner or later," Scalia continued, "so you define the market as food. Therefore everybody is in the market; therefore you can make people buy broccoli."[48] It was the same issue that troubled the Eleventh Circuit in 2011, which struck down the mandate because the government had failed to articulate a "generally applicable, judicially enforceable limiting principle."[49]

Nor did liberal Justice Stephen Breyer do the government's case any favors when he chimed in to say that "yes, of course," Congress can "create commerce where previously none existed," which could include forcing all Americans "to buy cell phones"[50] to facilitate the provision of emergency services (a hypothetical posed by Roberts). Verrilli hastened to clarify that the government was not in fact endorsing a cell phone mandate, but the damage seemed to have been done.

To make matters worse for the government, after Verrilli suggested that a ruling against the individual mandate would be tantamount to judicial activism because it would "import *Lochner*-style substantive due process,"[51] Roberts shot forward in his chair to forcefully dismiss the idea. Several minutes later, Roberts circled back and accused the government of inviting judicial activism by asking the Court to decide that a health insurance mandate is acceptable but that a broccoli or cell phone mandate is not. "It would be going back to *Lochner* if we were put in the position of saying, no, you can use your commerce power to regulate insurance, but you can't use your commerce power to regulate this market in other ways," Roberts declared. "I think that would be a very significant intrusion by the Court into Congress' power."[52]

Lochner, of course, is the 1905 case in which the Supreme Court struck down a state law limiting the working hours of bakers, saying it violated the Fourteenth Amendment right to liberty of contract. In the eyes of most liberal legal thinkers, *Lochner* stands as a notorious example of conservative judicial activism. But many conservative legal thinkers also dislike *Lochner,* and for the exact same reason. Among those conservatives is John Roberts. During his Senate confirmation hearings, the future chief justice said, "You go to a case like the *Lochner* case, you can read that opinion today, and it's quite clear that they're not interpreting the law; they're making the law."[53] So when Roberts told Verrilli that the government's theory of the Commerce Clause risked unleashing *Lochner*-style activism by the courts, he was raising a powerful objection, one that allowed him to wear the mantle of conservative judicial restraint. It was a sign of things to come.

"THE PRESIDENT SAID IT WASN'T A TAX"

The solicitor general was given a full hour to make his case that morning. With less than fifteen minutes left on the clock, he finally turned to his fallback position: The individual mandate may also be upheld under Congress's power to tax. "In terms of the tax power," Verrilli explained, "I think it's useful to separate this into two questions. One is a question of characterization. Can this be characterized as a tax; and second, is it a constitutional exercise of the power?"[54]

Once again, Verrilli ran into trouble. "The President said it wasn't a tax, didn't he?" asked Justice Scalia.

"The President said it wasn't a tax increase," Verrilli carefully responded, "because it ought to be understood as an incentive to get people to have insurance. I don't think it's fair to infer from that anything about whether that is an exercise of the tax power or not."

But the point of a tax is to raise revenue, objected Justice Ruth Bader Ginsburg, "and the purpose of this exaction is to get people into the health care risk—risk pool before they need medical care. . . . That's what the penalty is designed to do, not to raise revenue."[55]

"You're telling me they thought of it as a tax, they defended it on the tax power," added the chief justice. "Why didn't they say it was a tax?"[56]

As Verrilli continued fielding those objections, Scalia suddenly spoke back up. "You're saying that all the discussion we had earlier about how this is one big uniform scheme and the Commerce Clause blah, blah, blah, blah, it really doesn't matter," he told Verrilli. "This is a tax and the Federal Government could simply have said, without all the rest of this legislation, could simply have said, everybody who doesn't buy health insurance at a certain age will be taxed so much money, right?"

But Verrilli dodged the question. The government "used its powers together to solve the problem of the market not providing affordable coverage," he told Scalia.

"Yes, but you didn't need that," Scalia immediately shot back, his voice getting louder. "If it's a tax, it's only—raising money is enough."

Verrilli held his ground. "It is justifiable under its tax power," he insisted.

"Okay," Scalia responded. "Extraordinary,"[57] he added a few seconds later, the disbelief evident in his voice. Would the tax power end up deciding the outcome of this case, even after two years of courtroom battles over the scope of the Commerce Clause? Scalia appeared to be astounded at the thought.

"THE DEMOCRATICALLY ACCOUNTABLE
BRANCHES OF GOVERNMENT"

The next hour belonged to the legal challengers. Former Solicitor General Paul Clement, attorney for the twenty-six states, and conservative lawyer Michael Carvin, attorney for the National Federation of Independent Business, each had thirty minutes to lay siege to the individual mandate. Both came out with guns blazing. "The Commerce Clause gives Congress the power to regulate existing commerce," Clement declared. "It does not give Congress the far greater power to compel people to enter commerce, to create commerce essentially in the first place."[58]

Carvin amplified the point. "I'd like to begin with the Solicitor General's main premise," he told the Court, "which is that they can compel the purchase of health insurance in order to promote commerce in the health care market because it will reduce uncompensated care. If you accept that argument," he continued, "you have to fundamentally alter the text of the Constitution and give Congress plenary power."[59]

Things were not looking good for the government's Commerce Clause theory, as one conservative justice after another signaled varying degrees of sympathy for the legal challengers. Ironically, however, neither Clement nor Carvin spent any significant time rebutting Verrilli's second justification for the mandate, the tax power. In retrospect, it is a striking omission.

As day two began winding down, the solicitor general returned to the lectern to deliver a final, four-minute rebuttal. He made wise use of that time. "Congress confronted a grave problem when it enacted the Affordable Care Act: the 40 million Americans who can't get health insurance and suffered often very terrible consequences," Verrilli began. And to solve this grave national problem, he continued, Congress used its powers under the Commerce Clause to craft a comprehensive national solution. "That is the kind of choice,"[60] Verrilli emphasized, that must remain in the hands of elected lawmakers.

Turning next to the taxing power, Verrilli made perhaps the single most important argument of the entire three-day saga. "But if there is any doubt about that under the Commerce Clause, then I urge this Court to uphold the minimum coverage provision as an exercise of the taxing power," he said. According to the Court's own precedents, Verrilli stressed, the Supreme Court "has a solemn obligation to respect the judgments of the democratically accountable branches of government, and because this statute can be construed in a manner that allows it to be upheld that way, I respectfully submit that it is this Court's duty to do so."[61]

"Thank you, General," the chief justice responded, bringing the day's arguments to a close. "Counsel, we'll see you tomorrow."[62]

DAY THREE: "I WOULD URGE THIS COURT TO RESPECT THAT JUDGMENT"

The third and final day of arguments featured two separate sessions. First came the matter of severability. Did the entire ACA have to fall if the mandate was ruled unconstitutional? The justices appeared closely divided on the question. Then, after a short lunch break, came the Medicaid expansion. Was Congress coercing the states with a so-called gun to the head or merely spending money for the general welfare? A majority of the Court appeared hostile to Congress's tactics in this area and seemed willing to rule against the Medicaid expansion. Indeed, the government ultimately lost on this issue by a vote of seven to two. Once again, things were not looking good for the federal government.

In his final minutes at the lectern that afternoon, Solicitor General Verrilli took one last shot at saving the ACA. And once again, he made wise use of his time. "I'd like to take half a step back here,"[63] he told the

Court. "The Medicaid expansion that we're talking about this afternoon and the provisions we talked about yesterday, we've been talking about them in terms of their effect as measures that solve problems, problems in the economic marketplace."[64] But there is one more element to consider, he said. And that element is democracy. Health care reform "is something about which the people of the United States can deliberate and they can vote," Verrilli maintained, "and if they think it needs to be changed, they can change it." The Supreme Court should not usurp that power and displace the people's basic right to chart their own course. "This was a judgment of policy that democratically accountable branches of this government made by their best lights," he concluded. "And I would urge this Court to respect that judgment and ask that the Affordable Care Act, in its entirety, be upheld."[65]

At 2:24 p.m. that afternoon, the case was submitted. The fate of the Patient Protection and Affordable Care Act now rested in the hands of the U.S. Supreme Court.

THE BULLY PULPIT

In 1935, when President Franklin Roosevelt faced off against the Supreme Court over the constitutionality of the New Deal, he waited until four days after the Court invalidated his National Industrial Recovery Act before launching his famous attack on the "horse and buggy"[66] origins of the Commerce Clause. President Barack Obama, by contrast, could barely wait a week after the conclusion of oral arguments before lecturing the Supreme Court about its treatment of his health care law.

Speaking to the press on April 2, Obama said he was confident "the Supreme Court will not take what would be an unprecedented extraordinary step of overturning a law that was passed by a strong majority of Congress." Moreover, Obama added, "for years, what we've heard is the biggest problem on the bench was judicial activism, or a lack of judicial restraint. An unelected group of people would somehow overturn a duly constituted and passed law. Well," the president said, "this is a good example. And I'm pretty confident this court will recognize that and not take this step."[67]

The president's allies soon picked up on the theme. "I trust that [John Roberts] will be a chief justice for all of us and that he has a strong institutional sense of the proper role of the judicial branch," declared Democratic Senator Patrick Leahy of Vermont several weeks later. "It would be extraordinary for the Supreme Court not to defer to Congress in this matter that so clearly affects interstate commerce."[68]

Writing in *The New Republic* on May 4, legal affairs writer Jeffrey Rosen described the pending health care decision as "John Roberts's moment of truth." The chief justice "has to decide what kind of legal conservatism he wants to embrace," Rosen wrote. "Of course, if the Roberts Court strikes down health care reform by a 5–4 vote, then the chief justice's stated goal of presiding over a less divisive Court will be viewed as an irredeemable failure."[69]

In light of the chief justice's ultimate decision to uphold the health care law, the timing of these statements now appears suggestive. Was there a lobbying effort by liberal politicians and pundits designed to influence Roberts's opinion? Many conservatives thought so at the time. "It is cheeky of Rosen, a liberal, to lecture Roberts about jurisprudential conservatism," wrote *Washington Post* columnist George Will on May 25. "Such clumsy attempts to bend the chief justice are apt to reveal his spine of steel."[70]

On July 1, several days after the health care decision was released, Jan Crawford of CBS News, a veteran legal journalist and author of a respected book on the Supreme Court, reported that something had indeed been going on behind closed courtroom doors at that time. "Chief Justice John Roberts initially sided with the Supreme Court's four conservative justices to strike down the heart of President Obama's health care reform law," she reported, "but later changed his position and formed an alliance with liberals to uphold the bulk of the law, according to sources with specific knowledge of the deliberations." Why did Roberts change his vote? Crawford had no definitive answer from her sources. But she did note that "as Roberts began to craft the decision striking down the mandate, the external pressure began to grow. Roberts almost certainly was aware of it."[71]

For his part, Rosen has consistently denied participating in any sort of lobbying campaign, concerted or otherwise. "The idea that I was trying to 'intimidate' or 'bend' the Chief Justice came as a surprise to me," he wrote. "The justices have already voted in the health care case and are hardly influenced, in any event, by legal punditry."[72]

"TURNING FIRST TO
THE COMMERCE CLAUSE"

"I have the announcement in case number 11–393, *National Federation of Independent Business v. Sebelius,* and the related cases,"[73] Chief Justice Roberts announced on the morning of June 28, 2012, the last day of the Court's 2011–2012 term. After three months of waiting, the health care decision had finally arrived.

"In these cases," Roberts began, the packed courtroom fixed on his every word, "we consider claims that Congress lacked constitutional power to enact two provisions of the Patient Protection and Affordable Care Act of 2010." While most Americans may consider "affirmative restrictions such as contained in the Bill of Rights" to be the foremost "limits on government power," Roberts said, those restrictions only "come into play" when "the government possesses authority to act in the first place. And in our federal system, the national government possesses only those limited powers the Constitution assigns."

That opening description sounded very promising to the legal challengers. What came next sounded even better. "The question is whether Congress has the constitutional power to enact the individual mandate," Roberts explained. According to the federal government, it does have such power. "Turning first to the Commerce Clause," Roberts said, it turns out that Congress does not. "Congress has never before attempted to use the commerce power to order individuals not engaged in commerce to buy an unwanted product," he observed. "And nothing in the text of the Constitution suggests it can."

It was the very argument championed by Randy Barnett and his libertarian and conservative allies over the previous two years. Congress may regulate economic activity, they said, but Congress may not regulate inactivity. Now the chief justice of the United States was making the same point. "The Commerce Clause is not a general license to regulate an individual from cradle to grave simply because he will predictably engage in particular transactions," Roberts declared. In the 2010 *Citizens United* case, Roberts had struck down an act of Congress for exceeding the limits of the Constitution. To the horror of the Obama administration and its allies, he now appeared to be engaged in a repeat performance. But the show was not over yet. In fact, the final act had just begun.

"IT IS NOT OUR JOB"

"That brings us to the Government's second argument," Roberts continued, "that the mandate may be upheld under Congress' power to lay and collect taxes." According to this view, he explained, the mandate is not actually a command to purchase health insurance, but is instead only a tax levied on those who do not have health insurance. "Under that theory, the mandate makes going without insurance just another thing the government taxes like buying gasoline or earning income," Roberts said. Then came the kicker. "Under our precedent, if there are two possible interpretations of a statute and one of those interpretations violates the Constitution, the courts should adopt the interpretation that allows the statute to be upheld."

Roberts had just telegraphed the outcome of the case. In his fifty-nine-page opinion, he would spell out the reasoning in detail. "The

most straightforward reading of the mandate is that it commands individuals to purchase insurance," the chief justice wrote. "But for the
reasons explained above, the Commerce Clause does not give Congress that power. Under our precedent, it is therefore necessary to ask
whether the Government's alternative reading of the statute—that it
only imposes a tax on those without insurance—is a reasonable one."[74]

Among that precedent was a 1927 opinion by Justice Oliver Wendell Holmes, which Roberts proceeded to quote. "As between two possible interpretations of a statute," Holmes wrote, "by one of which
it would be unconstitutional and the other valid, our plain duty is
to adopt that which will save the Act."[75] Following Holmes's instruc-
tions, Roberts did his "duty" and saved the Affordable Care Act. "The
Government asks us to interpret the mandate as imposing a tax, if it
would otherwise violate the Constitution," Roberts wrote. "Granting
the Act the full measure of deference owed to federal statutes, it can so
be read."[76] Obamacare had survived.

Roberts would spend just over twenty minutes that morning summarizing his opinion from the bench, but he saved perhaps the most
important and revealing statement of all until the very last minute.
And once again, the chief justice of the United States turned to the
words of Justice Oliver Wendell Holmes for support. Today's ruling,
Roberts declared, has nothing to do with the Court's personal views as
to the wisdom or folly of the health care law. "That judgment is for the
people acting through their representatives," he said. Then, his voice
rising in emphasis, the chief justice reached his conclusion. "It is not
our job," Roberts declared, reading directly from his opinion, "to save
the people from the consequences of their political choices."[77]

Nearly a century earlier, Justice Holmes had first given expression
to that very sentiment. "If my fellow citizens want to go to Hell I will
help them," Holmes wrote about his role as a judge. "It's my job."[78]

EPILOGUE

NO PEACE

I N LATE APRIL 2012, BARELY A MONTH AFTER
the Supreme Court finished hearing oral arguments in the health
care case, Yale Law School hosted a weekend conference featuring a
group of distinguished legal scholars debating various forms of constitutional interpretation. Among the participants was Stanford law professor
Michael McConnell, a former judge on the U.S. Court of Appeals for the
Tenth Circuit and a respected legal conservative. McConnell, it turned
out, was none too thrilled about the prospects of a conservative Supreme
Court striking down the Affordable Care Act. In fact, he compared the
possibility to a feat of right-wing judicial activism.

"Democracy still seems to me to be a worthy project," McConnell
told the assembled legal experts. "I haven't quite given up on it." But he
also admitted to seeing little cause for optimism. The way things are
going now, he said, "everything is thrown into the courts," ultimately
leaving all political decisions in the hands of unelected judges. "It's
quite evident," McConnell concluded, "that, on the right side of the
legal world, the ascendancy is people like Randy Barnett who want a
more muscular judiciary."[1]

Was he right to worry? Just two months later, after all, Chief Justice John Roberts did what McConnell wanted and left the fate of health care reform in the hands of the voters and their elected representatives. It was the biggest Supreme Court case in decades, and the outcome ultimately hinged on the deferential philosophy of Justice Oliver Wendell Holmes. Perhaps the fear of the libertarian ascendancy was much ado about nothing.

But then again, perhaps McConnell was right to worry. *District of Columbia v. Heller,* the landmark 2008 ruling that recognized the Second Amendment as a core individual right, was certainly a libertarian win premised on the strenuous flexing of judicial muscle. So was the 2010 gun rights victory in *McDonald v. Chicago,* which applied the Second Amendment right to keep and bear arms against the states. Going forward, all firearm regulations must now contend with these forceful Supreme Court precedents. Like it or not, the Supreme Court has entered the political thicket of gun control.

Nor are the libertarian lawyers at the Institute for Justice showing any signs of fatigue in their long campaign to spark "judicial action"[2] on behalf of property rights and economic liberty. In fact, they're building momentum. In March 2013, for example, IJ scored another bull's-eye against the regulatory state when its lawyers convinced the U.S. Court of Appeals for the Fifth Circuit to strike down a Louisiana law that forbade a group of Benedictine monks from selling handmade wooden caskets without a license. "The great deference due state economic regulation does not demand judicial blindness," the Fifth Circuit declared, "nor does it require courts to accept nonsensical explanations for regulations."[3] With every such win, the Institute for Justice chips away further at the Progressive-era edifice upholding judicial deference and the rational-basis test.

As for the outcome of the 2012 health care case, the followers of Justice Holmes should not be too quick to drop their guards. Although it's true that Roberts saved the health care law, he also accepted the Commerce Clause arguments put forward by Barnett and the other legal challengers, thereby joining with the four dissenters—Scalia, Kennedy, Thomas, and Alito—to recognize the first new limits on congressional power since the stalled "federalism revolution" of *United States v. Lopez,* which invalidated the Gun-Free School Zones Act, and *United States v. Morrison,* which struck down a portion of the Violence Against Women Act. It remains to be seen how this aspect of the health care ruling will play out in future cases.

Finally, while Randy Barnett and his libertarian and conservative allies might have failed to nullify the Affordable Care Act, they only missed by a single vote. The next major test of government power may well produce a very different result. The long war for control of the Supreme Court rages on.

ACKNOWLEDGMENTS

WARM THANKS TO MY AGENT, DON Fehr, and to my editor, Karen Wolny, whose encouragement and wise counsel made this book possible.

Small portions of this work first appeared, in different form, in the pages of *Reason* magazine and online at Reason.com. I'm grateful to the editors who brought those pieces to life, particularly Nick Gillespie, Katherine Mangu-Ward, Jesse Walker, and Matt Welch. Thanks also to my other *Reason* colleagues, including Mike Alissi, Ronald Bailey, Meredith Bragg, Barb Burch, Brian Doherty, Jim Epstein, Matthew Feeney, Anthony Fisher, Jon Graff, Ed Krayewski, Chris Mitchell, Julian Morris, David Nott, Melissa Palmer, Scott Shackford, Peter Suderman, Jacob Sullum, Josh Swain, Mary Toledo, and J.D. Tuccille. And one more round of thanks to Nick for giving me my first real job in journalism.

As I look back now, I realize this book's origins are to be found in the classroom of Professor Herbert Sloan of the Barnard College History Department at Columbia University. His wonderful course "The Constitution in Historical Perspective" opened my eyes to some 200 years of landmark Supreme Court decisions. I remain in his debt.

My family is and always has been a deep source of friendship and support, and I lack the words to adequately express my love and gratitude to Mom, Amy, Alex, and Dan. Thanks also to my new family: Trish, Rick, Ellen, Charlotte, Alexander, Keith, Sara, Bill, Tom, and Maria. And very special thanks to my late, much beloved cat Orpheus, who always kept me company while I worked. I miss you.

Finally, to Allison, my partner in crime. None of this would be possible without you at my side.

NOTES

INTRODUCTION

1. *The Nomination of Elena Kagan to be an Associate Justice of the Supreme Court of the United States: Hearing Before the Senate Judiciary Committee*, 111th Cong., 2nd Sess., (2010) [hereinafter *Kagan Hearings*], 180.
2. *Kagan Hearings*, 181.
3. *Lochner v. New York*, 198 U.S. 45, 75.
4. Oliver Wendell Holmes Jr. to Harold Laski, March 4, 1920, in *Holmes-Laski Letters: The Correspondence of Mr. Justice Holmes and Harold J. Laski, 1916-1935*, ed. Mark De Wolfe Howe (Cambridge, Mass.: Harvard University Press, 1953), 249.
5. Felix Frankfurter, ed., *Mr. Justice Holmes* (New York: Coward-McCann, 1931), 166.
6. Frankfurter, *Mr. Justice Holmes*, 5.
7. Frankfurter, *Mr. Justice Holmes*, 2.
8. Frankfurter, *Mr. Justice Holmes*, 54.
9. *Department of Health and Human Services v. Florida*, 648 F.3d 1235 (11th Cir. 2011).
10. *Department of Health and Human Services v. Florida*, no. 11-398, transcript of oral argument, March 27, 2012, 11-12.
11. *National Federation of Independent Business v. Sebelius*, 132 S. Ct. 2566, 2594 (2012).
12. *Blodgett v. Holden*, 275 U.S. 142, 148 (1927).
13. *NFIB v. Sebelius*, 132 S. Ct. at 2579.
14. W. James Antle III, "John Roberts's Betrayal," *The American Conservative*, June 28, 2012.
15. See https://twitter.com/JackKingston/status/218359574539943937.
16. Robert H. Bork, *The Tempting of America: The Political Seduction of the Law* (New York: Touchstone, 1991), 139.
17. Stephen J. Field, *Personal Reminiscences of Early Days in California, with Other Sketches* (Birmingham, Ala.: Legal Classics Library, 1989; San Francisco, 1893), 44. Citation refers to the 1989 edition.
18. *The Slaughter-House Cases*, 83 U.S. 36, 88 (1873).
19. Stephen Macedo, *The New Right v. The Constitution* (Washington, D.C.: Cato Institute, 1986), 43.

CHAPTER ONE

1. Frederick Douglass, "To Thomas Auld," in *Frederick Douglass: Selected Speeches and Writings*, ed. Philip S. Foner (Chicago: Lawrence Hill Books, 1999), 113.
2. Douglass, "To Thomas Auld," 114.

3. Frederick Douglass, *My Bondage and My Freedom* (New York: Penguin Books, 2003), 256.

4. Cong. Globe, 42d Congress, 1st Sess., 86 (1871).

5. Ronald M. Labbe and Jonathan Lurrie, *The Slaughterhouse Cases: Regulation, Reconstruction, and the Fourteenth Amendment,* abr. ed. (Lawrence: University Press of Kansas, 2005), 72.

6. Charles Lofgren, *The Plessy Case* (New York: Oxford University Press, 1982), 67.

7. *Slaughter-House Cases,* 83 U.S. (16 Wall) 36, 62 (1873).

8. *Slaughter-House,* 83 U.S. at 78.

9. *Slaughter-House,* 83 U.S. at 110.

10. *Slaughter-House,* 83 U.S. at 89.

11. *Allen v. Tooley,* 80 Eng. Rep. 1055 (K.B. 1614).

12. Sir Edward Coke, "The Case of the Tailors of Ipswich," in *The Selected Writings and Speeches of Sir Edward Coke,* vol. 1, ed. Steve Sheppard (Indianapolis: Liberty Fund, 2003), 392.

13. Adam Smith, *An Inquiry Into the Nature and Causes of the Wealth of Nations,* vol. 1, eds. R. S. Campbell and A. S. Skinner (Indianapolis: Liberty Fund, 1981), 138.

14. James Madison, "Property," in Madison, *Writings* (New York: The Library of America, 1999), 516.

15. Thomas Jefferson, "First Inaugural Address," in Jefferson, *Writings* (New York: The Library of America, 1984), 494.

16. Charles Sumner, "The Barbarism of Slavery: Speech of Hon. Charles Sumner, on the Bill for the Admission of Kansas as a Free State, in the United States Senate, June 4, 1860." Available at https://archive.org/details/barbarismofslave00lcsumn.

17. William Goodell, "Lecture VII," *Antislavery Lecturer,* July 1, 1839.

18. *National Era,* March 25, 1847, quoted in Paul D. Moreno, *Black Americans and Organized Labor: A New History* (Baton Rouge: Louisiana State University Press, 2006), 13.

19. William E. Forbath, "The Ambiguities of Free Labor: Labor and Law in the Gilded Age," *Wisconsin Law Review* (1985), 770.

20. John C. Calhoun, "Speech on the Oregon Bill," in *John C. Calhoun: Selected Speeches and Writings,* ed. H. Lee Cheek Jr. (New York: Regnery, 2003), 683.

21. Calhoun, "Speech on the Oregon Bill," 684.

22. George Fitzhugh, *Sociology for the South, or The Failure of Free Society* (Richmond: A. Morris, 1854; Forgotten Books, 2012), 27. All citations refer to the 2012 reprint edition.

23. Quoted in C. Vann Woodward, "George Fitzhugh, *Sui Generis,*" introduction to *Cannibals All! Or Slaves Without Masters,* by George Fitzhugh (Cambridge, Mass.: Belknap Press, 1960), xv. First published in Richmond in 1857.

24. Fitzhugh, *Sociology for the South,* 27-28.

25. Fitzhugh, *Sociology for the South,* 7.

26. Fitzhugh, *Sociology for the South,* 13.

27. Fitzhugh, *Sociology for the South,* 29.

28. Eugene Genovese, *The World the Slaveholders Made* (New York: Pantheon, 1969), 190. Genovese is a peculiar figure. When he wrote this book, he was a prominent Marxist historian, recently infamous for telling the audience at a 1965 teach-in against the Vietnam War that he welcomed a Vietcong victory. Later in life, however, Genovese renounced the left and became a traditionalist conservative who praised the agrarian values of the South and attacked capitalism in language strikingly similar to that used by Fitzhugh. The one constant in Genovese's political odyssey was his hostility to capitalism.

29. Fitzhugh, *Sociology for the South,* 10.

30. Frederick Douglass, "The Meaning of the Fourth of July for the Negro," in *Frederick Douglass: Selected Speeches and Writings,* 195-196.

31. Douglass, "The Meaning of the Fourth of July for the Negro," 196.

32. Frederick Douglass, "Self-Made Men," in Jonathan Bean, ed., *Race and Liberty in America: The Essential Reader* (Lexington: University Press of Kentucky, 2009), 108.

33. Carl Schurz, *Speeches of Carl Schurz* (Philadelphia: J. B. Lippincott, 1865), 108.
34. Tony Horwitz, *Midnight Rising: John Brown and the Raid That Sparked the Civil War* (New York: Henry Holt, 2011), 54.
35. *Scott v. Sanford*, 60 U.S. 393, 407 (1857).
36. Frederick Douglass, "The Mission of the War," in *Frederick Douglass: Selected Speeches and Writings*, 566.
37. Theodore Brantner Wilson, *The Black Codes of the South* (Tuscaloosa: University of Alabama Press, 1965), 63.
38. W. E. B. DuBois, *Black Reconstruction* (New York: Harcourt, Brace, 1935), 168.
39. Wilson, *Black Codes*, 98.
40. Wilson, *Black Codes*, 75.
41. The Opelousas, Louisiana, ordinance is reproduced in Carl Schurz, "Report on the Conditions of the South," December 18, 1865, in Schurz, *Speeches, Correspondence and Political Papers of Carl Schurz*, vol. 1, ed. Frederic Bancroft (New York: G. P. Putnam's Sons, 1913), 324.
42. *Report of the Joint Committee on Reconstruction, At the First Session of the Thirty-Ninth Congress* (Westport, Conn.: Negro Universities Press, 1969; Washington, D.C.: Government Printing Office, 1866), part IV, 69. All citations refer to the 1969 reprint edition.
43. *Report of the Joint Committee on Reconstruction*, part IV, 64.
44. *Report of the Joint Committee on Reconstruction*, part II, 55.
45. *Report of the Joint Committee on Reconstruction*, part II, 56.
46. Wilson, *Black Codes*, 96.
47. Wilson, *Black Codes*, 143.
48. "Mississippi Black Code, 1866," in Bean, ed., *Race and Liberty in America*, 64.
49. DuBois, *Black Reconstruction*, 172.
50. *Report of the Joint Committee on Reconstruction*, part II, 57.
51. Civil Rights Act of 1866, 14 Stat. 27 (April 9, 1866).
52. Andrew Johnson, "Veto of Civil Rights Bill," in *The Papers of Andrew Johnson*, vol. 10, *February–July 1866*, ed. Paul H. Bergeron (Knoxville: University of Tennessee Press, 1992), 320.
53. Cong. Globe, 39th Cong., 1st Sess. 478 (1866).
54. *Barron v. Baltimore*, 32 U.S. 243, 249 (1833).
55. Paul Finkelman, "John Bingham and the Background to the Fourteenth Amendment," *Akron Law Review* 36 (2002-2003): 691.
56. Cong. Globe, 39th Cong., 1st Sess., 2542 (1866).
57. Michael Kent Curtis, *No State Shall Abridge: The Fourteenth Amendment and the Bill of Rights* (Durham, N.C.: Duke University Press, 1986), 6. See also Akhil Reed Amar, *The Bill of Rights: Creation and Reconstruction* (New Haven: Yale University Press, 1998).
58. Curtis, *No State Shall Abridge*, 7.
59. Curtis, *No State Shall Abridge*, 64-65.
60. Madison, *Writings*, 445.
61. Curtis, *No State Shall Abridge*, 64.
62. *Corfield v. Coryell*, 6 F. Cas. 546, 551 (C.C.E.D. Pa. 1823).
63. *Corfield*, 6 F. Cas. 551-552.
64. *Slaughter-House*, 83 U.S. at 97.
65. Cong. Globe, 39th Cong., 1st Sess., 2765-66 (1866).
66. Quoted in Curtis, *No State Shall Abridge*, 147-148.
67. Quoted in Curtis, *No State Shall Abridge*, 151.
68. *Slaughter-House*, 83 U.S. at 78.
69. *Slaughter-House*, 83 U.S. at 87.
70. *Slaughter-House*, 83 U.S. at 97.
71. *Slaughter-House*, 83 U.S. at 96.
72. *People v. Marx*, 2 N.E. 29, 33 (N.Y. 1885).
73. *In re Tie Loy* (Cal.), 26 Fed. Rep. 611, 613 (1886).

74. Ralph Hancock, "Margarine," in *The Oxford Companion to Food,* ed. Alan Davidson (New York: Oxford University Press, 1999), 478.

75. Paul D. Moreno, *The American State from the Civil War to the New Deal: The Twilight of Constitutionalism and the Triumph of Progressivism* (New York: Cambridge University Press, 2013), 78.

76. The statute is quoted in *Powell v. Pennsylvania,* 127 U.S. 678, 679 (1888).

77. *Powell,* 127 U.S. at 684 (internal quotations omitted).

78. *Powell,* 127 U.S. at 686.

79. *Powell,* 127 U.S. at 695.

80. *Powell,* 127 U.S. at 689.

81. *Powell,* 127 U.S. at 696.

82. *Powell,* 127 U.S. at 695.

83. Robert Green McCloskey, *American Conservatism in the Age of Enterprise, 1865-1910* (New York: Harper Torchbooks, 1951), 115.

84. McCloskey, *American Conservatism,* 116.

85. *Munn v. Illinois,* 94 U.S. 113, 126 (1877).

86. *Munn,* 94 U.S. at 132 (internal quotations omitted).

87. *Munn,* 94 U.S. at 134.

88. *Munn,* 94 U.S. at 139.

89. *Munn,* 94 U.S. at 140.

90. *Munn,* 94 U.S. at 148.

91. *Ah Kow v. Nunan,* 12 F. Cas. 252, 256 (C.C.D. Cal. 1879).

92. *Ah Kow,* 12 F. Cas. at 255.

93. *In re Quong Woo,* 13 Fed. 229 (C.C.D. Cal. 1882).

94. *Quong Woo,* 13 Fed. at 233.

95. *Quong Woo,* 13 Fed. at 232.

96. *Quong Woo,* 13 Fed. at 230.

97. *Allgeyer v. Louisiana,* 165 U.S. 578, 591 (1897).

CHAPTER TWO

1. Robert E. Lee to Jefferson Davis, September 8, 1862, in *The Wartime Papers of Robert E. Lee,* eds. Clifford Dowdey and Louis H. Manarin (New York: Da Capo Press, 1987), 301.

2. Abraham Lincoln to George B. McClellan, September 15, 1862, in *The Collected Works of Abraham Lincoln,* vol. 5, ed. Roy P. Basler (New Brunswick, N.J.: Rutgers University Press, 1953), 426.

3. Quoted in James McPherson, *Battle Cry of Freedom: The Civil War Years* (New York: Oxford University Press, 1988), 540.

4. Shelby Foote, *The Civil War: A Narrative, Fort Sumter to Perryville* (New York: Random House, 1958), 694.

5. Oliver Wendell Holmes Jr., *Touched with Fire: Civil War Letters and Diary of Oliver Wendell Holmes, Jr.,* ed. Mark De Wolfe Howe (New York: Fordham University Press, 2000), 64.

6. Holmes, *Touched with Fire,* 18.

7. Holmes, *Touched with Fire,* 92.

8. Holmes, *Touched with Fire,* 51.

9. Holmes, *Touched with Fire,* 56.

10. Holmes, *Touched with Fire,* 78.

11. Holmes, *Touched with Fire,* 135.

12. Louis Menand, *The Metaphysical Club* (New York: Farrar, Straus and Giroux, 2001), 4.

13. Oliver Wendell Holmes to Harold Laski, July 28, 1916, in *Holmes-Laski Letters: The Correspondence of Mr. Justice Holmes and Harold J. Laski, 1916-1935,* vol. 1, ed. Mark De Wolfe Howe (Cambridge, Mass.: Harvard University Press, 1953), 8.

14. Oliver Wendell Holmes Jr., "The Gas-Stoker's Strike," *American Law Review* 7 (1873): 583-584.
15. Oliver Wendell Holmes to Felix Frankfurter, March 24, 1914, in *Holmes and Frankfurter: Their Correspondence, 1912-1934,* eds. Robert M. Mennel and Christine L. Compston (Hanover, N.H.: University of New Hampshire Press, 1996), 19.
16. *Buck v. Bell,* 274 U.S. 200, 207 (1927).
17. *Buck,* 274 U.S. at 205.
18. *Buck,* 274 U.S. at 207.
19. *Powell v. Pennsylvania,* 127 U.S. 678, 696 (1888).
20. *Lochner v. New York,* 198 U.S. 45, 75 (1905).
21. David E. Bernstein, *Rehabilitating Lochner: Defending Individual Rights from Progressive Reform* (Chicago: University of Chicago Press, 2011).
22. Quoted in Bernstein, *Rehabilitating Lochner,* 24.
23. Bernstein, *Rehabilitating Lochner,* 25.
24. Quoted in Bernstein, *Rehabilitating Lochner,* 26.
25. *The Slaughter-House Cases,* 83 U.S. (16 Wall) 36, 110 (1873).
26. *Lochner,* 198 U.S. at 61.
27. *Lochner,* 198 U.S. at 53.
28. *Lochner,* 198 U.S. at 61.
29. *Lochner,* 198 U.S. at 57.
30. *Lochner,* 198 U.S. at 59.
31. *Lochner,* 198 U.S. at 64.
32. *Lochner,* 198 U.S. at 75.
33. Herbert Spencer, *Social Statics: The Conditions Essential to Human Happiness Specified, and the First of Them Developed* (London: J. Chapman, 1851; New York: Robert Schalkenbach Foundation, 1995), 95. Citation refers to the 1995 edition.
34. *Lochner,* 198 U.S. at 75-76.
35. Herbert Croly, *Progressive Democracy* (New York: Macmillan, 1914), 137.
36. Croly, *Progressive Democracy,* 138.
37. James Bradley Thayer, *The Origin and Scope of the American Doctrine of Constitutional Law* (Boston: Little, Brown, 1893), 18.
38. Thayer, *Origin and Scope,* 9.
39. Felix Frankfurter, "The Red Terror of Judicial Reform," *The New Republic,* October 1, 1924, 166-167.
40. *Olmstead v. United States,* 277 U.S. 438, 478 (1928).
41. *Olmstead v. United States,* 277 U.S. at 472.
42. Joseph Bucklin Bishop, ed., *Theodore Roosevelt and His Time: Shown in His Own Letters,* vol. 2 (New York: Charles Scribner's Son's, 1920), 301.
43. Theodore Roosevelt, "Judges and Progress," *The Outlook,* January 6, 1912, 43. For more on TR's Progressive critique of the judiciary, see Edmund Morris, *Colonel Roosevelt* (New York: Random House, 2010).
44. Roosevelt, "Judges and Progress," 48.
45. H. L. Mencken, *A Mencken Chrestomathy: His Own Selections of His Choicest Writings* (New York: Vintage Books, 1982), 260.
46. Mencken, *Chrestomathy,* 259.
47. Woodrow Wilson, *President Wilson's Great Speeches and Other History Making Documents* (Chicago: Stanton & Van Vliet, 1917), 94-95.
48. David M. Kennedy, *Over Here: The First World War and American Society* (New York: Oxford University Press, 1982), 67-68.
49. Quoted in Kennedy, *Over Here,* 68.
50. *Meyer v. State,* 187 N.W. 100 (1922).
51. *Meyer v. Nebraska,* 262 U.S. 390, 399 (1923).
52. *Bartels v. Iowa,* 262 U.S. 404, 412 (1923).

53. Felix Frankfurter to Learned Hand, June 5, 1923, quoted in Gerald Gunther, *Learned Hand: The Man and the Judge* (New York: Alfred A. Knopf, 1994), 378.

54. See Moorfield Storey and Marcial P. Lichauco, *The Conquest of the Philippines by the United States, 1898-1925* (New York: G. P. Putnam's Sons, 1926).

55. For more on the Gold Democrats, see David T. Beito and Linda Royster Beito, "Gold Democrats and the Decline of Classical Liberalism, 1896-1900," *The Independent Review* 4, no. 4 (Spring 2000.)

56. Moorfield Storey, *Charles Sumner* (New York: Houghton, Mifflin, 1900).

57. See William B. Hixson, Jr., *Moorfield Storey and the Abolitionist Tradition* (New York: Oxford University Press, 1972). Hixson described Storey's "intellectual outlook" as one that "included pacifism, anti-imperialism, and racial egalitarianism fully as much as it did laissez-faire and moral tone in government." Hixson, *Moorfield Storey,* 39.

58. The Louisville ordinance is quoted in *Buchanan v. Warley,* 245 U.S. 60, 70 (1917).

59. *Buchanan,* 245 U.S. at 62.

60. *Buchanan,* 245 U.S. at 64.

61. *Buchanan,* 245 U.S. at 65.

62. *Buchanan,* 245 U.S. at 67.

63. *Buchanan,* 245 U.S. at 74.

64. *Buchanan,* 245 U.S. at 75.

65. Quoted in Hixson, *Moorfield Storey and the Abolitionist Tradition,* 142.

66. Quoted in Alexander M. Bickel and Benno C. Schmidt Jr., *History of the Supreme Court of the United States,* vol. 9, *The Judiciary and Responsible Government, 1910-1921* (New York: Cambridge University Press, 2007), 816.

67. David E. Bernstein, "Philip Sober Controlling Philip Drunk: *Buchanan v. Warley* in Historical Perspective," *Vanderbilt Law Review* 51 (May 1998): 797.

68. Justice Holmes's undelivered *Buchanan* dissent is reproduced in Bickel and Schmidt, *The Judiciary and Responsible Government,* insert following 592.

69. Holmes, "The Gas-Stoker's Strike," 583.

70. Felix Frankfurter, ed., *Mr. Justice Holmes* (New York: Coward-McCann, 1931), 33.

71. Frankfurter, *Mr. Justice Holmes,* 125.

72. Frankfurter, *Mr. Justice Holmes,* 2.

73. Frankfurter, *Mr. Justice Holmes,* 5.

74. Frankfurter, *Mr. Justice Holmes,* 85.

75. *Adkins v. Children's Hospital,* 261 U.S. 525, 545 (1923).

76. See Hadley Arkes, *The Return of George Sutherland: Restoring a Jurisprudence of Natural Rights* (Princeton: Princeton University Press, 1994).

77. *Adkins v. Children's Hospital,* 261 U.S. 525, 553.

78. The Oklahoma statute is quoted in *New State Ice Co. v. Liebmann,* 285 U.S. 262, 271 (1932).

79. *New State Ice Co.,* 285 U.S. at 311.

80. *New State Ice Co.,* 285 U.S. at 280.

81. Franklin D. Roosevelt, "Address at Oglethorpe University in Atlanta, Georgia," May 22, 1932. Online by Gerhard Peters and John T. Woolley, *The American Presidency Project,* http://www.presidency.ucsb.edu/ws/?pid=88410.

82. *Nebbia v. New York,* 291 U.S. 502, 537 (1934).

83. *Munn v. Illinois,* 94 U.S. 113, 126 (1877).

84. *Nebbia,* 291 U.S. at 537.

85. Franklin D. Roosevelt: "Inaugural Address," March 4, 1933. Online by Gerhard Peters and John T. Woolley, *The American Presidency Project,* http://www.presidency.ucsb.edu/ws/?pid=14473.

86. Franklin D. Roosevelt, "Statement on Signing the National Industrial Recovery Act," June 16, 1933. Online by Gerhard Peters and John T. Woolley, *The American Presidency Project,* http://www.presidency.ucsb.edu/ws/?pid=14669.

87. The charges filed against the brothers are quoted in *Schechter Poultry Corp. v. United States*, 295 U.S. 495, 527-528 (1935).

88. *Louisville Bank v. Radford*, 295 U.S. 555 (1935).

89. *Humphrey's Executor v. United States*, 295 U.S. 602, 628 (1935).

90. *Schechter Poultry Corp.*, 295 U.S. at 548.

91. *Schechter Poultry Corp.*, 295 U.S. at 546.

92. *Schechter Poultry Corp.*, 295 U.S. at 528.

93. Melvin I. Urofsky, *Louis D. Brandeis: A Life* (New York: Pantheon Books, 2009), 705.

94. John T. Flynn, *Country Squire in the White House* (New York: Doubleday, Doran, 1940), 83.

95. Rexford Tugwell, *The Brains Trust* (New York: Viking Press, 1968), 100.

96. Raymond Moley, *The First New Deal* (New York: Harcourt, Brace & World, 1966), 295.

97. Melvin I. Urofsky, ed., *The Supreme Court Justices: A Biographical Dictionary* (New York: Taylor and Francis, 1994), 44.

98. Franklin D. Roosevelt, "Press Conference," May 31, 1935. Online by Gerhard Peters and John T. Woolley, *The American Presidency Project,* http://www.presidency.ucsb.edu /ws/?pid=15065.

99. Woodrow Wilson, *Woodrow Wilson: Essential Speeches and Writings of the Scholar-President,* ed. Mario R. DiNunzio (New York: New York University Press, 2006), 235-236.

100. Roosevelt, "Press Conference," May 31, 1935.

101. William E. Leuchtenburg, *The Supreme Court Reborn: The Constitutional Revolution in the Age of Roosevelt* (New York: Oxford University Press, 1995), 105.

102. "Roosevelt Indorses Recall of Judges," *New York Times,* February 22, 1912.

103. Franklin D. Roosevelt, "Message to Congress on the Reorganization of the Judicial Branch of the Government," February 5, 1937. Online by Gerhard Peters and John T. Woolley, *The American Presidency Project,* http://www.presidency.ucsb.edu/ ws/?pid=15360.

104. *West Coast Hotel Co. v. Parrish*, 300 U.S. 379, 391 (1937).

105. *West Coast Hotel*, 300 U.S. at 398.

106. *West Coast Hotel*, 300 U.S. at 402.

107. *West Coast Hotel*, 300 U.S. at 403.

108. *National Labor Relations Board v. Jones & Laughlin Steel Corp.*, 301 U.S. 1, 30 (1937).

109. *NLRB v. Jones & Laughlin*, 301 U.S. at 37.

110. Leuchtenburg, *The Supreme Court Reborn*, 219.

CHAPTER THREE

1. Ronald Reagan, "Remarks Announcing the Nomination of Robert H. Bork To Be an Associate Justice of the Supreme Court of the United States," July 1, 1987. Online by Gerhard Peters and John T. Woolley, *The American Presidency Project,* http://www.presi dency.ucsb.edu/ws/?pid=34503.

2. 133 Cong. Rec. S9188-S9189 (daily ed. July 1, 1987) (statement of Sen. Kennedy).

3. *Nomination of Robert H. Bork to be Associate Justice of the Supreme Court of the United States: Hearings Before the Senate Committee on the Judiciary,* 100th Cong., 1st Sess. (1987), 13 [hereinafter *Bork Hearings*].

4. *Bork Hearings*, 120.

5. *Bork Hearings*, 717.

6. *United States v. Carolene Products Co.*, 304 U.S. 144, 152 (1938).

7. Bryan A. Garner, ed., *Black's Law Dictionary*, 8th ed.; Abridged Edition (St. Paul, Minn.: Thomson/West, 2005), 1047.

8. *Carolene Products*, 304 U.S. at 146.

9. *Goesaert v. Cleary*, 335 U.S. 464, 466-47 (1948).

10. *Williamson v. Lee Optical Inc.*, 348 U.S. 483, 487 (1955).

11. *Lee Optical,* 348 U.S. at 488 (emphasis added).
12. *Ferguson v. Skrupa,* 372 U.S. 726, 732 (1963).
13. *Lehnhausen v. Lake Shore Auto Parts Co.,* 410 U.S. 356, 364 (1973).
14. *Carolene Products,* 304 U.S. at 153 n. 4.
15. *Brown v. Board of Education of Topeka, Kansas,* 347 U.S. 483, 495 (1954).
16. "Judge Learned Hand Dies," *New York Times,* August 19, 1961.
17. Learned Hand, *The Bill of Rights* (Cambridge, Mass.: Harvard University Press, 1958), 42.
18. Hand, *The Bill of Rights,* 51.
19. Hand, *The Bill of Rights,* 34.
20. Hand, *The Bill of Rights,* 55.
21. Hand, *The Bill of Rights,* 73.
22. Gerald Gunther, *Learned Hand: The Man and the Judge* (New York: Alfred A. Knopf, 1994), 655.
23. *Minersville School District v. Gobitis,* 310 U.S. 586, 598 (1940).
24. *Minersville v. Gobitis,* 310 U.S. at 600.
25. *West Virginia State Board of Education v. Barnette,* 319 U.S. 624, 634 (1943).
26. *Barnette,* 319 U.S. at 649.
27. *Barnette,* 319 U.S. at 666.
28. J. W. Peltason, "Baker v. Carr," in *The Oxford Companion to the Supreme Court of the United States,* 2nd ed., ed. Kermit L. Hall (New York: Oxford University Press, 2005), 67.
29. *Baker v. Carr,* 369 U.S. 186, 237 (1962).
30. *Reynolds v. Sims,* 377 U.S. 533, 562 (1964).
31. *Colegrove v. Green,* 328 U.S. 549, 556 (1946).
32. *Baker v. Carr,* 369 U.S. at 267.
33. *Baker v. Carr,* 369 U.S. at 270.
34. *Baker v. Carr,* 369 U.S. at 269.
35. *Baker v. Carr,* 369 U.S. at 270.
36. Noah Feldman, *Scorpions: The Battles and Triumphs of FDR's Great Supreme Court Justices* (New York: Twelve, 2010), 418.
37. The statute is quoted in *Griswold v. Connecticut,* 381 U.S. 479, 480 (1965).
38. *Griswold,* 381 U.S. at 484.
39. *Griswold,* 381 U.S. at 485.
40. *Griswold,* 381 U.S. at 485-486.
41. *Griswold,* 381 U.S. at 495.
42. To be sure, there was a feminist argument to be made that women's reproductive autonomy deserves extra judicial protection due to the history of sexist legal discrimination that has historically plagued American women, effectively qualifying them as a "discrete and insular minority." But no justice advanced that position in *Griswold.* Instead, most of the votes cast against the Connecticut law attempted to shoehorn the unenumerated right to privacy into Footnote Four's assertion that only enumerated rights deserve judicial attention.
43. *West Coast Hotel Co. v. Parrish,* 300 U.S. 379, 391 (1937).
44. *Griswold,* 381 U.S. at 481-482.
45. *Meyer v. Nebraska,* 262 U.S. 390, 399 (1923).
46. *Pierce v. Society of Sisters,* 268 U.S. 510, 535 (1925).
47. *Griswold,* 381 U.S. at 510.
48. Hugo Lafayette Black, *A Constitutional Faith* (New York: Alfred A. Knopf, 1968), 20.
49. Black, *Constitutional Faith,* 44-45.
50. Black, *Constitutional Faith,* 41.
51. *Griswold,* 381 U.S. at 522.
52. Black, *Constitutional Faith,* 11.
53. See Brian Doherty, *Radicals for Capitalism: A Freewheeling History of the Modern American Libertarian Movement* (New York: Public Affairs, 2007).

54. Alexander M. Bickel, *The Least Dangerous Branch: The Supreme Court at the Bar of Politics,* 2nd ed. (New Haven: Yale University Press, 1986), 16-18.
55. Bickel, *The Least Dangerous Branch,* 111.
56. *Bork Hearings,* 117 (statement of Robert H. Bork).
57. Robert H. Bork, "Neutral Principles and Some First Amendment Problems," *Indiana Law Journal* 47 (1971): 1-2.
58. Bork, "Neutral Principles," 9.
59. Oliver Wendell Holmes Jr., "The Gas-Stoker's Strike," *American Law Review* 7 (1873): 583-584.
60. Bork, "Neutral Principles," 10-11.
61. Bork, "Neutral Principles," 10.
62. Bork, "Neutral Principles," 11.
63. *Roe v. Wade,* 410 U.S. 113, 164 (1973).
64. *Roe,* 410 U.S. at 165.
65. *Roe,* 410 U.S. at 153.
66. *Roe,* 410 U.S. at 172.
67. *Roe,* 410 U.S. at 174.
68. Robert H. Bork, *The Tempting of America: The Political Seduction of the Law* (New York: Touchstone, 1991), 116.
69. Bork, *Tempting of America,* 110.
70. Bork, *Tempting of America,* 126.

CHAPTER FOUR

1. Charles Lane, "Roberts Listed in Federalist Society '97-98 Directory," *Washington Post,* July 25, 2005.
2. For a detailed account of the Federalist Society's origins, see Steven M. Teles, *The Rise of the Conservative Legal Movement: The Battle for Control of the Law* (Princeton: Princeton University Press, 2008).
3. For an excellent account of John Roberts's 2005 confirmation hearings, see Jan Crawford Greenburg, *Supreme Conflict: The Inside Story of the Struggle for Control of the United States Supreme Court* (New York: Penguin Books, 2007).
4. Jason DeParle, "Debating the Subtle Sway of the Federalist Society," *New York Times,* August 1, 2005.
5. Roger Pilon, "McCarthy Liberals," *New York Post,* July 29, 2005.
6. Steven Calabresi, Lee Liberman, and David McIntosh, "Proposal for a Symposium on the Legal Ramifications of the New Federalism," 1982, quoted in John J. Miller, *A Gift of Freedom: How the John M. Olin Foundation Changed America* (New York: Encounter Books, 2006), 89.
7. Interview with Eugene Meyer, March 2010.
8. Edwin M. Meese III, Speech to the American Bar Association, July 9, 1985. A transcript of the speech is available at http://www.justice.gov/ag/aghistory/meese/1985/07-09-1985.pdf.
9. Edwin M. Meese III, "A Return to Constitutional Interpretation from Judicial Law-Making," *New York Law School Law Review* 40 (1996): 925.
10. Robert H. Bork, *The Tempting of America: The Political Seduction of the Law* (New York: Touchstone, 1991), 2.
11. Bork, *Tempting of America,* 139.
12. Bernard H. Siegan, *Economic Liberties and the Constitution* (Chicago: University of Chicago Press, 1980), 6.
13. Siegan, *Economic Liberties,* 21.
14. Siegan, *Economic Liberties,* 324.
15. Siegan, *Economic Liberties,* 15.
16. Siegan, *Economic Liberties,* 114.

17. Siegan, *Economic Liberties,* 17.
18. Bork, *Tempting of America,* 224-225.
19. The statute is quoted in *Bowers v. Hardwick,* 478 U.S. 186, 200 (1986).
20. *Bowers,* 478 U.S. at 190.
21. *Bowers,* 478 U.S. at 194.
22. *Bowers,* 478 U.S. at 196.
23. Bork, *Tempting of America,* 117.
24. Interview with Roger Pilon, November 2013.
25. Roger Pilon, email to the author, March 17, 2010.
26. Pilon interview.
27. Roger Pilon, "On the Foundations of Justice," speech to the Philadelphia Society, April 10, 1981, in *The Intercollegiate Review* (Fall/Winter 1981): 5.
28. Pilon interview.
29. Roger Pilon, "Constitutional Visions," *Reason,* December 1990, 41.
30. Roger Pilon, "Rethinking Judicial Restraint," *Wall Street Journal,* February 1, 1991.
31. Pilon interview.
32. Antonin Scalia, "Economic Affairs as Human Affairs," *Cato Journal* vol. 4, no. 3 (Winter 1985): 705-706.
33. Richard A. Epstein, "Judicial Review: Reckoning on Two Kinds of Error," *Cato Journal* vol. 4, no. 3 (Winter 1985): 712.
34. Epstein, "Judicial Review," 714-715.
35. Epstein, "Judicial Review," 717-718.
36. Pilon, email to author.
37. Stephen Macedo, *The New Right v. The Constitution* (Washington, D.C.: Cato Institute, 1986), 27.
38. Richard A. Epstein, *Takings: Private Property and the Power of Eminent Domain* (Cambridge, Mass.: Harvard University Press, 1985), 331-332.
39. Epstein, *Takings,* x.
40. Bork, *Tempting of America,* 230.
41. Charles A. Fried, *Order and Law: Arguing the Reagan Revolution: A Firsthand Account* (New York: Simon & Schuster, 1991), 183.
42. *Cato 25: 25 Years at the Cato Institute: The 2001 Annual Report* (Washington, D.C.: The Cato Institute, 2001), 14.
43. Roger Pilon, "Proposal for a Center for Constitutional Studies to be Located at the Cato Institute, Washington, D.C., Under the Direction of Roger Pilon, Ph.D., J.D.," October 11, 1988, 4.
44. Pilon, "Proposal," 8.
45. Pilon, "Proposal," 4.
46. Pilon interview.
47. Brief of the Cato Institute as *Amicus Curiae* in Support of Petitioners, 2, *Lawrence v. Texas* 539 U.S. 558 (2003).
48. Cato Brief, *Lawrence v. Texas,* 9.
49. *Lawrence v. Texas,* 539 U.S. at 558, transcript of oral argument, March 26, 2003, 3-4.
50. *Lawrence* transcript, 16-17.
51. *Lawrence* transcript, 17.
52. *Lawrence* transcript, 9-10.
53. *Lawrence* transcript, 38.
54. *Lawrence* transcript, 42-43.
55. *Lawrence v. Texas,* 539 U.S. at 558, 562.
56. *Lawrence,* 539 U.S. at 578.
57. *Lawrence,* 539 U.S. at 602.
58. *Lawrence,* 539 U.S. at 592.
59. *Washington v. Glucksberg,* 521 U.S. 702, 721 (1997).

60. *Lawrence,* 539 U.S. at 603.
61. Jeffrey Rosen, "Second Opinions," *The New Republic,* May 4, 2012.
62. Randy E. Barnett, "Kennedy's Libertarian Revolution," *National Review* Online, July 10, 2003. Available at http://www.nationalreview.com/articles/207453/kennedys-liber tarian-revolution/randy-barnett.

CHAPTER FIVE

1. Dan Morgan, Sarah Cohen, and Gilbert M. Gaul, "Dairy Industry Crushed Innovator Who Bested Price-Control System," *Washington Post,* December 10, 2006.
2. *Hettinga v. United States,* 677 F.3d 471, 480 (D.C. Cir. 2012).
3. *United States v. Carolene Products Co.,* 304 U.S. 144, 152 (1938).
4. *Williamson v. Lee Optical Inc.,* 348 U.S. 483, 488 (1955).
5. *Hettinga,* 677 F.3d at 482-483.
6. *Lochner v. New York,* 198 U.S. 45, 75 (1905).
7. *Lehnhausen v. Lake Shore Auto Parts Co.,* 410 U.S. 356, 364 (1973).
8. Interview with William H. "Chip" Mellor, November 2013.
9. Clint Bolick, *Unfinished Business: A Civil Rights Strategy for America's Third Century* (San Francisco: Pacific Research Institute for Public Policy, 1990).
10. Jonathan W. Emord, *Freedom, Technology and the First Amendment* (San Francisco: Pacific Research Institute for Public Policy, 1991).
11. Mark L. Pollot, *Grand Theft and Petit Larceny: Property Rights in America* (San Francisco: Pacific Research Institute for Public Policy, 1993).
12. Bolick, *Unfinished Business,* 52.
13. Bolick, *Unfinished Business,* 76.
14. Interview with Clint Bolick, December 2013.
15. Clarence Thomas has also acknowledged an intellectual debt to Walter Williams. Meeting the libertarian economist in 1980 "was a landmark event for me," Thomas wrote in his memoir. "Very few black scholars were using that kind of research-driven thinking to study the everyday problems of blacks, and Dr. Williams' findings were as exciting to me as they were upsetting to those who still believed that government regulation was the only way to improve the lot of black people." Clarence Thomas, *My Grandfather's Son: A Memoir* (New York: Harper, 2007), 126.
16. Walter E. Williams, *The State against Blacks* (New York: McGraw-Hill, 1982), xvi.
17. Williams, *The State against Blacks,* 125.
18. Clint Bolick, *Changing Course: Civil Rights at the Crossroads* (New Brunswick, N.J.: Transaction Books, 1988), 123.
19. Bolick, *Changing Course,* 125.
20. Bolick, *Changing Course,* 122.
21. Mellor interview.
22. *Craigmiles v. Giles,* 312 F.3d 220, 225 (6th Cir. 2002) (internal quotations omitted).
23. *Craigmiles,* 318 F.3d at 229.
24. Mellor interview.
25. *Powers v. Harris,* 379 F.3d 1208, 1221-1222 (10th Cir. 2004).
26. *Powers,* 379 F.3d at 1218.
27. Petition for a Writ of Certiorari at 9-10, *Powers v. Harris,* no. 04-716, November 22, 2004.
28. *Carolene Products,* 304 U.S. at 144, 152 n. 4.
29. *Berman v. Parker,* 348 U.S. 26, 32 (1954).
30. *Berman,* 348 U.S. at 36.
31. "Donald Trump's House of Cards," *The Economist,* August 30, 1997.
32. David M. Herszenhorn, "Widowed Homeowner Foils Trump Bid in Atlantic City," *New York Times,* July 21, 1998.

33. For a superb account of the New London controversy, see Jeff Benedict, *Little Pink House: A True Story of Defiance and Courage* (New York: Grand Central Publishing, 2009).

34. Interview with Scott Bullock, November 2013. Ensuing Bullock quotes from same interview.

35. *Kelo v. City of New London,* 545 U.S. 469 (2005).

36. *Kelo v. City of New London,* 843 A.2d 500, 527 (Conn. 2004).

37. *Hawaii Housing Authority v. Midkiff,* 467 U.S. 229, 242-243 (1984).

38. Bullock interview.

39. Brief of Petitioners at 9, *Kelo,* 545 U.S. at 469.

40. Brief of Petitioners, *Kelo,* 11.

41. Brief of *Amici Curiae* National Association for the Advancement of Colored People, AARP, Hispanic Alliance of Atlantic County, Inc., Citizens in Action, Cramer Hill Resident Association, Inc., and the Southern Christian Leadership Conference in Support of Petitioners at 3-4, *Kelo,* 545 U.S. at 469.

42. *Kelo,* 545 U.S. at 469, transcript of oral argument, February 22, 2005, 3.

43. *Kelo* transcript, 3-4.

44. *Kelo* transcript, 6-7.

45. *Kelo* transcript, 9.

46. *Kelo* transcript, 10-11.

47. *Berman,* 348 U.S. at 32.

48. *Kelo* transcript, 12.

49. *Kelo* transcript, 14.

50. *Kelo* transcript, 14-15.

51. Bullock interview.

52. *United States v. James Daniel Good Real Prop.,* 510 U.S. 43, 61 (1993).

53. *Kelo* transcript, 26-27.

54. *Kelo* transcript, 28-29.

55. Bullock interview.

56. *Kelo* transcript, 30.

57. Bullock interview.

58. *Kelo* transcript, 37.

59. *Kelo* transcript, 55.

60. Bullock interview.

61. *Kelo,* 545 U.S. at 469, 480.

62. *Kelo,* 545 U.S. at 483.

63. *Kelo,* 545 U.S. at 494.

64. *Kelo,* 545 U.S. at 521-522.

65. "Congress Assails Domain Ruling," *Washington Times,* July 1, 2005.

66. The results of the 2008 Associated Press/National Constitution Center Poll are available at http://www.constitutioncenter.org/media/files/poll-ap-ncc-poll-2008.pdf.

67. Mellor interview.

68. *Norwood v. Horney,* 110 St.3d 353 (Ohio, 2006).

69. *Nomination of Sonia Sotomayor to be Associate Justice of the Supreme Court of the United States: Hearings Before the Senate Committee on the Judiciary,* 111th Cong., 1st Sess. (2009).

70. *Kelo,* 545 U.S. at 483.

71. Jeff Benedict, "Apology Adds an Epilogue to Kelo Case," *Hartford Courant,* September 18, 2011.

CHAPTER SIX

1. J. Harvie Wilkinson III, "Of Guns, Abortions, and the Unraveling Rule of Law," *Virginia Law Review* 95, vol. 2 (April 2009): 254.

2. Interview with Clark Neily, December 2013.
3. Sanford Levinson, "The Embarrassing Second Amendment," *Yale Law Journal* 99 (1989): 642.
4. Adam Liptak, "A Liberal Case for Gun Rights Sways Judiciary," *New York Times,* May 6, 2007.
5. Neily interview. Ensuing Neily quotes from same interview.
6. Interview with William H. "Chip" Mellor, November 2013.
7. Neily interview.
8. Interview with Alan Gura, December 2013.
9. Neily interview.
10. Gura interview.
11. Neily interview.
12. *Parker v. District of Columbia,* 478 F.3d 370 (D.C. Cir. 2007).
13. Neily interview.
14. *District of Columbia v. Heller,* 554 U.S. 570 (2008), transcript of oral argument, March 18, 2008, 3-4.
15. *Heller* transcript, 6.
16. *Heller* transcript, 4.
17. *Heller* transcript, 14.
18. *Heller* transcript, 5-6.
19. *Heller* transcript, 8.
20. Neily interview.
21. *Heller* transcript, 18-19.
22. Neily interview.
23. John Ashcroft, attorney general of the United States, to James Jay Baker, executive director, National Rifle Association, May 17, 2001, Office of the Attorney General.
24. Brief for the United States as *Amicus Curiae* at 8, *Heller,* 554 U.S. at 570.
25. *Heller* transcript, 40.
26. *Heller* transcript, 44.
27. Neily interview.
28. *Heller* transcript, 50-53.
29. *Heller* transcript, 54.
30. *Heller* transcript, 57-58.
31. See Ralph Ketcham, ed., *The Anti-Federalist Papers and the Constitutional Convention Debates* (New York: Mentor, 1986).
32. *Heller* transcript, 73.
33. *Heller* transcript, 73-74.
34. *District of Columbia v. Heller,* 128 S. Ct. 2783, 2799 (2008).
35. *Heller,* 128 S. Ct. at 2801.
36. *Heller,* 128 S. Ct. at 2817.
37. *Heller,* 128 S. Ct. at 2816-2817.
38. *Heller,* 128 S. Ct. at 2822.
39. *Heller,* 128 S. Ct. at 2828.
40. *Heller,* 128 S. Ct. at 2846-2847.
41. *Colegrove v. Green,* 328 U.S. 549, 556 (1946).
42. *Heller,* 128 S. Ct. at 2846 n. 39.
43. Gura interview.
44. *Gitlow v. United States,* 268 U.S. 652, 666 (1925).
45. Gura interview.
46. Eric Foner, *Reconstruction: America's Unfinished Revolution, 1863-1877,* Francis Parkman Prize Edition (New York: History Book Club, 2005), 530.
47. *Heller,* 128 S. Ct. at 2813 n. 23.
48. Gura interview.
49. Neily interview.

50. Antonin Scalia, *A Matter of Interpretation: Federal Courts and the Law* (Princeton: Princeton University Press, 1997), 46-47.
51. Marcia Coyle, *The Roberts Court: The Struggle for the Constitution* (New York: Simon & Schuster, 2013), 163.
52. *Chicago v. Morales,* 527 U.S. 41, 85 (1999).
53. Scalia, *A Matter of Interpretation,* 25.
54. Gura interview.
55. Robert Bork, *The Tempting of America: The Political Seduction of the Law* (New York: Touchstone, 1991), 37-39.
56. Antonin Scalia, "Economic Affairs as Human Affairs," *Cato Journal* vol. 4, no. 3 (Winter 1985): 706.
57. Gura interview.
58. Brief of the American Civil Rights Union, Let Freedom Ring, Committee for Justice, and the Family Research Council as *Amici Curiae* in Support of Petitioners at 6-7, *McDonald v. Chicago,* 561 U.S. 3025 (2010).
59. Ken Klukowski and Ken Blackwell, "A Gun Case or Pandora's Box?," *Washington Times,* December 11, 2009.
60. Gura interview.
61. Motion of Respondents-Supporting-Petitioners for Divided Argument at 2, *McDonald,* 561 U.S. at 3025.
62. Opposition to Motion of National Rifle Association, Et. Al., for Divided Argument at 1, *McDonald,* 561 U.S. at 3025.
63. Gura interview.
64. *McDonald,* 561 U.S. at 3025, transcript of oral argument, March 2, 2010, 3-4.
65. *McDonald* transcript, 6-7.
66. *McDonald v. Chicago,* 130 S. Ct. 3020, 3062 (2010).
67. A lifelong advocate of armed self-defense, Frederick Douglass once wrote, "the liberties of the American people were dependent upon the ballot-box, the jury-box, and the cartridge-box," and added, "without these no class of people could live and flourish in this country." Frederick Douglass, *Life and Times of Frederick Douglass,* in Douglass, *Writings* (New York: Library of America, 1994), 816-817.
68. *McDonald,* 130 S. Ct. at 3088.
69. *McDonald,* 130 S. Ct. at 3086.
70. Gura interview.
71. Clint Bolick, *Unfinished Business: A Civil Rights Strategy for America's Third Century* (San Francisco: Pacific Research Institute for Public Policy, 1990), 86.

CHAPTER SEVEN

1. *Gonzales v. Raich,* 545 U.S. 1 (2005), transcript of oral argument, November 29, 2004, 25.
2. *Raich,* 545 U.S. at 1, 9.
3. Interview with Randy Barnett, March 2012.
4. *Raich,* 57-58.
5. *Department of Health and Human Services v. Florida,* no. 11-398, transcript of oral argument, March 27, 2012, 54.
6. Orin Kerr, email to author, February 22, 2012.
7. Interview with Ilya Shapiro, February 2012.
8. Matt Cover, "When Asked Where the Constitution Authorizes Congress to Order Americans to Buy Health Insurance, Pelosi Says: 'Are You Serious?'" *CNS News,* October 22, 2009. Available at http://www.cnsnews.com/node/55971.
9. *Dept. of HHS v. Florida,* transcript, March 27, 2012, 11-12.
10. James Madison, *Federalist 42,* in *The Federalist Papers,* ed. Clinton Rossiter (New York: Mentor, 1961), 267.

11. Alexander Hamilton, *Federalist* 17, in *The Federalist Papers,* ed. Rossiter, 118.

12. *Wickard v. Filburn,* 317 U.S. 111, 125 (1942).

13. The Patient Protection and Affordable Care Act of 2010, 42 U.S. Code § 18091 (2010).

14. Roger Pilon, email to the author, March 17, 2010.

15. Glenn Harlan Reynolds, "Kids, Guns, and the Commerce Clause: Is the Court Ready for Constitutional Government?" Cato Institute Policy Analysis, no. 216, October 10, 1994, 1.

16. Richard A. Epstein, "The Proper Scope of the Commerce Power," *Virginia Law Review* 73 (1987): 1388.

17. Pilon, email to author.

18. *United States v. Lopez,* 514 U.S. 549 (1995). Audio of the November 8, 1994 oral argument is available at http://www.oyez.org/cases/1990-1999/1994/1994_93_1260.

19. *United States v. Lopez,* 514 U.S. 549, 567-568 (1995).

20. Interview with Randy Barnett, March 2012.

21. Randy E. Barnett, *Restoring the Lost Constitution: The Presumption of Liberty* (Princeton: Princeton University Press, 2004), x-xi.

22. Barnett interview.

23. *United States v. Morrison,* 529 U.S. 598, 613 (2000).

24. Randy Barnett, Nathaniel Stewart, and Todd Gaziano, "Why the Personal Mandate to Buy Health Insurance Is Unprecedented and Unconstitutional," Heritage Foundation Legal Memorandum, no. 49, December 9, 2009. See also Josh Blackman, *Unprecedented: The Constitutional Challenge to Obamacare* (New York: Public Affairs, 2013).

25. Barnett interview.

26. Complaint at 4, *Florida v. Department of Health and Human Services,* no. 3:10-cv-91, N.D. Fla., March 23, 2010.

27. *Florida v. Department of Health and Human Services,* 780 F. Supp. 2d 1256 (N.D. Fla. 2011).

28. *Department of Health and Human Services v. Florida,* 648 F.3d 1235 (11th Cir. 2011).

29. *Thomas More Law Center v. Obama,* 651 F.3d 529, 566 (6th Cir. 2011).

30. The Anti-Injunction Act, 26 U.S.C. § 7421(a) (1867).

31. David Weigel, "Into the Void: How the Democrats Gave a Conservative Judge an Opening to Invalidate the Health Care Law," *Slate,* January 31, 2011. Available at http://www.slate.com/articles/news_and_politics/politics/2011/01/into_the_void.html.

32. *Time,* June 18, 2012.

33. *Confirmation Hearings on the Nomination of John G. Roberts, Jr. to be Chief Justice of the United States, Hearing Before the Senate Judiciary Committee,* 109th Cong., 1st Sess. (2005), 145 [hereinafter *Roberts Hearings*].

34. *Roberts Hearings,* 284-285.

35. *Roberts Hearings,* 285-286.

36. *Citizens United v. Federal Election Commission,* 130 S. Ct. 876, 917 (2010).

37. *Citizens United,* 130 S. Ct. at 919.

38. *Citizens United,* 130 S. Ct. at 921.

39. Damon Root, "Strict Scrutiny," Reason.com, August 18, 2011. Available at http://www.reason.com/archives/2011/08/18/strict-scrutiny.

40. *Dept. of HHS v. Florida,* transcript, no. 11-398, transcript of oral argument, March 26, 2012, 3.

41. *Dept. of HHS v. Florida* transcript, March 26, 2012, 31-32.

42. *Dept. of HHS v. Florida* transcript, March 26, 2012, 44-45.

43. Jason DeParle, "In Battle to Pick Next Justice, Right Says, Avoid a Kennedy," *New York Times,* June 27, 2005.

44. *Raich,* 545 U.S. at 1. That same year, Justice Kennedy also voted against the libertarian Institute for Justice in *Kelo v. City of New London,* 545 U.S. 469 (2005). For the argument that Kennedy practices a "modestly libertarian jurisprudence," see Helen J.

Knowles, *The Tie Goes to Freedom: Justice Anthony Kennedy on Liberty* (Lanham, Md.: Rowman & Littlefied, 2009), 3.

45. *Dept. of HHS v. Florida* transcript, March 27, 2012, 31.
46. *Dept. of HHS v. Florida* transcript, March 27, 2012, 104.
47. *Dept. of HHS v. Florida* transcript, March 27, 2012, 39-40.
48. *Dept. of HHS v. Florida* transcript, March 27, 2012, 12-13.
49. *Dept. of HHS v. Florida* 648 F.3d at 1235.
50. *Dept. of HHS v. Florida* transcript, March 27, 2012, 15-16.
51. *Dept. of HHS v. Florida* transcript, March 27, 2012, 30.
52. *Dept. of HHS v. Florida* transcript, March 27, 2012, 39.
53. *Roberts Hearings,* 162.
54. *Dept. of HHS v. Florida* transcript, March 27, 2012, 46.
55. *Dept. of HHS v. Florida* transcript, March 27, 2012, 47-48.
56. *Dept. of HHS v. Florida* transcript, March 27, 2012, 50.
57. *Dept. of HHS v. Florida* transcript, March 27, 2012, 52-53.
58. *Dept. of HHS v. Florida* transcript, March 27, 2012, 54.
59. *Dept. of HHS v. Florida* transcript, March 27, 2012, 81.
60. *Dept. of HHS v. Florida* transcript, March 27, 2012, 108-109.
61. *Dept. of HHS v. Florida* transcript, March 27, 2012, 110-11.
62. *Dept. of HHS v. Florida* transcript, March 27, 2012, 111.
63. *Florida v. Department of Health and Human Services,* no. 11-400, transcript of oral argument, March 28, 2012, 81.
64. *Florida v. Dept. of HHS* transcript, March 28, 2012, 82.
65. *Florida v. Dept. of HHS* transcript, March 28, 2012, 83.
66. Franklin D. Roosevelt, "Press Conference," May 31, 1935. Online by Gerhard Peters and John T. Woolley, *The American Presidency Project,* http://www.presidency.ucsb.edu/ws/?pid=15065.
67. Jake Tapper and Mary Bruce, "President Obama Seems to Prepare Arguments for a Supreme Court Defeat," ABC News, April 2, 2012. Available at http://abcnews.go.com/blogs/politics/2012/04/president-obama-seems-to-prepare-arguments-for-a-supreme-court-defeat/.
68. Statement of Senator Patrick Leahy (D-Vt.), Chairman, Senate Judiciary Committee, On the Supreme Court's Review of the Affordable Care Act, May 14, 2012. Available at http://www.leahy.senate.gov/press/on-senate-floor-leahy-shares-observations-about-scotus-arguments-on-affordable-care-act.
69. Jeffrey Rosen, "Second Opinions," *The New Republic,* May 4, 2012. Available at http://www.newrepublic.com/article/politics/103090/magazine/conservative-judges-justices-supreme-court-obama.
70. George Will, "Liberals Put the Squeeze to Justice Roberts," *Washington Post,* May 25, 2012.
71. Jan Crawford, "Roberts Switched Views to Uphold Health Care Law," CBS News, July 2, 2012. Available at http://www.cbsnews.com/news/roberts-switched-views-to-uphold-health-care-law/.
72. Jeffrey Rosen, "Are Liberals Trying to Intimidate John Roberts?" *The New Republic,* May 28, 2012. Available at http://www.newrepublic.com/article/politics/103656/obamacare-affordable-care-act-critics-response.
73. Audio of the June 28, 2012 opinion announcement in *National Federation of Independent Business v. Sebelius* 132 S. Ct. 2566 (2012) is available at http://www.oyez.org/cases/2010-2019/2011/2011_11_400. All quotes from the opinion announcement are taken from my transcription.
74. *National Federation of Independent Business v. Sebelius,* 132 S. Ct. 2566, 2593 (2012).
75. *Blodgett v. Holden,* 275 U.S. 142, 148 (1927).
76. *NFIB v. Sebelius,* 132 S. Ct. at 2594.
77. *NFIB v. Sebelius,* 132 S. Ct. at 2579.

78.   Oliver Wendell Holmes to Harold Laski, March 4, 1920, in *Holmes-Laski Letters: The Correspondence of Mr. Justice Holmes and Harold J. Laski, 1916-1935,* vol. 1, ed. Mark De Wolfe Howe (Cambridge, Mass.: Harvard University Press, 1953), 249.

EPILOGUE

1.   Video of the Yale conference is available at http://www.law.yale.edu/intellectuallife/constinterp12.htm.
2.   Clint Bolick, *Changing Course: Civil Rights at the Crossroads* (New Brunswick, N.J.: Transaction Books, 1988), 122.
3.   *St. Joseph Abbey v. Castille,* 712 F.3 215, 226 (5th Cir. 2013).

SELECT
BIBLIOGRAPHY

Arkes, Hadley. *The Return of George Sutherland: Restoring a Jurisprudence of Natural Rights.*
Princeton: Princeton University Press, 1994.

Barnett, Randy E. "Kennedy's Libertarian Revolution." *National Review* Online, July 10,
2003. http://www.nationalreview.com/articles/207453/kennedys-libertarian-revolution
/randy-barnett.

Barnett, Randy E. *Restoring the Lost Constitution: The Presumption of Liberty.* Princeton:
Princeton University Press, 2004.

Bean, Jonathan, ed. *Race and Liberty in America: The Essential Reader.* Lexington: University
Press of Kentucky, 2009.

Beito, David T., and Linda Royster Beito. "Gold Democrats and the Decline of Classical Liberalism, 1896–1900." *The Independent Review,* vol. 4, no. 4, Spring 2000.

Benedict, Jeff. *Little Pink House: A True Story of Defiance and Courage.* New York: Grand
Central Publishing, 2009.

Bernstein, David E. "Philip Sober Controlling Philip Drunk: *Buchanan v. Warley* in Historical
Perspective." *Vanderbilt Law Review* 51, May 1998.

Bernstein, David E. *Rehabilitating Lochner: Defending Individual Rights from Progressive Reform.* Chicago: University of Chicago Press, 2011.

Bickel, Alexander M. *The Least Dangerous Branch: The Supreme Court at the Bar of Politics.* 2nd
ed. New Haven: Yale University Press, 1986.

Bickel, Alexander M., and Benno C. Schmidt Jr. *History of the Supreme Court of the United
States.* Vol. 9, *The Judiciary and Responsible Government, 1910–1921.* New York: Cambridge University Press, 2007.

Bishop, Joseph Bucklin, ed. *Theodore Roosevelt and His Time: Shown in His Own Letters.* Vol.
2. New York: Charles Scribner's Son's, 1920.

Black, Hugo Lafayette. *A Constitutional Faith.* New York: Alfred A. Knopf, 1968.

Blackman, Josh. *Unprecedented: The Constitutional Challenge to Obamacare.* New York: Public
Affairs, 2013.

Bolick, Clint. *Changing Course: Civil Rights at the Crossroads.* New Brunswick, N.J.: Transaction Books, 1988.

Bolick, Clint. *Unfinished Business: A Civil Rights Strategy for America's Third Century.* San
Francisco: Pacific Research Institute for Public Policy, 1990.

Bork, Robert H. "Neutral Principles and Some First Amendment Problems." *Indiana Law
Journal* 47, 1971.

Bork, Robert H. *The Tempting of America: The Political Seduction of the Law.* New York:
Touchstone, 1991.

Calhoun, John C. *John C. Calhoun: Selected Speeches and Writings.* Edited by H. Lee Cheek Jr. New York: Regnery, 2003.

Coke, Sir Edward. *The Selected Writings and Speeches of Sir Edward Coke.* 2 vols. Edited by Steve Sheppard. Indianapolis: Liberty Fund, 2003.

Coyle, Marcia. *The Roberts Court: The Struggle for the Constitution.* New York: Simon & Schuster, 2013.

Crawford, Jan. "Roberts Switched Views to Uphold Health Care Law." CBS News, July 2, 2012. http://www.cbsnews.com/news/roberts-switched-views-to-uphold-health-care-law/.

Croly, Herbert. *Progressive Democracy.* New York: Macmillan, 1914.

Curtis, Michael Kent. *No State Shall Abridge: The Fourteenth Amendment and the Bill of Rights.* Durham, N.C.: Duke University Press, 1986.

Davidson, Alan, ed. *The Oxford Companion to Food.* New York: Oxford University Press, 1999.

Doherty, Brian. *Radicals for Capitalism: A Freewheeling History of the Modern American Libertarian Movement.* New York: Public Affairs, 2007.

Douglass, Frederick. *Frederick Douglass: Selected Speeches and Writings,* Edited by Philip S. Foner. Chicago: Lawrence Hill Books, 1999.

Douglass, Frederick. *My Bondage and My Freedom.* New York: Penguin Books, 2003. First published in 1855 by Miller, Orton & Mulligan.

Douglass, Frederick. *Writings.* New York: Library of America, 1994.

DuBois, W. E. B. *Black Reconstruction.* New York: Harcourt, Brace, 1935.

Epstein, Richard A. "Judicial Review: Reckoning on Two Kinds of Error." *Cato Journal,* vol. 4, no. 3, Winter 1985.

Epstein, Richard A. *Takings: Private Property and the Power of Eminent Domain.* Cambridge, Mass.: Harvard University Press, 1985.

Epstein, Richard A. "The Proper Scope of the Commerce Power." *Virginia Law Review* 73, 1987.

Feldman, Noah. *Scorpions: The Battles and Triumphs of FDR's Great Supreme Court Justices.* New York: Twelve, 2010.

Field, Stephen J. *Personal Reminiscences of Early Days in California, with Other Sketches.* Birmingham, Ala.: Legal Classics Library, 1989. First published privately in 1893.

Finkelman, Paul. "John Bingham and the Background to the Fourteenth Amendment." *Akron Law Review* 36, 2002–2003.

Fitzhugh, George. *Sociology for the South, or The Failure of Free Society.* London: Forgotten Books, 2012. First published in 1854 by A. Morris.

Flynn, John T. *Country Squire in the White House.* New York: Doubleday, Doran, 1940.

Foner, Eric. *Reconstruction: America's Unfinished Revolution, 1863–1877.* Francis Parkman Prize Edition. New York: History Book Club, 2005.

Foote, Shelby. *The Civil War: A Narrative, Fort Sumter to Perryville.* New York: Random House, 1958.

Forbath, William E. "The Ambiguities of Free Labor: Labor and Law in the Gilded Age." *Wisconsin Law Review,* 1985.

Frankfurter, Felix, ed. *Mr. Justice Holmes.* New York: Coward-McCann, 1931.

Frankfurter, Felix. "The Red Terror of Judicial Reform." *The New Republic,* October 1, 1924.

Fried, Charles A. *Order and Law: Arguing the Reagan Revolution: A Firsthand Account.* New York: Simon & Schuster, 1991.

Genovese, Eugene. *The World the Slaveholders Made.* New York: Pantheon, 1969.

Greenburg, Jan Crawford. *Supreme Conflict: The Inside Story of the Struggle for Control of the United States Supreme Court.* New York: Penguin Books, 2007.

Gunther, Gerald. *Learned Hand: The Man and the Judge.* New York: Alfred A. Knopf, 1994.

Hall, Kermit L., ed. *The Oxford Companion to the Supreme Court of the United States.* 2nd ed. New York: Oxford University Press, 2005.

Hamilton, Alexander, James Madison, and John Jay. *The Federalist Papers.* Edited by Clinton Rossiter. New York: Mentor, 1961.

Hand, Learned. *The Bill of Rights.* Cambridge, Mass.: Harvard University Press, 1958.

Hixson, William B., Jr. *Moorfield Storey and the Abolitionist Tradition.* New York: Oxford University Press, 1972.

Holmes, Oliver Wendell, Jr. "The Gas-Stoker's Strike." *American Law Review* 7, 1873.

Holmes, Oliver Wendell, Jr. *Touched with Fire: Civil War Letters and Diary of Oliver Wendell Holmes, Jr.* Edited by Mark De Wolfe Howe. New York: Fordham University Press, 2000.

Holmes, Oliver Wendell, Jr., and Felix Frankfurter. *Holmes and Frankfurter: Their Correspondence, 1912–1934.* Edited by Robert M. Mennel and Christine L. Compston. Hanover: University of New Hampshire Press, 1996.

Holmes, Oliver Wendell, Jr., and Harold Laski. *Holmes-Laski Letters: The Correspondence of Mr. Justice Holmes and Harold J. Laski, 1916–1935.* 2 vols. Edited by Mark De Wolfe Howe. Cambridge, Mass.: Harvard University Press, 1953.

Horwitz, Tony. *Midnight Rising: John Brown and the Raid that Sparked the Civil War.* New York: Henry Holt, 2011.

Jefferson, Thomas. *Writings.* New York: Library of America, 1984.

Johnson, Andrew. *The Papers of Andrew Johnson.* Vol. 10, *February–July 1866.* Edited by Paul H. Bergeron. Knoxville: University of Tennessee Press, 1992.

Kennedy, David M. *Over Here: The First World War and American Society.* New York: Oxford University Press, 1982.

Ketcham, Ralph, ed. *The Anti-Federalist Papers and the Constitutional Convention Debates.* New York: Mentor, 1986.

Knowles, Helen J. *The Tie Goes to Freedom: Justice Anthony Kennedy on Liberty.* Lanham, Md.: Rowman & Littlefield, 2009.

Labbe, Ronald M., and Jonathan Lurrie. *The Slaughterhouse Cases: Regulation, Reconstruction, and the Fourteenth Amendment.* Abridged edition. Lawrence: University Press of Kansas, 2005.

Lee, Robert E. *The Wartime Papers of Robert E. Lee.* Edited by Clifford Dowdey and Louis H. Manarin. New York: Da Capo Press, 1987.

Leuchtenburg, William E. *The Supreme Court Reborn: The Constitutional Revolution in the Age of Roosevelt.* New York: Oxford University Press, 1995.

Levinson, Sanford. "The Embarrassing Second Amendment." *Yale Law Journal* 99, 1989.

Lincoln, Abraham. *The Collected Works of Abraham Lincoln.* Vol. 5. Edited by Roy P. Basler. New Brunswick, N.J.: Rutgers University Press, 1953.

Lofgren, Charles. *The Plessy Case.* New York: Oxford University Press, 1982.

Macedo, Stephen. *The New Right v. The Constitution.* Washington, D.C.: Cato Institute, 1986.

Madison, James. *Writings.* New York: Library of America, 1999.

McCloskey, Robert Green. *American Conservatism in the Age of Enterprise, 1865–1910.* New York: Harper Torchbooks, 1951.

McPherson, James. *Battle Cry of Freedom: The Civil War Years.* New York: Oxford University Press, 1988.

Meese, Edwin M., III. "A Return to Constitutional Interpretation from Judicial Law-Making." *New York Law School Law Review* 40, 1996.

Menand, Louis. *The Metaphysical Club.* New York: Farrar, Straus and Giroux, 2001.

Mencken, H. L. *A Mencken Chrestomathy: His Own Selections of His Choicest Writings.* New York: Vintage Books, 1982.

Miller, John J. *A Gift of Freedom: How the John M. Olin Foundation Changed America.* New York: Encounter Books, 2006.

Moley, Raymond. *The First New Deal.* New York: Harcourt, Brace & World, 1966.

Moreno, Paul D. *Black Americans and Organized Labor: A New History.* Baton Rouge: Louisiana State University Press, 2006.

Moreno, Paul D. *The American State from the Civil War to the New Deal: The Twilight of Constitutionalism and the Triumph of Progressivism.* New York: Cambridge University Press, 2013.

Morris, Edmund. *Colonel Roosevelt.* New York: Random House, 2010.

Pilon, Roger. "Constitutional Visions." *Reason,* December 1990.

Pilon, Roger. "On the Foundations of Justice." *The Intercollegiate Review,* Fall/Winter 1981.

Pilon, Roger. "Rethinking Judicial Restraint." *Wall Street Journal,* February 1, 1991.

Roosevelt, Theodore. "Judges and Progress." *The Outlook,* January 6, 1912.

Scalia, Antonin. "Economic Affairs As Human Affairs." *Cato Journal,* vol. 4, no. 3, Winter 1985.

Scalia, Antonin. *A Matter of Interpretation: Federal Courts and the Law.* Princeton: Princeton University Press, 1997.

Schurz, Carl. *Speeches, Correspondence and Political Papers of Carl Schurz.* Vol 1. Edited by Frederic Bancroft. New York: G. P. Putnam's Sons, 1913.

Schurz, Carl. *Speeches of Carl Schurz.* Philadelphia: J. B. Lippincott, 1865.

Siegan, Bernard H. *Economic Liberties and the Constitution.* Chicago: University of Chicago Press, 1980.

Smith, Adam. *An Inquiry Into the Nature and Causes of the Wealth of Nations.* 2 vols. Edited by R. S. Campbell and A. S. Skinner. Indianapolis: Liberty Fund, 1981.

Spencer, Herbert. *Social Statics: The Conditions Essential to Human Happiness Specified, and the First of Them Developed.* New York: Robert Schalkenbach Foundation, 1995. First published in 1851 by J. Chapman.

Storey, Moorfield. *Charles Sumner.* New York: Houghton, Mifflin, 1900.

Storey, Moorfield, and Marcial P. Lichauco. *The Conquest of the Philippines by the United States, 1898–1925.* New York: G. P. Putnam's Sons, 1926.

Teles, Steven M. *The Rise of the Conservative Legal Movement: The Battle for Control of the Law.* Princeton: Princeton University Press, 2008.

Thayer, James Bradley. *The Origin and Scope of the American Doctrine of Constitutional Law.* Boston: Little, Brown, 1893.

Thomas, Clarence. *My Grandfather's Son: A Memoir.* New York: Harper, 2007.

Tugwell, Rexford. *The Brains Trust.* New York: Viking Press, 1968.

Urofsky, Melvin I. *Louis D. Brandeis: A Life.* New York: Pantheon Books, 2009.

Urofsky, Melvin I., ed. *The Supreme Court Justices: A Biographical Dictionary.* New York: Taylor and Francis, 1994.

Wilkinson, J. Harvie, III. "Of Guns, Abortions, and the Unraveling Rule of Law." *Virginia Law Review* 95, vol. 2, April 2009.

Williams, Walter E. *The State against Blacks.* New York: McGraw-Hill, 1982.

Wilson, Theodore Brantner. *The Black Codes of the South.* Tuscaloosa: University of Alabama Press, 1965.

Wilson, Woodrow. *President Wilson's Great Speeches and Other History Making Documents.* Chicago: Stanton & Van Vliet, 1917.

Wilson, Woodrow. *Woodrow Wilson: Essential Speeches and Writings of the Scholar-President.* Edited by Mario R. DiNunzio. New York: New York University Press, 2006.

Woodward, C. Vann. "George Fitzhugh, *Sui Generis.*" Introduction to George Fitzhugh, *Cannibals All! Or Slaves Without Masters.* Cambridge, Mass.: Belknap Press, 1960.

INDEX